जीवन [illegible]

स्वयं ही भगवान
शिव बनारस में हैं।

ॐ

Bhagavad Gita

SHUBHA VILAS

BEL!EF

Published by
FiNGERPRINT! BEL!EF
An imprint of Prakash Books India Pvt. Ltd.

113/A, Darya Ganj, New Delhi-110 002,
Tel: (011) 2324 7062 – 65, Fax: (011) 2324 6975
Email: info@prakashbooks.com/sales@prakashbooks.com

facebook www.facebook.com/fingerprintpublishing
twitter www.twitter.com/FingerprintP
www.fingerprintpublishing.com

ISBN: 978 93 8653 867 3

Processed & printed in India

TO THAT TEACHER WHO TAUGHT ME TO VALUE, UNDERSTAND, AND RELISH THE WISDOM OF THE BHAGAVAD GITA, APPLY IT PERSONALLY, AND SHARE IT WITH THE WORLD. I WOULD LIKE TO DEDICATE THIS BOOK TO MY ETERNAL MASTER AND GUIDE H.D.G. A.C. BHAKTIVEDANTA SWAMI SRILA PRABHUPADA FROM WHOSE BOOK BHAGAVAD GITA AS IT IS, I LEARNT EVERYTHING I KNOW ABOUT THE GITA. THIS BOOK IS A GRATITUDE TO HIS UNLIMITED WISDOM AND KINDNESS UPON ME.

Contents

Chapter

01

Arjuna Vishada Yoga

The Bhagavad Gita begins with a question by Dhritarashtra, the blind king and father of the hundred Kauravas. He poses this question to his advisor and charioteer Sanjaya, as to what is going on in the war field of Kurukshetra between his sons and the sons of Pandu, the two warring factions. This very question reveals Dhritarashtra's offensive outlook towards his nephews and partiality for his own sons.

What follows is Sanjaya's reply to this question, a narration of events going on in the holy Kurukshetra.

Sanjaya says that the Pandava army's formation has deeply troubled the eldest Kuru son, Duryodhana, and he approaches Dronacharya, his guru. Duryodhana sarcastically informs his guru that the enemy army is led by Dronacharya's very own disciple, the son of Drupada. He painstakingly names all the stalwarts fighting on behalf of the Pandavas and then enumerates his own. This he does only to inspire and motivate his own commanders to be able to fight against their kith and kin and not give up.

Bhishma, Duryodhana's grandfather, understands that Duryodhana's morale is at an all-time low and so, he proceeds to blow his conch shell which sounds like a lion's roar.

Both Krishna and Arjuna then follow suit with their transcendental conch shells, in turn followed by

Bhima, Yudhishthir, Nakula and Sahadeva as well as their commanders.

In the beginning itself, Sanjaya, very wisely, has given Dhritarashtra an inkling of who is going to win the war. The signs of victory for the Pandavas are multiple, chiefly, presence of Krishna with the Pandavas; presence of Hanuman on Arjuna's flag; divine conchshells; and Arjuna's chariot which is a gift from Agnideva.

Meanwhile, Arjuna, mounted on a chariot displaying a flag bearing Hanuman, requests Krishna to take him ahead, in between the two armies, so that he can have a good look at the enemy strength.

Krishna obliges and the chariot stops at a strategic location from where Arjuna observes a sea of familiar faces, fathers and grandfathers, teachers, maternal uncles, brothers, sons, grandsons on one side, blurring with faces of friends, fathers-in-law and well-wishers on the other.

This scene evokes such intense emotions in Arjuna that he is overwhelmed and speaks to Krishna in despair. To justify his despair, he gives Krishna five reasons that make it impossible for him to fight the war.

The first reason he cites is compassion. At the thought of fighting his near and dear ones, his limbs have started to quiver and his mouth has dried up.

His mind is so disturbed that his Gandiva bow is sliding off his hand.

The second reason is that he fails to see how he can enjoy a kingdom by killing his own people. He wants neither victory nor kingdom nor the associated happiness. In fact he cannot fight the battle even if it means control of all the three worlds, let alone one measly kingdom.

If he kills his own friends and family members, then certainly he is sinning. Surely he does not want to commit any sin knowing its consequences. This is the next justification Arjuna gives.

And even if the family wants to fight out of greed, Krishna and he himself know better than that. Shouldn't they cease from engaging in this activity of destroying a dynasty? With destruction of a dynasty, family traditions are eternally lost; and irreligious practices prevail. Consequently, the women are taken advantage of and there is disorder in society. He'd rather die unarmed than raise his weapons in the war. This is the fourth plea from Arjuna.

These reasons point not towards Arjuna's weakness but his softheartedness, his saintliness and his high caliber and character.

And finally, not convinced with his own reasoning, he admits that he is confused. Absolutely undecided, he slumps in his chariot casting aside his bow and arrows, his mind highly distressed at the very thought of fighting the war.

1

धृतराष्ट्र उवाच
धर्मक्षेत्रे कुरुक्षेत्रे समवेता युयुत्सवः ।
मामकाः पाण्डवाश्चैव किमकुर्वत सञ्जय ॥

dhṛtarāṣṭra uvāca
dharma-kṣetre kuru-kṣetre
samavetā yuyutsavaḥ
māmakāḥ pāṇḍavāś caiva
kim akurvata sañjaya

Dhritarashtra said –
O Sanjaya, tell me what did my sons and the sons of Pandu (who were eager to fight) do after assembling in the sacred field of Kurukshetra?

2

सञ्जय उवाच
दृष्ट्वा तु पाण्डवानीकं व्यूढं दुर्योधनस्तदा ।
आचार्यमुपसङ्गम्य राजा वचनमब्रवीत् ॥

sañjaya uvāca
dṛṣṭvā tu pāṇḍavānīkaṁ
vyūḍhaṁ duryodhanas tadā
ācāryam upasaṅgamya
rājā vacanam abravīt

Sanjaya said –
On seeing the Pandava army's formation, Duryodhana approached Dronacharya and this is what he said.

3

पश्यैतां पाण्डुपुत्राणामाचार्य महतीं चमूम् ।
व्यूढां द्रुपदपुत्रेण तव शिष्येण धीमता ॥

paśyaitāṁ pāṇḍu-putrāṇām
ācārya mahatīṁ camūm
vyūḍhāṁ drupada-putreṇa
tava śiṣyeṇa dhīmatā

O master, see this great army of the sons of Pandu arrayed in a military formation by your wise disciple, the son of Drupada.

4

अत्र शूरा महेष्वसा भीमार्जुनसमा युधि ।
युयुधानो विराटश्च द्रुपदश्च महारथ: ॥

atra śūrā maheṣvāsā
bhīmārjuna-samā yudhi
yuyudhāno virāṭaś ca
drupadaś ca mahā-rathaḥ

Here are heroes and powerful archers that match Bhima and Arjuna's strength, like Yuyudhana, Virata and the ace fighter Drupada.

5

धृष्टकेतुश्चेकितान: काशिराजश्च वीर्यवान् ।
पुरुजित्कुन्तिभोजश्च शैब्यश्च नरपुङ्गव: ॥

dhṛṣṭaketuś cekitānaḥ
kāśirājaś ca vīryavān
purujit kuntibhojaś ca
śaibyaś ca nara-puṅgavaḥ

Dhristaketu, Chekitana, the heroic king of Kashi, Purojit, Kuntibhoja and Saibya are the best amongst men.

6

युधामन्युश्च विक्रान्त उत्तमौजाश्च वीर्यवान् ।
सौभद्रो द्रौपदेयाश्च सर्व एव महारथाः ॥

yudhāmanyuś ca vikrānta
uttamaujāś ca vīryavān
saubhadro draupadeyāś ca
sarva eva mahā-rathāḥ

The mighty Yudhamanyu and the heroic Uttamaujas, both sons of Subhadra, along with sons of Draupadi, are all expert fighters.

7

अस्माकं तु विशिष्टा ये तान्निबोध द्विजोत्तम ।
नायका मम सैन्यस्य संज्ञार्थं तान्ब्रवीमि ते ॥

asmākaṁ tu viśiṣṭā ye
tān nibodha dvijottama
nāyakā mama sainyasya
saṁjñārthaṁ tān bravīmi te

But there are especially powerful captains on our side whom you must take note of, O best of *brahmanas*. For your information let me tell you about those who lead my forces.

8

भवान्भीष्मश्च कर्णश्च कृपश्च समितिंजयः ।
अश्वत्थामा विकर्णश्च सौमदत्तिस्तथैव च ॥

bhavān bhīṣmaś ca karṇaś ca
kṛpaś ca samitiṁ-jayaḥ
aśvatthāmā vikarṇaś ca
saumadattis tathaiva ca

There are personalities like yourself, Bhishma, Karna and Krpa who are always victorious in battle. In addition there are people like Ashwatthama, Vikarna and Bhurisrava, the son of Somadatta.

9

अन्ये च बहवः शूरा मदर्थे त्यक्तजीविताः ।
नानाशस्त्रप्रहरणाः सर्वे युद्धविशारदाः ॥

anye ca bahavaḥ śūrā
mad-arthe tyakta-jīvitāḥ
nānā-śastra-praharaṇāḥ
sarve yuddha-viśāradāḥ

There are numerous heroes who are willing to sacrifice their lives for my cause. Each of them wield various weapons and are experts in the science of warfare.

10

अपर्याप्तं तदस्माकं बलं भीष्माभिरक्षितम् ।
पर्याप्तं त्विदमेतेषां बलं भीमाभिरक्षितम् ॥

aparyāptaṁ tad asmākaṁ
balaṁ bhīṣmābhirakṣitam
paryāptaṁ tv idam eteṣāṁ
balaṁ bhīmābhirakṣitam

Our strength is unfathomable, carefully protected by Bhishma. But their forces are limited under the protection of Bhima.

11

अयनेषु च सर्वेषु यथाभागमवस्थिताः ।
भीष्ममेवाभिरक्षन्तु भवन्तः सर्व एव हि ॥

ayaneṣu ca sarveṣu
yathā-bhāgam avasthitāḥ
bhīṣmam evābhirakṣantu
bhavantaḥ sarva eva hi

From your assigned strategic positions, each one of you should certainly protect and support Bhishma.

12

तस्य सञ्जनयन्हर्षं कुरुवृद्धः पितामहः ।
सिंहनादं विनद्योच्चैः शङ्खं दध्मौ प्रतापवान् ॥

tasya sañjanayan harṣaṁ
kuru-vṛddhaḥ pitāmahaḥ
siṁha-nādaṁ vinadyoccaiḥ
śaṅkhaṁ dadhmau pratāpavān

To rouse the morale of Duryodhana, the eldest of the Kuru dynasty, the valiant grandsire Bhishma blew his conch shell which sounded like a lion's roar.

13

ततः शङ्खाश्च भेर्यश्च पणवानकगोमुखाः ।
सहसैवाभ्यहन्यन्त स शब्दस्तुमुलोऽभवत् ॥

tataḥ śaṅkhāś ca bheryaś ca
paṇavānaka-gomukhāḥ
sahasaivābhyahanyanta
sa śabdas tumulo 'bhavat

Thereafter, conches, large drums, kettle drums, bugles, trumpets and horns were all suddenly and simultaneously sounded, resulting in a combined tumultuous sound.

14

तत: श्वेतैर्हयैर्युक्ते महति स्यन्दने स्थितौ ।
माधव: पाण्डवश्चैव दिव्यौ शङ्खौ प्रदध्मतु: ॥

tataḥ śvetair hayair yukte
mahati syandane sthitau
mādhavaḥ pāṇḍavaś caiva
divyau śaṅkhau pradadhmatuḥ

Stationed on a great chariot yoked with swift white horses, both Krishna and Arjuna then sounded their transcendental conch shells.

15

पाञ्चजन्यं हृषीकेशो देवदत्तं धनञ्जय: ।
पौण्ड्रं दध्मौ महाशङ्खं भीमकर्मा वृकोदर: ॥

pāñcajanyaṁ hṛṣīkeśo
devadattaṁ dhanañjayaḥ
pauṇḍraṁ dadhmau mahā-śaṅkhaṁ
bhīma-karmā vṛkodaraḥ

Krishna blew Panchajanya conch, Arjuna blew Devadutta conch, the terrific conch named Paundra was blown by the performer of Herculean deeds, the voracious eater Bhima.

16

अनन्तविजयं राजा कुन्तीपुत्रो युधिष्ठिरः ।
नकुलः सहदेवश्च सुघोषमणिपुष्पकौ ॥

anantavijayaṁ rājā
kuntī-putro yudhiṣṭhiraḥ
nakulaḥ sahadevaś ca
sughoṣa-maṇipuṣpakau

The son of Kunti, Yudhishthir, blew Anantavijaya conch. Nakula and Sahadeva blew their conches named Sughosha and Manipushpaka respectively.

17 – 18

काश्यश्च परमेष्वासः शिखण्डी च महारथः ।
धृष्टद्युम्नो विराटश्च सात्यकिश्चापराजितः ॥
द्रुपदो द्रौपदेयाश्च सर्वशः पृथिवीपते ।
सौभद्रश्च महाबाहुः शङ्खान्दध्मुः पृथक्पृथक् ॥

kāśyaś ca parameṣv-āsaḥ
śikhaṇḍī ca mahā-rathaḥ
dhṛṣṭadyumno virāṭaś ca
sātyakiś cāparājitaḥ
drupado draupadeyāś ca
sarvaśaḥ pṛthivī-pate

saubhadraś ca mahā-bāhuḥ
śaṅkhān dadhmuḥ pṛthak pṛthak

Also, the super excellent bowman, the King of Kashi, the mighty warrior Shikhandi, Dhrstadyumna, Virata, the unconquerable Satyaki, Drupada, the sons of Draupadi, the mighty-armed son of Subhadra, all of them blew their respective conches one after the other.

19

स घोषो धार्तराष्ट्राणां हृदयानि व्यदारयत् ।
नभश्च पृथिवीं चैव तुमुलोऽभ्यनुनादयन् ॥

sa ghoṣo dhārtarāṣṭrāṇāṁ
hṛdayāni vyadārayat
nabhaś ca pṛthivīṁ caiva
tumulo 'bhyanunādayan

The combined vibrations of all these conches shattered the hearts of the sons of Dhritarashtra and an uproarious sound echoed through the sky and earth.

20

अथ व्यवस्थितान्दृष्ट्वा धार्तराष्ट्रान्कपिध्वज: ।
प्रवृत्ते शस्त्रसम्पाते धनुरुद्यम्य पाण्डव: ।
हृषीकेशं तदा वाक्यमिदमाह महीपते ॥

atha vyavasthitān dṛṣṭvā
dhārtarāṣṭrān kapi-dhvajaḥ
pravṛtte śastra-sampāte
dhanur udyamya pāṇḍavaḥ
hṛṣīkeśaṁ tadā vākyam
idam āha mahī-pate

A chariot displaying a flag banner of Hanuman carried the son of Pandu, Arjuna, who looked over the army of the sons of Dhritarashtra, arrayed in a battle formation with readied weapons. Raising his bow, he then spoke the following words to Krishna.

21 – 22

अर्जुन उवाच ।
सेनयोरुभयोर्मध्ये रथं स्थापय मेऽच्युत ॥
यावदेतान्निरीक्षेऽहं योद्धुकामानवस्थितान् ।
कैर्मया सह योद्धव्यमस्मिन्रणसमुद्यमे ॥

arjuna uvāca
senayor ubhayor madhye

rathaṁ sthāpaya me 'cyuta
yāvad etān nirīkṣe 'haṁ
yoddhu-kāmān avasthitān
kair mayā saha yoddhavyam
asmin raṇa-samudyame

Arjuna said –
Kindly station my chariot between the two armies, O Achyuta, so that I can observe those who have assembled here desiring to fight and those with whom I have to fight in this great battle.

23

योत्स्यमानानवेक्षेऽहं य एतेऽत्र समागताः ।
धार्तराष्ट्रस्य दुर्बुद्धेर्युद्धे प्रियचिकीर्षवः ॥

yotsyamānān avekṣe 'haṁ
ya ete 'tra samāgatāḥ
dhārtarāṣṭrasya durbuddher
yuddhe priya-cikīrṣavaḥ

Let me have a look at those who have assembled here as well-wishers of the evil-minded sons of Dhritarashtra.

24

सञ्जय उवाच
एवमुक्तो हृषीकेशो गुडाकेशेन भारत ।
सेनयोरुभयोर्मध्ये स्थापयित्वा रथोत्तमम् ॥

sañjaya uvāca
evam ukto hṛṣīkeśo
guḍākeśena bhārata
senayor ubhayor madhye
sthāpayitvā rathottamam

Sanjaya said –
Thus being instructed by Arjuna, O descendent of Bharata, Krishna stationed the best of the chariots between the two armies.

25

भीष्मद्रोणप्रमुखतः सर्वेषां च महीक्षिताम् ।
उवाच पार्थ पश्यैतान्समवेतान्कुरूनिति॥

bhīṣma-droṇa-pramukhataḥ
sarveṣāṁ ca mahī-kṣitām
uvāca pārtha paśyaitān
samavetān kurūn iti

Facing Bhishma, Drona and all the chiefs of the world, Krishna said, "Just see, O Partha, assembled here are the members of the Kuru clan."

26

तत्रापश्यत्स्थितान्पार्थः पितॄनथ पितामहान् ।
आचार्यान्मातुलान्भ्रातॄन्पुत्रान्पौत्रान्सखींस्तथा ।
श्वशुरान्सुहृदश्चैव सेनयोरुभयोरपि ॥

tatrāpaśyat sthitān pārthaḥ
pitṝn atha pitāmahān
ācāryān mātulān bhrātṝn
putrān pautrān sakhīṁs tathā
śvaśurān suhṛdaś caiva
senayor ubhayor api

Standing there, Arjuna saw fathers and grandfathers, teachers, maternal uncles, brothers, sons, grandsons from one army juxtaposed with friends, fathers-in-law and well-wishers with another.

27

तान्समीक्ष्य स कौन्तेय: सर्वान्बन्धूनवस्थितान् ।
कृपया परयाविष्टो विषीदन्निदमब्रवीत् ॥

tān samīkṣya sa kaunteyaḥ
sarvān bandhūn avasthitān
kṛpayā parayāviṣṭo
viṣīdann idam abravīt

After seeing all kinds of relatives assembled there, the son of Kunti, overwhelmed with intense compassion, spoke in despair.

28

अर्जुन उवाच
दृष्ट्वेमं स्वजनं कृष्ण युयुत्सुं समुपस्थितम् ।
सीदन्ति मम गात्राणि मुखं च परिशुष्यति ॥

arjuna uvāca
dṛṣṭvemaṁ sva-janaṁ kṛṣṇa
yuyutsuṁ samupasthitam
sīdanti mama gātrāṇi
mukhaṁ ca pariśuṣyati

Arjuna said –
After seeing my near and dear ones present before me, enthusiastic to fight with one another, the limbs of my body are quaking and my mouth is drying up.

29

वेपथुश्च शरीरे मे रोमहर्षश्च जायते ।
गाण्डीवं स्रंसते हस्तात्त्वक्चैव परिदह्यते ॥

vepathuś ca śarīre me
roma-harṣaś ca jāyate
gāṇḍīvaṁ sraṁsate hastāt
tvak caiva paridahyate

My body is trembling, my hair is standing on end, my Gandiva bow is sliding off my hand and my skin is burning.

30

न च शक्नोम्यवस्थातुं भ्रमतीव च मे मनः ।
निमित्तानि च पश्यामि विपरीतानि केशव ॥

na ca śaknomy avasthātuṁ
bhramatīva ca me manaḥ
nimittāni ca paśyāmi
viparītāni keśava

I am unable to retain my composure. My mind is whirling. I can clearly see that the end result will only be misfortune, O Keshava.

31

न च श्रेयोऽनुपश्यामि हत्वा स्वजनमाहवे ।
न काङ्क्षे विजयं कृष्ण न च राज्यं सुखानि च ॥

na ca śreyo 'nupaśyāmi
hatvā sva-janam āhave
na kāṅkṣe vijayaṁ kṛṣṇa
na ca rājyaṁ sukhāni ca

I do not foresee any good in killing my own people in this battle. O Krishna, I desire neither victory, nor a kingdom, nor happiness itself.

32 – 35

किं नो राज्येन गोविन्द किं भोगैर्जीवितेन वा ।
येषामर्थे काङ्क्षितं नो राज्यं भोगाः सुखानि च ॥
त इमेऽवस्थिता युद्धे प्राणांस्त्यक्त्वा धनानि च ।
आचार्याः पितरः पुत्रास्तथैव च पितामहाः ॥
मातुलाः श्वशुराः पौत्राः श्यालाः सम्बन्धिनस्तथा ।
एतान्न हन्तुमिच्छामि घ्नतोऽपि मधुसूदन ॥

अपि त्रैलोक्यराज्यस्य हेतोः किं नु महीकृते ।
निहत्य धार्तराष्ट्रान्नः का प्रीतिः स्याज्जनार्दन ॥

kiṁ no rājyena govinda
kiṁ bhogair jīvitena vā
yeṣām arthe kāṅkṣitaṁ no
rājyaṁ bhogāḥ sukhāni ca
ta ime 'vasthitā yuddhe
prāṇāṁs tyaktvā dhanāni ca
ācāryāḥ pitaraḥ putrās
tathaiva ca pitāmahāḥ
mātulāḥ śvaśurāḥ pautrāḥ
śyālāḥ sambandhinas tathā
etān na hantum icchāmi
ghnato 'pi madhusūdana
api trailokya-rājyasya
hetoḥ kiṁ nu mahī-kṛte
nihatya dhārtarāṣṭrān naḥ
kā prītiḥ syāj janārdana

O Govinda, what is the use of a kingdom, enjoyment or even life itself when those whom we aspire for are standing on this battlefield ready to fight, at the risk of their lives and wealth? Teachers, fathers, sons, grandfathers, maternal uncles, fathers-in-law, grandsons, brothers-in-law and all other relatives . . . all these I have no desire to kill, even though they might desire to kill me, O Madhusudana. I am unprepared to fight with them for sovereignty of the three worlds, let alone a mere earthly kingdom. In killing the sons of Dhritarashtra, what pleasure will I derive, O Janardhana?

36

पापमेवाश्रयेदस्मान्हत्वैतानाततायिनः ।
तस्मान्नार्हा वयं हन्तुं धार्तराष्ट्रान्सबान्धवान् ।
स्वजनं हि कथं हत्वा सुखिनः स्याम माधव ॥

pāpam evāśrayed asmān
hatvaitān ātatāyinaḥ
tasmān nārhā vayaṁ hantuṁ
dhārtarāṣṭrān sa-bāndhavān
sva-janaṁ hi kathaṁ hatvā
sukhinaḥ syāma mādhava

Sin will certainly accrue on us by killing these aggressors. Therefore it is unjustifiable to kill the sons of Dhritarashtra along with our friends. How can anyone achieve happiness after killing his own family members, O Madhava?

37 – 38

यद्यप्येते न पश्यन्ति लोभोपहतचेतसः ।
कुलक्षयकृतं दोषं मित्रद्रोहे च पातकम् ॥
कथं न ज्ञेयमस्माभिः पापादस्मान्निवर्तितुम् ।
कुलक्षयकृतं दोषं प्रपश्यद्भिर्जनार्दन ॥

yady apy ete na paśyanti
lobhopahata-cetasaḥ
kula-kṣaya-kṛtaṁ doṣaṁ
mitra-drohe ca pātakam
kathaṁ na jñeyam asmābhiḥ
pāpād asmān nivartitum
kula-kṣaya-kṛtaṁ doṣaṁ
prapaśyadbhir janārdana

Even if these people with their hearts overpowered by greed, do not perceive any fault in killing one's own family or anything wrong in deceiving one's friends, why should we, who know better and can see clearly, not cease from engaging in this sin of destroying a dynasty, O Janardhana?

39

कुलक्षये प्रणश्यन्ति कुलधर्माः सनातनाः ।
धर्मे नष्टे कुलं कृत्स्नमधर्मोऽभिभवत्युत ॥

kula-kṣaye praṇaśyanti
kula-dharmāḥ sanātanāḥ
dharme naṣṭe kulaṁ kṛtsnam
adharmo 'bhibhavaty uta

With destruction of a dynasty, family traditions are eternally lost. With destruction of traditions, the rest of the family is overcome by irreligious practices.

40

अधर्माभिभवात्कृष्ण प्रदुष्यन्ति कुलस्त्रियः ।
स्त्रीषु दुष्टासु वार्ष्णेय जायते वर्णसङ्करः ॥

adharmābhibhavāt kṛṣṇa
praduṣyanti kula-striyaḥ
strīṣu duṣṭāsu vārṣṇeya
jāyate varṇa-saṅkaraḥ

When irreligion increases O Krishna, the women of the family are taken advantage of. When women are degraded, there's disorder in society.

41

सङ्करो नरकायैव कुलघ्नानां कुलस्य च ।
पतन्ति पितरो ह्येषां लुप्तपिण्डोदकक्रियाः ॥

saṅkaro narakāyaiva
kula-ghnānāṁ kulasya ca
patanti pitaro hy eṣāṁ
lupta-piṇḍodaka-kriyāḥ

Such disorder in society brings about a hellish experience for both the destroyers of the family traditions as well as for the family. Even the ancestors of families fall, being deprived of their ritual offerings of food and water.

42

दोषैरेतैः कुलघ्नानां वर्णसङ्करकारकैः ।
उत्साद्यन्ते जातिधर्माः कुलधर्माश्च शाश्वताः ॥

doṣair etaiḥ kula-ghnānāṁ
varṇa-saṅkara-kārakaiḥ
utsādyante jāti-dharmāḥ
kula-dharmāś ca śāśvatāḥ

The acts of the destroyers of family traditions cause utter chaos in society; the result of which is that all community projects and family welfare activities are destroyed.

43

उत्सन्नकुलधर्माणां मनुष्याणां जनार्दन ।
नरके नियतं वासो भवतीत्यनुशुश्रुम ॥

utsanna-kula-dharmāṇāṁ
manuṣyāṇāṁ janārdana
narake niyataṁ vāso
bhavatīty anuśuśruma

Those men whose family tradition and values have been spoiled, undergo a permanent hellish experience. O Janardhana, all this I have heard from reliable sources.

44

अहो बत महत्पापं कर्तुं व्यवसिता वयम् ।
यद्राज्यसुखलोभेन हन्तुं स्वजनमुद्यताः ॥

aho bata mahat pāpaṁ
kartuṁ vyavasitā vayam
yad rājya-sukha-lobhena
hantuṁ sva-janam udyatāḥ

Alas! How is it that we have committed to perform this great sin of trying to kill our own people driven by our greed for royal pleasures?

45

यदि मामप्रतीकारमशस्त्रं शस्त्रपाणयः ।
धार्तराष्ट्रा रणे हन्युस्तन्मे क्षेमतरं भवेत् ॥

yadi mām apratīkāram
aśastraṁ śastra-pāṇayaḥ
dhārtarāṣṭrā raṇe hanyus
tan me kṣemataraṁ bhavet

I would prefer that the armed sons of Dhritarashtra kill me unresisting and unarmed in the battlefield.

46

सञ्जय उवाच
एवमुक्त्वार्जुनः संख्ये रथोपस्थ उपाविशत् ।
विसृज्य सशरं चापं शोकसंविग्नमानसः ॥

sañjaya uvāca
evam uktvārjunaḥ saṅkhye
rathopastha upāviśat
visṛjya sa-śaraṁ cāpaṁ
śoka-saṁvigna-mānasaḥ

Sanjaya said –
Having thus spoken, Arjuna sat down in his chariot casting aside his bow and arrows, with his mind highly distressed.

Chapter 02

Sankhya Yoga

Arjuna continues to plead with Krishna to stop the war. Krishna answers by questioning Arjuna's compassion. According to Krishna, Arjuna's compassion is misplaced; showing compassion for the body and not for the soul. And neither is he acting in accordance to his high birth and dynasty.

When all reasons and logic get exhausted, Arjuna, with tears in his eyes, admits that his mind has become weak and in a highly confused state about his duties. Even if he fights the war and wins, how can he enjoy a victory achieved by bloodshed; on the other hand if he does not fight, he has no alternative but to beg for sustenance.

Krishna happily accepts Arjuna as his disciple and a discussion begins.

Krishna gives Arjuna three reasons to fight. First reason is to fight for material gains and pleasures. The second is to fight based on the knowledge that soul is eternal and cannot be killed. And thirdly, fight for the pleasure of God.

Krishna goads Arjuna to fight the war citing material gains. If he fights and wins, he enjoys the kingdom; and if he dies while fighting, the gates of heaven open for him. If he turns his back on the war, he faces loss of reputation by neglecting his duties. And for a respectable person, isn't dishonour and ridicule worse than death?

The second route Krishna takes is that of knowledge. A truly learned person does not lament the destruction of the body for what is valuable is not the body but the soul. True knowledge is realizing the body to be different from the soul. The soul never dies; it migrates into another body. Because we're attached to the body, we mourn the loss of loved ones. When facing such sorrow, one should remember that joy and sorrow come and go just like summer and winter. One must learn to tolerate these non-permanent dualities.

Even if Arjuna refuses to kill the Kauravas or Bhishma or Drona, they will still die; no one has ever escaped death. At the time of death, the soul changes the body just as one changes a dress. The soul does not get destroyed under any circumstance. Krishna is introducing his audience to the concept of reincarnation. He goes on to assure Arjuna that this killing will not accrue any sinful reaction because he is doing it under Krishna's directions. Religious duties ought not be sacrificed for material considerations. Neglecting duties tantamounts to sinful acts. Krishna explains that one who executes his duties in proper consciousness does not incur sin. Performing prescribed duties is a prerequisite for spiritual advancement and liberation.

Living beings are part and parcel of the Supreme whole and will remain so till eternity. The soul is unborn, indestructible, immeasurable, unchangeable, invisible, inconceivable and eternal. It cannot be cut, burnt, dried or wet. Just like the sun pervades the universe, the conscious of the soul maintains the material body.

Once born, death is certain and after death, birth is certain. Since this is an inevitable fact, one need not lament. Thus on the basis of this knowledge, Krishna concludes that Arjuna, a Kshatriya, cannot disregard his prescribed duties for fear of killing his family and superiors.

Those with little knowledge, use vedic sacrifices to please the demigods and gain material benefits. But Arjuna, by avoiding this mentality, can rise to a higher level of transcending the three modes of material nature.

This entails action free from attachment (to result) and also free from reactions. Attachment to results implies that you are the doer. And doership brings along with it enjoyment or suffering. Freedom from reactions means freedom from bondage, whether negative or positive, while still permitting active engagement.

Arjuna asks how does one recognize a person situated in higher divine consciousness. How does he respond to praise and criticism? How does he control his senses?

A self-realized person is one who has given up desire for sense gratification. Free from fear and anger, he is calm and composed in the face of distress or happiness. Like a tortoise with limbs withdrawn inside, he is in complete control of his senses.

It is possible to develop this higher taste by fixing the consciousness on Krishna. When a person dwells on sense objects, he develops attachment to them. From that attachment develops desire. When desires are unfulfilled, anger manifests. From anger arises delusion. From delusion arises bewilderment with loss of memory and discrimination. Leading to complete downfall.

In the absence of this consciousness, the mind is like a strong wind that can carry away the boat of intelligence. A person who remains steady in spite of an incessant stream of desires attains peace and not the one who tries to fulfill all those desires.

In this path of devotional endeavor, there is no loss. And finally Krishna ends by concluding that for one situated in this consciousness, he is on a divine platform even in the material world and at the time of death, he attains the kingdom of God.

1

सञ्जय उवाच
तं तथा कृपयाविष्टमश्रुपूर्णाकुलेक्षणम् ।
विषीदन्तमिदं वाक्यमुवाच मधुसूदनः ॥

sañjaya uvāca
taṁ tathā kṛpayāviṣṭam
aśru-pūrṇākulekṣaṇam
viṣīdantam idaṁ vākyam
uvāca madhusūdanaḥ

Sanjaya said –
On seeing Arjuna overwhelmed by compassion, with downcast tear-filled eyes, Krishna spoke the following words.

2

श्रीभगवानुवाच
कुतस्त्वा कश्मलमिदं विषमे समुपस्थितम् ।
अनार्यजुष्टमस्वर्ग्यमकीर्तिकरमर्जुन ॥

śrī-bhagavān uvāca
kutas tvā kaśmalam idaṁ
viṣame samupasthitam
anārya-juṣṭam asvargyam
akīrti-karam arjuna

"Wherefrom has this impurity come upon you at this most crucial hour? It does not befit a person who lives by higher values; and does not lead to a higher destination but rather leads to infamy, O Arjuna."

3

क्लैब्यं मा स्म गमः पार्थ नैतत्त्वय्युपपद्यते ।
क्षुद्रं हृदयदौर्बल्यं त्यक्त्वोत्तिष्ठ परन्तप ॥

klaibyaṁ mā sma gamaḥ pārtha
naitat tvayy upapadyate
kṣudraṁ hṛdaya-daurbalyaṁ
tyaktvottiṣṭha parantapa

"Do not yield to this impotency, O Arjuna. This is inappropriate for you. Give up this petty weakness of heart and rise up."

4

अर्जुन उवाच
कथं भीष्ममहं संख्ये द्रोणं च मधुसूदन ।
इषुभिः प्रतियोत्स्यामि पूजार्हावरिसूदन ॥

arjuna uvāca
kathaṁ bhīṣmam ahaṁ saṅkhye

droṇaṁ ca madhusūdana
iṣubhiḥ pratiyotsyāmi
pūjārhāv ari-sūdana

Arjuna said –

How do you expect me to use my arrows on Bhishma and Drona, the very people whom I worship, O Madhusudan, killer of the enemies?

5

गुरूनहत्वा हि महानुभावान्
श्रेयो भोक्तुं भैक्ष्यमपीह लोके ।
हत्वार्थकामांस्तु गुरूनिहैव
भुञ्जीय भोगान्रुधिरप्रदिग्धान् ॥

gurūn ahatvā hi mahānubhāvān
śreyo bhoktuṁ bhaikṣyam apīha loke
hatvārtha-kāmāṁs tu gurūn ihaiva
bhuñjīya bhogān rudhira-pradigdhān

Rather than killing venerable superiors, it is better to survive by begging in this world. Even if these elders desire worldly gains, why should I kill them with a desire to enjoy worldly things contaminated with their blood?

6

न चैतद्विद्मः कतरन्नो गरीयो
यद्वा जयेम यदि वा नो जयेयुः ।
यानेव हत्वा न जिजीविषाम-
स्तेऽवस्थिताः प्रमुखे धार्तराष्ट्राः ॥

na caitad vidmaḥ kataran no garīyo
yad vā jayema yadi vā no jayeyuḥ
yān eva hatvā na jijīviṣāmas
te 'vasthitāḥ pramukhe dhārtarāṣṭrāḥ

I am unable to understand what is better for us; our conquering them or them conquering us. Certainly, after killing the sons of Dhritarashtra who are standing before us, we should not care to live.

7

कार्पण्यदोषोपहतस्वभावः
पृच्छामि त्वां धर्मसम्मूढचेताः ।
यच्छ्रेयः स्यान्निश्चितं ब्रूहि तन्मे
शिष्यस्तेऽहं शाधि मां त्वां प्रपन्नम् ॥

kārpaṇya-doṣopahata-svabhāvaḥ
pṛcchāmi tvāṁ dharma-saṁmūḍha-cetāḥ
yac chreyaḥ syān niścitaṁ brūhi tan me
śiṣyas te 'haṁ śādhi māṁ tvāṁ prapannam

My mind has become weak and I am in a highly confused state of heart about my duties. Please consider me to be a disciple and a soul surrendered unto You. Now instruct me giving clarity on what would be the best thing for me to do?

8

न हि प्रपश्यामि ममापनुद्याद्
यच्छोकमुच्छोषणमिन्द्रियाणाम् ।
अवाप्य भूमावसपत्नमृद्धं
राज्यं सुराणामपि चाधिपत्यम् ॥

na hi prapaśyāmi mamāpanudyād
yac chokam ucchoṣaṇam indriyāṇām
avāpya bhūmāv asapatnam ṛddhaṁ
rājyaṁ surāṇām api cādhipatyam

Even if I achieve an unrivaled prosperous kingdom with supremacy like the demigods, I do not see any way to drive away the grief that is literally drying up my senses.

9

सञ्जय उवाच
एवमुक्त्वा हृषीकेशं गुडाकेशः परन्तपः ।
न योत्स्य इति गोविन्दमुक्त्वा तूष्णीं बभूव ह ॥

sañjaya uvāca
evam uktvā hṛṣīkeśaṁ
guḍākeśaḥ parantapaḥ
na yotsya iti govindam
uktvā tūṣṇīṁ babhūva ha

Sanjaya said –
Having thus spoken to Hrishikesha, Arjuna concluded by saying, "I will not fight, O Govinda." And then he became completely silent.

10

तमुवाच हृषीकेशः प्रहसन्निव भारत ।
सेनयोरुभयोर्मध्ये विषीदन्तमिदं वचः ॥

tam uvāca hṛṣīkeśaḥ
prahasann iva bhārata
senayor ubhayor madhye
viṣīdantam idaṁ vacaḥ

With a smile on His face, Krishna, stationed between the two armies, spoke the following words to the grief-stricken Arjuna.

11

श्रीभगवानुवाच
अशोच्यानन्वशोचस्त्वं प्रज्ञावादांश्च भाषसे ।
गतासूनगतासूंश्च नानुशोचन्ति पण्डिताः ॥

śrī-bhagavān uvāca
aśocyān anvaśocas tvaṁ
prajñā-vādāṁś ca bhāṣase
gatāsūn agatāsūṁś ca
nānuśocanti paṇḍitāḥ

Sri Bhagavan said –
While speaking learned words, you are lamenting for that which is not worthy of lamentation. A learned person laments neither for the living nor for the dead.

12

न त्वेवाहं जातु नासं न त्वं नेमे जनाधिपाः ।
न चैव न भविष्यामः सर्वे वयमतः परम् ॥

na tv evāhaṁ jātu nāsaṁ
na tvaṁ neme janādhipāḥ
na caiva na bhaviṣyāmaḥ
sarve vayam ataḥ param

There was never a time when I did not exist, neither you, not all these kings. And certainly never in the future will any of us cease to exist.

13

देहिनोऽस्मिन्यथा देहे कौमारं यौवनं जरा ।
तथा देहान्तरप्राप्तिर्धीरस्तत्र न मुह्यति ॥

dehino 'smin yathā dehe
kaumāraṁ yauvanaṁ jarā
tathā dehāntara-prāptir
dhīras tatra na muhyati

The embodied soul while in the body passes from childhood to adulthood to old age; similarly it passes into another body after death. The wise are never bewildered about such changes.

14

मात्रास्पर्शास्तु कौन्तेय शीतोष्णसुखदुःखदाः ।
आगमापायिनोऽनित्यास्तांस्तितिक्षस्व भारत ॥

mātrā-sparśās tu kaunteya
śītoṣṇa-sukha-duḥkha-dāḥ
āgamāpāyino 'nityās
tāṁs titikṣasva bhārata

Pleasures and pains experienced by the senses coming in contact with sense objects are temporary and transitory. They come and go like the summer and winter seasons. One must learn to tolerate such temporary experiences, O scion of Bharata.

15

यं हि न व्यथयन्त्येते पुरुषं पुरुषर्षभ ।
समदुःखसुखं धीरं सोऽमृतत्वाय कल्पते ॥

yaṁ hi na vyathayanty ete
puruṣaṁ puruṣarṣabha
sama-duḥkha-sukhaṁ dhīraṁ
so 'mṛtatvāya kalpate

A wise person who is never afflicted by such dualities and perceives happiness and distress equally is eligible for liberation.

16

नासतो विद्यते भावो नाभावो विद्यते सतः ।
उभयोरपि दृष्टोऽन्तस्त्वनयोस्तत्त्वदर्शिभिः ॥

nāsato vidyate bhāvo
nābhāvo vidyate sataḥ
ubhayor api dṛṣṭo 'ntas
tv anayos tattva-darśibhiḥ

For that which is temporary (the material body) there is no permanence. For that which is permanent (the soul) there is no change. Both these facts have been observed and concluded by those who are seers of the truth.

17

अविनाशि तु तद्विद्धि येन सर्वमिदं ततम् ।
विनाशमव्ययस्यास्य न कश्चित्कर्तुमर्हति ॥

avināśi tu tad viddhi
yena sarvam idaṁ tatam
vināśam avyayasyāsya
na kaścit kartum arhati

You should know, that which pervades the body is imperishable. No one can destroy that indestructible soul.

18

अन्तवन्त इमे देहा नित्यस्योक्ताः शरीरिणः ।
अनाशिनोऽप्रमेयस्य तस्माद्युध्यस्व भारत ॥

antavanta ime dehā
nityasyoktāḥ śarīriṇaḥ
anāśino 'prameyasya
tasmād yudhyasva bhārata

The body is perishable. But the eternal soul residing in the body can never be destroyed and is immeasurable. Therefore, fight, O scion of Bharata.

19

य एनं वेत्ति हन्तारं यश्चैनं मन्यते हतम् ।
उभौ तौ न विजानीतो नायं हन्ति न हन्यते ॥

ya enaṁ vetti hantāraṁ
yaś cainaṁ manyate hatam
ubhau tau na vijānīto
nāyaṁ hanti na hanyate

Anyone who thinks that the soul kills or can be killed, is not in knowledge of the fact that the soul neither slays nor can be slain.

20

न जायते म्रियते वा कदाचि-
न्नायं भूत्वा भविता वा न भूयः ।
अजो नित्यः शाश्वतोऽयं पुराणो
न हन्यते हन्यमाने शरीरे ॥

na jāyate mriyate vā kadācin
nāyaṁ bhūtvā bhavitā vā na bhūyaḥ
ajo nityaḥ śāśvato 'yaṁ purāṇo
na hanyate hanyamāne śarīre

The soul has neither birth nor death. Nor has it come into being in the past nor will it come into being in the future. It is unborn, eternal, permanent and the oldest. It can never be killed even when the body is slain.

21

वेदाविनाशिनं नित्यं य एनमजमव्ययम् ।
कथं स पुरुषः पार्थ कं घातयति हन्ति कम् ॥

vedāvināśinaṁ nityaṁ
ya enam ajam avyayam
kathaṁ sa puruṣaḥ pārtha
kaṁ ghātayati hanti kam

One who knows the indestructible, eternal, unborn and imperishable nature of the self, how can that person kill anyone or cause anyone to be killed, O Partha?

22

वासांसि जीर्णानि यथा विहाय
नवानि गृह्णाति नरोऽपराणि ।
तथा शरीराणि विहाय जीर्णा-
न्यन्यानि संयाति नवानि देही ॥

vāsāṁsi jīrṇāni yathā vihāya
navāni gṛhṇāti naro 'parāṇi
tathā śarīrāṇi vihāya jīrṇāny
anyāni saṁyāti navāni dehī

Just as clothes once old are discarded and new ones accepted, similarly when the body gets old, the soul discards it and accepts a new body.

23

नैनं छिन्दन्ति शस्त्राणि नैनं दहति पावकः ।
न चैनं क्लेदयन्त्यापो न शोषयति मारुतः ॥

nainaṁ chindanti śastrāṇi
nainaṁ dahati pāvakaḥ
na cainaṁ kledayanty āpo
na śoṣayati mārutaḥ

Weapons cannot pierce the soul, it cannot be burnt by fire, it cannot also be wet by water, nor can it be withered by the wind.

24

अच्छेद्योऽयमदाह्योऽयमक्लेद्योऽशोष्य एव च ।
नित्यः सर्वगतः स्थाणुरचलोऽयं सनातनः ॥

acchedyo 'yam adāhyo 'yam
akledyo 'śoṣya eva ca
nityaḥ sarva-gataḥ sthāṇur
acalo 'yaṁ sanātanaḥ

The soul is indivisible, uninflammable, insoluble and un-dryable. It is eternal, present everywhere, changeless, immovable and primeval.

25

अव्यक्तोऽयमचिन्त्योऽयमविकार्योऽयमुच्यते ।
तस्मादेवं विदित्वैनं नानुशोचितुमर्हसि ॥

avyakto 'yam acintyo 'yam
avikāryo 'yam ucyate
tasmād evaṁ viditvainaṁ
nānuśocitum arhasi

The soul is said to be invisible, inconceivable and unchangeable. Knowing this, one should not lament.

26

अथ चैनं नित्यजातं नित्यं वा मन्यसे मृतम् ।
तथापि त्वं महाबाहो नैनं शोचितुमर्हसि ॥

atha cainaṁ nitya-jātaṁ
nityaṁ vā manyase mṛtam
tathāpi tvaṁ mahā-bāho
nainaṁ śocitum arhasi

If however, you believe that the soul constantly goes through birth and death, even then, O mighty-armed one, you still have no reason to lament.

27

जातस्य हि ध्रुवो मृत्युर्ध्रुवं जन्म मृतस्य च ।
तस्मादपरिहार्येऽर्थे न त्वं शोचितुमर्हसि ॥

jātasya hi dhruvo mṛtyur
dhruvaṁ janma mṛtasya ca
tasmād aparihārye 'rthe
na tvaṁ śocitum arhasi

Of those born, death is certain and of those who die, birth is certain. Since this is an inevitable fact, one should not lament.

28

अव्यक्तादीनि भूतानि व्यक्तमध्यानि भारत ।
अव्यक्तनिधनान्येव तत्र का परिदेवना ॥

avyaktādīni bhūtāni
vyakta-madhyāni bhārata
avyakta-nidhanāny eva
tatra kā paridevanā

All created beings were unmanifest in the beginning, manifested in the middle and again unmanifest in the end. Thus where is the cause for lamentation?

29

आश्चर्यवत्पश्यति कश्चिदेन-
माश्चर्यवद्वदति तथैव चान्य: ।
आश्चर्यवच्चैनमन्य: शृणोति
श्रुत्वाप्येनं वेद न चैव कश्चित् ॥

āścarya-vat paśyati kaścid enam
āścarya-vad vadati tathaiva cānyaḥ
āścarya-vac cainam anyaḥ śṛṇoti
śrutvāpy enaṁ veda na caiva kaścit

Some perceive the soul as amazing. Others describe it as amazing. Yet others hear about it as amazing. But even on hearing about it, no one knows about it truly.

30

देही नित्यमवध्योऽयं देहे सर्वस्य भारत ।
तस्मात्सर्वाणि भूतानि न त्वं शोचितुमर्हसि ॥

dehī nityam avadhyo 'yaṁ
dehe sarvasya bhārata
tasmāt sarvāṇi bhūtāni
na tvaṁ śocitum arhasi

The eternal soul residing within the body of all beings is indestructible, O Bharata. Therefore you need not lament for any living being.

31

स्वधर्ममपि चावेक्ष्य न विकम्पितुमर्हसि ।
धर्म्याद्धि युद्धाच्छ्रेयोऽन्यत्क्षत्रियस्य न विद्यते ॥

sva-dharmam api cāvekṣya
na vikampitum arhasi
dharmyād dhi yuddhāc chreyo 'nyat
kṣatriyasya na vidyate

Also considering your own duties as a warrior, you should never hesitate to fight. Other than fighting for righteousness, there is no better engagement for a warrior.

32

यदृच्छया चोपपन्नं स्वर्गद्वारमपावृतम् ।
सुखिनः क्षत्रियाः पार्थ लभन्ते युद्धमीदृशम् ॥

yadṛcchayā copapannaṁ
svarga-dvāram apāvṛtam

sukhinaḥ kṣatriyāḥ pārtha
labhante yuddham īdṛśam

By good fortune, the doors to the heavens have become wide open. Happy are those warriors who achieve the opportunity to fight in a war like this.

33

अथ चेत्त्वमिमं धर्म्यं सङ्ग्रामं न करिष्यसि ।
ततः स्वधर्मं कीर्तिं च हित्वा पापमवाप्स्यसि ॥

atha cet tvam imaṁ dharmyaṁ
saṅgrāmaṁ na kariṣyasi
tataḥ sva-dharmam kīrtiṁ ca
hitvā pāpam avāpsyasi

However, if you do not perform this religious duty of fighting, then you will lose your reputation by neglecting your duties and incur sins.

34

अकीर्तिं चापि भूतानि कथयिष्यन्ति तेऽव्ययाम् ।
सम्भावितस्य चाकीर्तिर्मरणादतिरिच्यते ॥

akīrtiṁ cāpi bhūtāni
kathayiṣyanti te 'vyayām
sambhāvitasya cākīrtir
maraṇād atiricyate

People will speak about your infamy constantly and for a respectable person, infamy is worse than death.

35

भयाद्रणादुपरतं मंस्यन्ते त्वां महारथाः ।
येषां च त्वं बहुमतो भूत्वा यास्यसि लाघवम् ॥

bhayād raṇād uparataṁ
maṁsyante tvāṁ mahā-rathāḥ
yeṣāṁ ca tvaṁ bahu-mato
bhūtvā yāsyasi lāghavam

Great warriors will assume that you have retreated from the battlefield out of fear. Those who have held you in high esteem will then take you lightly.

36

अवाच्यवादांश्च बहून्वदिष्यन्ति तवाहिताः ।
निन्दन्तस्तव सामर्थ्यं ततो दुःखतरं नु किम् ॥

avācya-vādāṁś ca bahūn
vadiṣyanti tavāhitāḥ
nindantas tava sāmarthyaṁ
tato duḥkhataraṁ nu kim

Your enemies, while vilifying your abilities, will speak many unkind words about you. What could be more painful than that?

37

हतो वा प्राप्स्यसि स्वर्गं जित्वा वा भोक्ष्यसे महीम् ।
तस्मादुत्तिष्ठ कौन्तेय युद्धाय कृतनिश्चयः ॥

hato vā prāpsyasi svargaṁ
jitvā vā bhokṣyase mahīm
tasmād uttiṣṭha kaunteya
yuddhāya kṛta-niścayaḥ

Either you will attain the heavens by being killed or you will enjoy the earthly kingdom by being victorious. Both ways you benefit from fighting the war. Therefore get up with a resolve to fight.

38

सुखदुःखे समे कृत्वा लाभालाभौ जयाजयौ ।
ततो युद्धाय युज्यस्व नैवं पापमवाप्स्यसि ॥

sukha-duḥkhe same kṛtvā
lābhālābhau jayājayau
tato yuddhāya yujyasva
naivaṁ pāpam avāpsyasi

Considering happiness and distress, gain and loss, victory and defeat with equanimity, fight for the sake of fighting. In this way you will never accrue sin.

39

एषा तेऽभिहिता सांख्ये बुद्धिर्योगे त्विमां शृणु ।
बुद्ध्या युक्तो यया पार्थ कर्मबन्धं प्रहास्यसि ॥

eṣā te 'bhihitā sāṅkhye
buddhir yoge tv imāṁ śṛṇu
buddhyā yukto yayā pārtha
karma-bandhaṁ prahāsyasi

So far I have described this wisdom to you through analysis or *sankhya*. Now hear about it as I explain in terms of working without attachment to result. When you act in such knowledge, O Partha, you are freed from the bondage resulting from action.

40

नेहाभिक्रमनाशोऽस्ति प्रत्यवायो न विद्यते ।
स्वल्पमप्यस्य धर्मस्य त्रायते महतो भयात् ॥

nehābhikrama-nāśo 'sti
pratyavāyo na vidyate
sv-alpam apy asya dharmasya
trāyate mahato bhayāt

In this endeavor there is no loss nor is there any diminution. Even a very little progress on this path protects one from greatest types of fear.

41

व्यवसायात्मिका बुद्धिरेकेह कुरुनन्दन ।
बहुशाखा ह्यनन्ताश्च बुद्धयोऽव्यवसायिनाम् ॥

vyavasāyātmikā buddhir
ekeha kuru-nandana
bahu-śākhā hy anantāś ca
buddhayo 'vyavasāyinām

Those who are resolute in purpose, their intelligence is fixed only on this path; but for those whose intelligence is unlimitedly multi-branched are irresolute in their purpose.

42

यामिमां पुष्पितां वाचं प्रवदन्त्यविपश्चितः ।
वेदवादरताः पार्थ नान्यदस्तीति वादिनः ॥

yām imāṁ puṣpitāṁ vācaṁ
pravadanty avipaścitaḥ
veda-vāda-ratāḥ pārtha
nānyad astīti vādinaḥ

Men with such irresolute intelligence who take delight in the flowery words of the Vedas, O Partha, proclaim that nothing else matters.

43

कामात्मानः स्वर्गपरा जन्मकर्मफलप्रदाम् ।
क्रियाविशेषबहुलां भोगैश्वर्यगतिं प्रति ॥

kāmātmānaḥ svarga-parā
janma-karma-phala-pradām
kriyā-viśeṣa-bahulāṁ
bhogaiśvarya-gatiṁ prati

Being full of desires, aiming to achieve the heavens, wanting a good birth and other selfish results, such people take up various ritualistic performances aimed towards progressive enjoyment and opulence.

44

भोगैश्वर्यप्रसक्तानां तयापहृतचेतसाम् ।
व्यवसायात्मिका बुद्धिः समाधौ न विधीयते ॥

bhogaiśvarya-prasaktānāṁ
tayāpahṛta-cetasām
vyavasāyātmikā buddhiḥ
samādhau na vidhīyate

For those who are too attached to sense enjoyment and opulence, their minds are bewildered and the resolute determination to focus the mind on one path does not take place.

45

त्रैगुण्यविषया वेदा निस्त्रैगुण्यो भवार्जुन ।
निर्द्वन्द्वो नित्यसत्त्वस्थो निर्योगक्षेम आत्मवान् ॥

trai-guṇya-viṣayā vedā
nistrai-guṇyo bhavārjuna
nirdvandvo nitya-sattva-stho
niryoga-kṣema ātmavān

The main subject matter that the Vedas speak about is the three modes of material nature. You should transcend the three modes and become free from dualities, remain in a pure state of spiritual existence, free from concerns for gain and security and establish oneself in self-realization.

46

यावानर्थ उदपाने सर्वतः सम्प्लुतोदके ।
तावान्सर्वेषु वेदेषु ब्राह्मणस्य विजानतः ॥

yāvān artha udapāne
sarvataḥ samplutodake
tāvān sarveṣu vedeṣu
brāhmaṇasya vijānataḥ

All purposes that are fulfilled by a well and more can be fulfilled by a great reservoir of water. Similarly, one who knows the essence of the Vedas can fulfill all purposes of the Vedas.

47

कर्मण्येवाधिकारस्ते मा फलेषु कदाचन ।
मा कर्मफलहेतुर्भूर्मा ते सङ्गोऽस्त्वकर्मणि ॥

karmaṇy evādhikāras te
mā phaleṣu kadācana

mā karma-phala-hetur bhūr
mā te saṅgo 'stv akarmaṇi

You have claim over the right of doing your prescribed duty, but never over the result of action. Never become motivated by hope of enjoying the result of action nor become attached to not doing your duty.

48

योगस्थः कुरु कर्माणि सङ्गं त्यक्त्वा धनञ्जय ।
सिद्ध्यसिद्ध्योः समो भूत्वा समत्वं योग उच्यते ॥

yoga-sthaḥ kuru karmāṇi
saṅgaṁ tyaktvā dhanañjaya
siddhy-asiddhyoḥ samo bhūtvā
samatvaṁ yoga ucyate

Being equipoised, perform your duty giving up attachment to success and failure, O Dhananjaya. Such equanimity of the mind is called yoga.

49

दूरेण ह्यवरं कर्म बुद्धियोगाद्धनञ्जय ।
बुद्धौ शरणमन्विच्छ कृपणाः फलहेतवः ॥

dūreṇa hy avaraṁ karma
buddhi-yogād dhanañjaya
buddhau śaraṇam anviccha
kṛpaṇāḥ phala-hetavaḥ

By far, action with attachment to results is inferior to disciplined intelligence, O Dhananjaya. Seek refuge in this wisdom. Those motivated by fruits of work are miserly.

50

बुद्धियुक्तो जहातीह उभे सुकृतदुष्कृते ।
तस्माद्योगाय युज्यस्व योगः कर्मसु कौशलम् ॥

buddhi-yukto jahātīha
ubhe sukṛta-duṣkṛte
tasmād yogāya yujyasva
yogaḥ karmasu kauśalam

One who is disciplined by wisdom rids himself of both good and bad reactions. Therefore devote yourself to practice of yoga, the art of right action.

51

कर्मजं बुद्धियुक्ता हि फलं त्यक्त्वा मनीषिण: ।
जन्मबन्धविनिर्मुक्ता: पदं गच्छन्त्यनामयम् ॥

karma-jaṁ buddhi-yuktā hi
phalaṁ tyaktvā manīṣiṇaḥ
janma-bandha-vinirmuktāḥ
padaṁ gacchanty anāmayam

The wise that are established in yogic wisdom certainly renounce the fruits born of action. Being liberated from the bondage of rebirth, they attain the abode that is free from miseries.

52

यदा ते मोहकलिलं बुद्धिर्व्यतितरिष्यति ।
तदा गन्तासि निर्वेदं श्रोतव्यस्य श्रुतस्य च ॥

yadā te moha-kalilaṁ
buddhir vyatitariṣyati
tadā gantāsi nirvedaṁ
śrotavyasya śrutasya ca

When your intelligence emerges out of the thick forest of illusion, at that time you will become indifferent to all that is to be heard and all that has already been heard.

53

श्रुतिविप्रतिपन्ना ते यदा स्थास्यति निश्चला ।
समाधावचला बुद्धिस्तदा योगमवाप्स्यसि ॥

śruti-vipratipannā te
yadā sthāsyati niścalā
samādhāv acalā buddhis
tadā yogam avāpsyasi

When your intellect is no longer influenced by the flowery language of the Vedas and remains fixed and unperplexed, you will attain the perfection of yoga.

54

अर्जुन उवाच
स्थितप्रज्ञस्य का भाषा समाधिस्थस्य केशव ।
स्थितधीः किं प्रभाषेत किमासीत व्रजेत किम् ॥

arjuna uvāca
sthita-prajñasya kā bhāṣā
samādhi-sthasya keśava
sthita-dhīḥ kiṁ prabhāṣeta
kim āsīta vrajeta kiṁ

Arjuna said –

What are the characteristics of one who is situated in higher consciousness and steady in intelligence, O Keshava? How does he speak? How does he sit? How does he move about?

55

श्रीभगवानुवाच
प्रजहाति यदा कामान्सर्वान्पार्थ मनोगतान् ।
आत्मन्येवात्मना तुष्टः स्थितप्रज्ञस्तदोच्यते ॥

śrī-bhagavān uvāca
prajahāti yadā kāmān
sarvān pārtha mano-gatān
ātmany evātmanā tuṣṭaḥ
sthita-prajñas tadocyate

Sri Bhagavan said –

One who has renounced all desires that are born out of the mind, O Partha, and is self-satisfied, such a person is situated in higher consciousness.

56

दु:खेष्वनुद्विग्नमना: सुखेषु विगतस्पृह: ।
वीतरागभयक्रोध: स्थितधीर्मुनिरुच्यते ॥

duḥkheṣv anudvigna-manāḥ
sukheṣu vigata-spṛhaḥ
vīta-rāga-bhaya-krodhaḥ
sthita-dhīr munir ucyate

One who in misery does not get agitated and in joy does not get deluded, and who is free from attachment, fear and anger, such a person is called a sage of steady mind.

57

य: सर्वत्रानभिस्नेहस्तत्तत्प्राप्य शुभाशुभम् ।
नाभिनन्दति न द्वेष्टि तस्य प्रज्ञा प्रतिष्ठिता ॥

yaḥ sarvatrānabhisnehas
tat tat prāpya śubhāśubham
nābhinandati na dveṣṭi
tasya prajñā pratiṣṭhitā

One who always remains unaffected by pleasant or unpleasant things and neither praises them nor despises them, such a person is firmly fixed in perfect consciousness.

58

यदा संहरते चायं कूर्मोऽङ्गानीव सर्वशः ।
इन्द्रियाणीन्द्रियार्थेभ्यस्तस्य प्रज्ञा प्रतिष्ठिता ॥

yadā saṁharate cāyaṁ
kūrmo 'ṅgānīva sarvaśaḥ
indriyāṇīndriyārthebhyas
tasya prajñā pratiṣṭhitā

Just as a tortoise draws its limbs into a shell, one who is able to withdraw his senses from the sense objects, such a person is fixed in perfect consciousness.

59

विषया विनिवर्तन्ते निराहारस्य देहिनः ।
रसवर्जं रसोऽप्यस्य परं दृष्ट्वा निवर्तते ॥

viṣayā vinivartante
nirāhārasya dehinaḥ
rasa-varjaṁ raso 'py asya
paraṁ dṛṣṭvā nivartate

When one refrains from the objects of selfish enjoyment by artificial restriction, the taste for the sense enjoyment still remains. But along with such restriction, if one experiences a higher taste, then the lower taste fades away.

60

यततो ह्यपि कौन्तेय पुरुषस्य विपश्चितः ।
इन्द्रियाणि प्रमाथीनि हरन्ति प्रसभं मनः ॥

yatato hy api kaunteya
puruṣasya vipaścitaḥ
indriyāṇi pramāthīni
haranti prasabhaṁ manaḥ

Even for a man of intelligence who is striving to control, the senses are so strong that they can forcibly carry away his mind.

61

तानि सर्वाणि संयम्य युक्त आसीत मत्परः ।
वशे हि यस्येन्द्रियाणि तस्य प्रज्ञा प्रतिष्ठिता ॥

tāni sarvāṇi saṁyamya
yukta āsīta mat-paraḥ
vaśe hi yasyendriyāṇi
tasya prajñā pratiṣṭhitā

While keeping all the senses under control, one who fixes his consciousness upon Me is a man of steady intelligence.

62

ध्यायतो विषयान्पुंसः सङ्गस्तेषूपजायते ।
सङ्गात्सञ्जायते कामः कामात्क्रोधोऽभिजायते ॥

dhyāyato viṣayān puṁsaḥ
saṅgas teṣūpajāyate
saṅgāt sañjāyate kāmaḥ
kāmāt krodho 'bhijāyate

When a person dwells on sense objects, he develops attachment to them. From that attachment develops desire. From unfulfilled desires, anger manifests.

63

क्रोधाद्भवति सम्मोहः सम्मोहात्स्मृतिविभ्रमः ।
स्मृतिभ्रंशाद्बुद्धिनाशो बुद्धिनाशात्प्रणश्यति ॥

krodhād bhavati saṁmohaḥ
saṁmohāt smṛti-vibhramaḥ
smṛti-bhraṁśād buddhi-nāśo
buddhi-nāśāt praṇaśyati

From anger arises delusion. From delusion arises bewilderment of memory. From loss of memory power of discrimination is lost. As a result of loss of discrimination, one becomes completely destroyed.

64

रागद्वेषविमुक्तैस्तु विषयानिन्द्रियैश्चरन् ।
आत्मवश्यैर्विधेयात्मा प्रसादमधिगच्छति ॥

rāga-dveṣa-vimuktais tu
viṣayān indriyaiś caran
ātma-vaśyair vidheyātmā
prasādam adhigacchati

One who has become free from attachment and aversion even when the senses are in contact with sense objects, by following the regulative principles of freedom, can attain God's grace.

65

प्रसादे सर्वदुःखानां हानिरस्योपजायते ।
प्रसन्नचेतसो ह्याशु बुद्धिः पर्यवतिष्ठते ॥

prasāde sarva-duḥkhānāṁ
hānir asyopajāyate
prasanna-cetaso hy āśu
buddhiḥ paryavatiṣṭhate

For one who has achieved the grace of the Lord, all miseries cease to exist. In such a pleasant state of mind, one's intelligence becomes steady.

66

नास्ति बुद्धिरयुक्तस्य न चायुक्तस्य भावना ।
न चाभावयतः शान्तिरशान्तस्य कुतः सुखम् ॥

nāsti buddhir ayuktasya
na cāyuktasya bhāvanā
na cābhāvayataḥ śāntir
aśāntasya kutaḥ sukham

One who is not connected to higher consciousness can neither have a steady intelligence nor a controlled mind, without which peace is impossible. And without peace where is the question of happiness?

67

इन्द्रियाणां हि चरतां यन्मनोऽनुविधीयते ।
तदस्य हरति प्रज्ञां वायुर्नावमिवाम्भसि ॥

indriyāṇāṁ hi caratāṁ
yan mano 'nuvidhīyate
tad asya harati prajñāṁ
vāyur nāvam ivāmbhasi

Even one of the roaming senses the mind runs after, can carry away a man's intelligence just like a strong wind carries away a boat on water.

68

तस्माद्यस्य महाबाहो निगृहीतानि सर्वशः ।
इन्द्रियाणीन्द्रियार्थेभ्यस्तस्य प्रज्ञा प्रतिष्ठिता ॥

tasmād yasya mahā-bāho
nigṛhītāni sarvaśaḥ
indriyāṇīndriyārthebhyas
tasya prajñā pratiṣṭhitā

Therefore, O mighty-armed one, one whose senses are withdrawn from their objects is a person of steady intelligence.

69

या निशा सर्वभूतानां तस्यां जागर्ति संयमी ।
यस्यां जाग्रति भूतानि सा निशा पश्यतो मुनेः ॥

yā niśā sarva-bhūtānāṁ
tasyāṁ jāgarti saṁyamī
yasyāṁ jāgrati bhūtāni
sā niśā paśyato muneḥ

What is night for all living beings is time of wakefulness for a self-controlled person and what is the time of awakening for all living beings is like night for an introspective sage.

70

आपूर्यमाणमचलप्रतिष्ठं
समुद्रमापः प्रविशन्ति यद्वत् ।
तद्वत्कामा यं प्रविशन्ति सर्वे
स शान्तिमाप्नोति न कामकामी ॥

āpūryamāṇam acala-pratiṣṭhaṁ
samudram āpaḥ praviśanti yadvat
tadvat kāmā yaṁ praviśanti sarve
sa śāntim āpnoti na kāma-kāmī

Just like the ocean remains still and unaffected in spite of being filled by river waters, similarly a person who remains steady in spite of an incessant stream of desires attains peace and not the one who tries to fulfill all those desires.

71

विहाय कामान्यः सर्वान्पुमांश्चरति निःस्पृहः ।
निर्ममो निरहङ्कारः स शान्तिमधिगच्छति ॥

vihāya kāmān yaḥ sarvān
pumāṁś carati niḥspṛhaḥ
nirmamo nirahaṅkāraḥ
sa śāntim adhigacchati

Abandoning all desires for sense indulgence, a person who lives free from desires, without a sense of proprietorship and devoid of egotism, such a person attains lasting peace.

72

एषा ब्राह्मी स्थितिः पार्थ नैनां प्राप्य विमुह्यति ।
स्थित्वास्यामन्तकालेऽपि ब्रह्मनिर्वाणमृच्छति ॥

eṣā brāhmī sthitiḥ pārtha
naināṁ prāpya vimuhyati
sthitvāsyām anta-kāle 'pi
brahma-nirvāṇam ṛcchati

Having attained this divine state, one is never bewildered. If one is situated in this consciousness at the time of death, then one attains the kingdom of God.

Chapter 03

Karma Yoga

Arjun is still in confusion, and asks Krishna to explain what he means. If knowledge was superior to action, then why indulge in this ghastly war? Why was Krishna giving two apparently contradictory instructions?

Krishna explains that there are two classes of men, one that takes the path of knowledge preferred by philosophers and the other, who chooses the path of action that devotees prefer. Simply abstaining from action or renunciation does not lead to freedom from reaction. In fact no one can remain inactive even for a second, since the modes of nature drive everyone into action.

Even though physically inactive, if one is always active mentally, contemplating on the objects of the senses, such a person is considered a hypocrite. But one who controls his senses with his mind and performs actions without any attachment to the results is by far superior to one not acting at all.

To remain free from the bondage of reactions, one must carry out assigned duties for the satisfaction of Vishnu. Therefore it is better to perform one's duty in this consciousness.

By performing work as a sacrifice for Vishnu, one can satisfy the gods who in turn supply all necessities to those who nourish them through sacrifices. For instance, living beings survive on food grains which are in turn produced by rains. Rains are simply a product of performance of sacrifices to please gods. Such mutual cooperation leads to the greatest good. But one who has a thief mentality will not be grateful to acknowledge the gifts bestowed by the gods.

Assigned duties are those prescribed in the Vedas and the Vedas originate from the Supreme Lord himself. This implies that in every act of sacrifice, the Supreme Lord is manifested himself. If one only understands the purpose and intention of work and duties, he does not get bound by it.

But for someone who is free from desires and lives a life of self-realization, there is no need to perform any assigned duties. He has nothing to gain by performing the assigned duties and nothing to lose by not performing them. He depends on no other, having no obligations to anyone.

In the past, King Janaka had taken this path of performing assigned duties without attachment to results and attained perfection of his life. Because whatever a great man does, common men emulate. Whatever standards he sets, becomes a worldwide trend.

For Krishna himself, there is no prescribed duty within the three worlds and neither does he have any material desires; but he still engaged himself in carrying out assigned duties. Else the common men will use His example as an excuse to abandon their duties, with resultant social chaos. And Krishna would be then responsible for the mayhem.

It is the ignorant who performs his duties with attachment to results; the intelligent are expected to perform with no such attachment, and set the right trend for this world to follow.

The ignorant, attached to the results of his duties, should not be misled into giving up duties. Instead, he should be inspired to carry out duties without attachment to results.

Because he is under influence of false ego, he works thinking that he is the doer of the action that is in effect, carried out by the three modes of material nature. Under the influence of the modes of nature, ignorant persons are absorbed in mundane action.

On the other hand, the intelligent person knows very well the influence of the three modes of nature on his actions. He knows very well the difference between work done in spirit of devotion and work done with expectation of results.

Krishna then sums up his instructions to Arjuna step-by-step—to offer all his work to him; in complete knowledge of him, without any desire for profit; without claiming ownership; and without any lethargy. This is the spirit, the consciousness in which Krishna wants Arjuna to fight. To perform his duty, even if imperfectly rather than perform another's duty perfectly.

Arjuna now asks a very relevant question. What drives one to act wrongly, to sin, even though he knows he is doing wrong? Which force propels one to act against his own will?

Krishna replies it is nothing but the influence of lust that dictates unwilling action; it is lust that is borne of the mode of passion that eventually morphs into anger, the greatest enemy of the world.

Lust covers each living entity in varying degrees just like smoke envelopes fire, or dust covers a mirror or a womb seals an embryo.

It finds a seat in the senses, mind and intelligence from where it strategically influences the soul.

The senses are superior to matter; the mind is higher than the senses; the intelligence is much higher than the mind; and the soul is much more superior to even intelligence. The only way to free the soul from the clutches of lust is by using the intellect to control the mind so the mind in turn regulates the senses. This is the wisest way of killing this enemy of knowledge and self-realization.

1

अर्जुन उवाच
ज्यायसी चेत्कर्मणस्ते मता बुद्धिर्जनार्दन ।
तत्किं कर्मणि घोरे मां नियोजयसि केशव ॥

arjuna uvāca
jyāyasī cet karmaṇas te
matā buddhir janārdana
tat kiṁ karmaṇi ghore
māṁ niyojayasi keśava

Arjuna said –
According to you, if knowledge is superior to mere action, then why are you pushing me to indulge in this ghastly action, Krishna?

2

व्यामिश्रेणेव वाक्येन बुद्धिं मोहयसीव मे ।
तदेकं वद निश्चित्य येन श्रेयोऽहमाप्नुयाम् ॥

vyāmiśreṇeva vākyena
buddhiṁ mohayasīva me
tad ekaṁ vada niścitya
yena śreyo 'ham āpnuyām

You are confusing me by giving me two completely opposing instructions. Could you please tell me clearly which the most beneficial path is?

3

श्रीभगवानुवाच
लोकेऽस्मिन्द्विविधा निष्ठा पुरा प्रोक्ता मयानघ ।
ज्ञानयोगेन साङ्ख्यानां कर्मयोगेन योगिनाम् ॥

śrī-bhagavān uvāca
loke 'smin dvi-vidhā niṣṭhā
purā proktā mayānagha
jnāna-yogena sāṅkhyānāṁ
karma-yogena yoginām

Sri Bhagavan said –
Arjuna, as already explained, there are two types of faith in this world. The path of knowledge that philosophers prefer and the path of action that devotees prefer.

4

न कर्मणामनारम्भान्नैष्कर्म्यं पुरुषोऽश्नुते ।
न च सन्न्यसनादेव सिद्धिं समधिगच्छति ॥

na karmaṇām anārambhān
naiṣkarmyaṁ puruṣo 'śnute
na ca sannyasanād eva
siddhiṁ samadhigacchati

Neither by abstaining from action can one attain freedom from reaction nor attain perfection by mere renunciation.

5

न हि कश्चित्क्षणमपि जातु तिष्ठत्यकर्मकृत् ।
कार्यते ह्यवशः कर्म सर्वः प्रकृतिजैर्गुणैः ॥

na hi kaścit kṣaṇam api
jātu tiṣṭhaty akarma-kṛt
kāryate hy avaśaḥ karma
sarvaḥ prakṛti-jair guṇaiḥ

No one can remain inactive even for a fraction of a second, since the modes of nature helplessly push everyone into action.

6

कर्मेन्द्रियाणि संयम्य य आस्ते मनसा स्मरन् ।
इन्द्रियार्थान्विमूढात्मा मिथ्याचारः स उच्यते ॥

karmendriyāṇi saṁyamya
ya āste manasā smaran
indriyārthān vimūḍhātmā
mithyācāraḥ sa ucyate

A person who remains physically inactive but mentally active by contemplating on the objects of the senses, is called a hypocrite.

7

यस्त्विन्द्रियाणि मनसा नियम्यारभतेऽर्जुन ।
कर्मेन्द्रियैः कर्मयोगमसक्तः स विशिष्यते ॥

yas tv indriyāṇi manasā
niyamyārabhate 'rjuna
karmendriyaiḥ karma-yogam
asaktaḥ sa viśiṣyate

On the other hand, one who controls his senses with his mind and performs actions without any attachment to the results is by far superior.

8

नियतं कुरु कर्म त्वं कर्म ज्यायो ह्यकर्मणः ।
शरीरयात्रापि च ते न प्रसिद्ध्येदकर्मणः ॥

niyataṁ kuru karma tvaṁ
karma jyāyo hy akarmaṇaḥ
śarīra-yātrāpi ca te
na prasiddhyed akarmaṇaḥ

Therefore it is better to perform one's duty. This is much superior to not acting at all. The fact is that, one cannot even maintain one's body without work.

9

यज्ञार्थात्कर्मणोऽन्यत्र लोकोऽयं कर्मबन्धनः ।
तदर्थं कर्म कौन्तेय मुक्तसङ्गः समाचर ॥

yajñārthāt karmaṇo 'nyatra
loko 'yaṁ karma-bandhanaḥ
tad-arthaṁ karma kaunteya
mukta-saṅgaḥ samācara

Work that is performed as a sacrifice for the pleasure of Vishnu does not bind one to this world. Therefore one who carries out his assigned duties for the satisfaction of Vishnu, always remains free from the bondage of reactions.

10

सहयज्ञाः प्रजाः सृष्ट्वा पुरोवाच प्रजापतिः ।
अनेन प्रसविष्यध्वमेष वोऽस्त्विष्टकामधुक् ॥

saha-yajñāḥ prajāḥ sṛṣṭvā
purovāca prajāpatiḥ
anena prasaviṣyadhvam
eṣa vo 'stv iṣṭa-kāma-dhuk

At the beginning of creation, the creator had ordained that one could obtain everything desirable for a happy living in this world by performing work as a sacrifice for Vishnu.

11

देवान्भावयतानेन ते देवा भावयन्तु वः ।
परस्परं भावयन्तः श्रेयः परमवाप्स्यथ ॥

devān bhāvayatānena
te devā bhāvayantu vaḥ
parasparaṁ bhāvayantaḥ
śreyaḥ param avāpsyatha

By such sacrifices, one can satisfy the gods who in turn will satisfy the performers. This mutual cooperation will lead to the greatest good.

12

इष्टान्भोगान्हि वो देवा दास्यन्ते यज्ञभाविताः ।
तैर्दत्तानप्रदायैभ्यो यो भुङ्क्ते स्तेन एव सः ॥

iṣṭān bhogān hi vo devā
dāsyante yajña-bhāvitāḥ
tair dattān apradāyaibhyo
yo bhuṅkte stena eva saḥ

The satisfied gods will supply all necessities to those who nourish them by performing sacrifices. But one who has a thief mentality will not be grateful to acknowledge the gifts bestowed by the gods.

13

यज्ञशिष्टाशिनः सन्तो मुच्यन्ते सर्वकिल्बिषैः ।
भुञ्जते ते त्वघं पापा ये पचन्त्यात्मकारणात् ॥

yajña-śiṣṭāśinaḥ santo
mucyante sarva-kilbiṣaiḥ
bhuñjate te tv agham pāpā
ye pacanty ātma-kāraṇāt

A saintly person does not even eat food without first offering it to the Lord. Just by eating such purified food he is released from the sin cycle while the wicked that eat only for their enjoyment end up eating only sin.

14

अन्नाद्भवन्ति भूतानि पर्जन्यादन्नसम्भवः ।
यज्ञाद्भवति पर्जन्यो यज्ञः कर्मसमुद्भवः ॥

annād bhavanti bhūtāni
parjanyād anna-sambhavaḥ
yajñād bhavati parjanyo
yajñaḥ karma-samudbhavaḥ

Living beings survive on food grains which are in turn produced by rains. Rains are simply a product of performance of sacrifices. While sacrifices are borne as a result of carrying out assigned duties.

15

कर्म ब्रह्मोद्भवं विद्धि ब्रह्माक्षरसमुद्भवम् ।
तस्मात्सर्वगतं ब्रह्म नित्यं यज्ञे प्रतिष्ठितम् ॥

karma brahmodbhavaṁ viddhi
brahmākṣara-samudbhavam
tasmāt sarva-gataṁ brahma
nityaṁ yajñe pratiṣṭhitam

Assigned duties are those prescribed in the Vedas and the Vedas originate from the Supreme Lord. Which only means that in every act of sacrifice, the Supreme Lord himself is manifested.

16

एवं प्रवर्तितं चक्रं नानुवर्तयतीह यः ।
अघायुरिन्द्रियारामो मोघं पार्थ स जीवति ॥

evaṁ pravartitaṁ cakraṁ
nānuvartayatīha yaḥ
aghāyur indriyārāmo
moghaṁ pārtha sa jīvati

My dear Arjuna, one who fails to acknowledge and follow this divine cycle simply lives a life of indulgence, irresponsibility and sin.

17

यस्त्वात्मरतिरेव स्यादात्मतृप्तश्च मानवः ।
आत्मन्येव च सन्तुष्टस्तस्य कार्यं न विद्यते ॥

yas tv ātma-ratir eva syād
ātma-tṛptaś ca mānavaḥ
ātmany eva ca santuṣṭas
tasya kāryaṁ na vidyate

But for someone who is self-satisfied and lives a life only aimed at self-realization, for such a person there is no need to perform any assigned duties.

18

नैव तस्य कृतेनार्थो नाकृतेनेह कश्चन ।
न चास्य सर्वभूतेषु कश्चिदर्थव्यपाश्रयः ॥

naiva tasya kṛtenārtho
nākṛteneha kaścana
na cāsya sarva-bhūteṣu
kaścid artha-vyapāśrayaḥ

Such a person has nothing to gain by performing his assigned duties and nothing to lose by not performing them. In fact he depends on no one in this world.

19

तस्मादसक्तः सततं कार्यं कर्म समाचर ।
असक्तो ह्याचरन्कर्म परमाप्नोति पूरुषः ॥

tasmād asaktaḥ satataṁ
kāryaṁ karma samācara
asakto hy ācaran karma
param āpnoti pūruṣaḥ

What is recommended for you, however, is to work without attachment to the results of your action. Such action without attachment leads to attainment of perfection of the highest consciousness.

20

कर्मणैव हि संसिद्धिमास्थिता जनकादयः ।
लोकसङ्ग्रहमेवापि सम्पश्यन्कर्तुमर्हसि ॥

karmaṇaiva hi saṁsiddhim
āsthitā janakādayaḥ
loka-saṅgraham evāpi
sampaśyan kartum arhasi

Many kings in the past like King Janaka have followed this path of performing assigned duties without attachment to results and have attained perfection of their lives. You should also take up this path to set a standard that the world can follow.

21

यद्यदाचरति श्रेष्ठस्तत्तदेवेतरो जनः ।
स यत्प्रमाणं कुरुते लोकस्तदनुवर्तते ॥

yad yad ācarati śreṣṭhas
tat tad evetaro janaḥ
sa yat pramāṇaṁ kurute
lokas tad anuvartate

Whatever a great man does, common men emulate. Whatever standards he sets, becomes a worldwide trend.

22

न मे पार्थास्ति कर्तव्यं त्रिषु लोकेषु किञ्चन ।
नानवाप्तमवाप्तव्यं वर्त एव च कर्मणि ॥

na me pārthāsti kartavyaṁ
triṣu lokeṣu kiñcana
nānavāptam avāptavyaṁ
varta eva ca karmaṇi

Look at Me! Though there is no duty prescribed for Me within the three worlds and neither am I in want of anything, I still engage in carrying out My assigned duties.

23

यदि ह्यहं न वर्तेयं जातु कर्मण्यतन्द्रितः ।
मम वर्त्मानुवर्तन्ते मनुष्याः पार्थ सर्वशः ॥

yadi hy ahaṁ na varteyaṁ
jātu karmaṇy atandritaḥ
mama vartmānuvartante
manuṣyāḥ pārtha sarvaśaḥ

Because I know that if I fail in carrying out My duties, people will use My example as an excuse to abandon their duties.

24

उत्सीदेयुरिमे लोका न कुर्यां कर्म चेदहम् ।
सङ्करस्य च कर्ता स्यामुपहन्यामिमा: प्रजा: ॥

utsīdeyur ime lokā
na kuryāṁ karma ced aham
saṅkarasya ca kartā syām
upahanyām imāḥ prajāḥ

By not setting the right standards, I will be responsible for chaos in this world.

25

सक्ता: कर्मण्यविद्वांसो यथा कुर्वन्ति भारत ।
कुर्याद्विद्वांस्तथासक्तश्चिकीर्षुर्लोकसङ्ग्रहम् ॥

saktāḥ karmaṇy avidvāṁso
yathā kurvanti bhārata
kuryād vidvāṁs tathāsaktaś
cikīrṣur loka-saṅgraham

While the ignorant carry out their duties with attachment to results, the intelligent are expected to perform their duties with no such attachment, just to set the right trend for this world to follow.

26

न बुद्धिभेदं जनयेदज्ञानां कर्मसङ्गिनाम् ।
जोषयेत्सर्वकर्माणि विद्वान्युक्तः समाचरन् ॥

na buddhi-bhedaṁ janayed
ajñānāṁ karma-saṅginām
joṣayet sarva-karmāṇi
vidvān yuktaḥ samācaran

Do not mislead the minds of the ignorant that are attached to the results of their duties. Rather than inspiring them to give up their duties, you should be inspiring them to carry out their duties without attachment to results.

27

प्रकृतेः क्रियमाणानि गुणैः कर्माणि सर्वशः ।
अहङ्कारविमूढात्मा कर्ताहमिति मन्यते ॥

prakṛteḥ kriyamāṇāni
guṇaiḥ karmāṇi sarvaśaḥ
ahaṅkāra-vimūḍhātmā
kartāham iti manyate

An ignorant person influenced by the false ego works thinking that he is the doer of the action which in reality is carried out by the three modes of material nature.

28

तत्त्ववित्तु महाबाहो गुणकर्मविभागयोः ।
गुणा गुणेषु वर्तन्त इति मत्वा न सज्जते ॥

tattva-vit tu mahā-bāho
guṇa-karma-vibhāgayoḥ
guṇā guṇeṣu vartanta
iti matvā na sajjate

A knowledgeable person knows very well the influence of the three modes of nature on one's actions. He knows very well the difference between work done in spirit of devotion and work done with expectation of results.

29

प्रकृतेर्गुणसम्मूढाः सज्जन्ते गुणकर्मसु ।
तानकृत्स्नविदो मन्दान्कृत्स्नविन्न विचालयेत् ॥

prakṛter guṇa-saṁmūḍhāḥ
sajjante guṇa-karmasu
tān akṛtsna-vido mandān
kṛtsna-vin na vicālayet

Under the influence of the modes of nature, ignorant persons are absorbed in mundane action. The wise do not venture into disturbing these ignorant fools.

30

मयि सर्वाणि कर्माणि सन्न्यस्याध्यात्मचेतसा ।
निराशीर्निर्ममो भूत्वा युध्यस्व विगतज्वरः ॥

mayi sarvāṇi karmāṇi
sannyasyādhyātma-cetasā
nirāśīr nirmamo bhūtvā
yudhyasva vigata-jvaraḥ

Therefore offer all your work to Me, with complete knowledge of Me, without any desire for results, without claiming any ownership and without being lethargic. In this spirit, fight, Arjuna.

31

ये मे मतमिदं नित्यमनुतिष्ठन्ति मानवाः ।
श्रद्धावन्तोऽनसूयन्तो मुच्यन्ते तेऽपि कर्मभिः ॥

ye me matam idaṁ nityam
anutiṣṭhanti mānavāḥ
śraddhāvanto 'nasūyanto
mucyante te 'pi karmabhiḥ

Those who follow My proposed principles with full faith and without envy, attain freedom from reactions.

32

ये त्वेतदभ्यसूयन्तो नानुतिष्ठन्ति मे मतम् ।
सर्वज्ञानविमूढांस्तान्विद्धि नष्टानचेतस: ॥

ye tv etad abhyasūyanto
nānutiṣṭhanti me matam
sarva-jñāna-vimūḍhāṁs tān
viddhi naṣṭān acetasaḥ

Those who disregard My teachings out of envy, do not achieve perfection and are lost on their path.

33

सदृशं चेष्टते स्वस्या: प्रकृतेर्ज्ञानवानपि ।
प्रकृतिं यान्ति भूतानि निग्रह: किं करिष्यति ॥

sadṛśaṁ ceṣṭate svasyāḥ
prakṛter jñānavān api
prakṛtiṁ yānti bhūtāni
nigrahah kiṁ kariṣyati

Even wise people act according to the nature they have acquired by the influence of the three modes. Therefore one should never try to suppress one's inner nature.

34

इन्द्रियस्येन्द्रियस्यार्थे रागद्वेषौ व्यवस्थितौ ।
तयोर्न वशमागच्छेत्तौ ह्यस्य परिपन्थिनौ ॥

indriyasyendriyasyārthe
rāga-dveṣau vyavasthitau
tayor na vaśam āgacchet
tau hy asya paripanthinau

Both attachment and aversion are obstacles on the path of progress. The senses get attached to mundane things and are averse to spiritual teachings. One desiring progress should not come under the influence of either.

35

श्रेयान्स्वधर्मो विगुणः परधर्मात्स्वनुष्ठितात् ।
स्वधर्मे निधनं श्रेयः परधर्मो भयावहः ॥

śreyān sva-dharmo viguṇaḥ
para-dharmāt sva-nuṣṭhitāt
sva-dharme nidhanaṁ śreyaḥ
para-dharmo bhayāvahaḥ

It is more beneficial to perform one's assigned duty imperfectly than to perform another's duty perfectly.

Destruction in the course of discharging one's own duty is beneficial whereas there are dangers on the path of performing another's duty.

36

अर्जुन उवाच
अथ केन प्रयुक्तोऽयं पापं चरति पूरुषः ।
अनिच्छन्नपि वार्ष्णेय बलादिव नियोजितः ॥

arjuna uvāca
atha kena prayukto 'yaṁ
pāpaṁ carati pūruṣaḥ
anicchann api vārṣṇeya
balād iva niyojitaḥ

Arjuna said –
What influences one to act wrongly even though unwilling as if by force?

37

श्रीभगवानुवाच
काम एष क्रोध एष रजोगुणसमुद्भवः ।
महाशनो महापाप्मा विद्ध्येनमिह वैरिणम् ॥

śrī-bhagavān uvāca
kāma eṣa krodha eṣa

rajo-guṇa-samudbhavaḥ
mahā-śano mahā-pāpmā
viddhy enam iha vairiṇam

Sri Bhagavan said –
It is lust that is borne of the mode of passion that eventually morphs into anger, the greatest enemy of the world.

38

धूमेनाव्रियते वह्निर्यथादर्शो मलेन च ।
यथोल्बेनावृतो गर्भस्तथा तेनेदमावृतम् ॥

dhūmenāvriyate vahnir
yathādarśo malena ca
yatholbenāvṛto garbhas
tathā tenedam āvṛtam

Just like fire is enveloped by smoke, a mirror is covered by dust and an embryo is sealed by a womb, similarly a person is covered by varying degrees of this lust.

39

आवृतं ज्ञानमेतेन ज्ञानिनो नित्यवैरिणा ।
कामरूपेण कौन्तेय दुष्पूरेणानलेन च ॥

āvṛtaṁ jñānam etena
jñānino nitya-vairiṇā
kāma-rūpeṇa kaunteya
duṣpūreṇānalena ca

Even the pure consciousness of a knowledgeable person is covered by this lust, which is insatiable and burns uncontrollably like fire.

40

इन्द्रियाणि मनो बुद्धिरस्याधिष्ठानमुच्यते ।
एतैर्विमोहयत्येष ज्ञानमावृत्य देहिनम् ॥

indriyāṇi mano buddhir
asyādhiṣṭhānam ucyate
etair vimohayaty eṣa
jñānam āvṛtya dehinam

The senses, mind and intelligence are the strategic places where lust is seated from which it influences the soul, bewilders and covers the wisdom.

41

तस्मात्त्वमिन्द्रियाण्यादौ नियम्य भरतर्षभ ।
पाप्मानं प्रजहि ह्येनं ज्ञानविज्ञाननाशनम् ॥

tasmāt tvam indriyāṇy ādau
niyamya bharatarṣabha
pāpmānaṁ prajahi hy enaṁ
jñāna-vijñāna-nāśanam

Regulating the senses right in the beginning is the wisest way of killing this enemy of knowledge and self-realization.

42

इन्द्रियाणि पराण्याहुरिन्द्रियेभ्यः परं मनः ।
मनसस्तु परा बुद्धिर्यो बुद्धेः परतस्तु सः ॥

indriyāṇi parāṇy āhur
indriyebhyaḥ paraṁ manaḥ
manasas tu parā buddhir
yo buddheḥ paratas tu saḥ

The senses are superior to matter; the mind is higher than the senses; the intelligence is much higher than the mind; and the soul is much more superior to even intelligence.

43

एवं बुद्धेः परं बुद्ध्वा संस्तभ्यात्मानमात्मना ।
जहि शत्रुं महाबाहो कामरूपं दुरासदम् ॥

evaṁ buddheḥ paraṁ buddhvā
saṁstabhyātmānam ātmanā
jahi śatruṁ mahā-bāho
kāma-rūpaṁ durāsadam

Knowing oneself to be superior to intellect, control the mind using the intellect. In this way, by deliberate intelligence conquer the insatiable enemy known as lust.

Chapter 04

Jnana Karma Sannyasa Yoga

Krishna reveals that he had earlier spoken this timeless wisdom of yoga to Vivasvan, the sun god, who in turn shared it with Manu, and Manu disseminated it to Ikshvaku. Through disciplic succession of a chain of saintly kings this supreme science was preserved unbroken. But under the influence of time, this knowledge had been lost. And today he was once again sharing the lost ancient science of yoga with Arjuna who was well qualified to understand that secret science being his devotee and friend.

A baffled Arjuna enquires how is it possible for Krishna to instruct Vivasvan as Vivasvan was born much before Krishna.

Krishna explains that both Arjuna and he himself have taken birth many times in the past. The only difference between them was that Krishna remembers each birth, whereas Arjuna does not.

Krishna, out of his own will, chooses to appear in this world in every millennium, as and when righteousness declines and unrighteousness reaches a pinnacle. He himself appears to protect the saintly people, eliminate the evil ones and reestablish *dharma*. Those who understand his transcendental birth and activities get purified; are freed from attachment, greed and fear; attain perfection; and do not take another birth again, attaining his eternal abode.

Krishna shares with Arjuna how he reciprocates. His reciprocation depending on how he is approached. Those who seek success prefer to approach demigods to obtain quick results. Ultimately whether one approaches Krishna directly or via demigods indirectly, everyone reaches some form of Krishna himself.

He also clarifies that he has created the four divisions of human society according to people's qualities and activities. Though he created the system, he is not part of it. He is neither affected by any work in this world nor is he interested in the results of work. One who understands this truth does not get bound by the reactions of his own actions. Liberated souls in the past who understood this, engaged in action and therefore Arjuna should also act in their footsteps in *parampara*.

Krishna then explains what is action and what is inaction, a highly confusing subject matter. There is right action (*karma*) and then there is wrong action (*vikarma*) and lastly there is inaction (*akarma*). Inaction can free one from reactions whereas inappropriate inaction can result in sinful reactions. Even learned people in the past have tried to understand this concept in an effort to get liberated from negativity.

Inaction or *akarma* is difficult to understand. Though externally doing a lot of action, a person who has no attachment to the results of action, who is always satisfied and not dependent on others, is considered to be doing nothing at all (*akarma*).

He works without desires to enjoy the results of action; in the fire of knowledge he burns the reactions of all his actions. Without a sense of proprietorship, he incurs no reaction for his actions. Content with what comes of its own accord, free from envy and unaffected by success or failure; he is not bound by reactions of his actions. An unattached liberated soul absorbed in knowledge; he does not accrue reactions for his actions.

Such a yogi, fully absorbed in higher activities, attains the spiritual kingdom because his actions are completely spiritual. Some yogis worship the demigods by offering sacrifices to them; celibate students sacrifice by constantly hearing the glories of lord with a controlled mind; the regulated householders sacrifice desires; the controlled yogis sacrifice their life for self-realization through modes of charity, austerity, eight-fold yogic process and the study of Vedas.

The result of such sacrificial performance purifies them from sinful reactions of their actions and leads them to attain the eternal spiritual abode. Those who do not perform sacrifices can never be happy either in this life or the next.

All these sacrifices, approved by the Vedas, stem from different types of actions of the body, mind and words and lead to liberation. Of them, sacrifice based on knowledge is superior to sacrifice based on giving up material possessions because all sacrifices of work culminate in divine knowledge.

To acquire this divine knowledge, Krishna explains further, one begins by approaching a bonafide spiritual master with humility. With genuine desire to enquire submissively and by rendering service unto him, one can please the spiritual master. Self-realized souls then impart this knowledge because they have seen the truth. By dint of this knowledge one learns that each and every living being is a part of God.

The material world is an ocean of miseries and this knowledge serves as a boat that even the most sinful of the sinners can use to cross over. Like fire reduces wood to ashes, this divine knowledge burns away all reactions of actions performed in this world.

A person who acquires this knowledge with faith achieves success in his efforts and attains supreme peace. The faithless and doubting souls experience happiness or success neither in this world nor in the next and eventually perish.

Once again Krishna appeals to Arjuna to use the sword of knowledge to slash the doubts that have arisen in his heart out of ignorance. He inspires him to stand up and fight by understanding the science of action.

1

श्रीभगवानुवाच
इमं विवस्वते योगं प्रोक्तवानहमव्ययम् ।
विवस्वान्मनवे प्राह मनुरिक्ष्वाकवेऽब्रवीत् ॥

śrī-bhagavān uvāca
imaṁ vivasvate yogaṁ
proktavān aham avyayam
vivasvān manave prāha
manur ikṣvākave 'bravīt

Sri Bhagavan said –
Previously I spoke this timeless wisdom of yoga to Vivasvan, the Sun God, who in turn shared it with Manu and Manu disseminated it to Ikshvaku.

2

एवं परम्पराप्राप्तमिमं राजर्षयो विदु: ।
स कालेनेह महता योगो नष्ट: परन्तप ॥

evaṁ paramparā-prāptam
imaṁ rājarṣayo viduḥ
sa kāleneha mahatā
yogo naṣṭaḥ parantapa

This knowledge was passed down through a chain of saintly kings and thus this supreme science was preserved by an unbroken disciplic succession. But under the influence of time, this knowledge has been lost.

3

स एवायं मया तेऽद्य योगः प्रोक्तः पुरातनः ।
भक्तोऽसि मे सखा चेति रहस्यं ह्येतदुत्तमम् ॥

sa evāyaṁ mayā te 'dya
yogaḥ proktaḥ purātanaḥ
bhakto 'si me sakhā ceti
rahasyaṁ hy etad uttamam

Today I'm sharing with you that lost ancient science of yoga because you are My devotee as well as a friend and you are thus qualified to understand that secret science.

4

अर्जुन उवाच
अपरं भवतो जन्म परं जन्म विवस्वतः ।
कथमेतद्विजानीयां त्वमादौ प्रोक्तवानिति ॥

arjuna uvāca
aparaṁ bhavato janma

paraṁ janma vivasvataḥ
katham etad vijānīyāṁ
tvam ādau proktavān iti

Arjuna said –
When I know for a fact that you were born much after Vivasvan, how do you expect me to believe that you instructed him in this ancient science?

5

श्रीभगवानुवाच
बहूनि मे व्यतीतानि जन्मानि तव चार्जुन ।
तान्यहं वेद सर्वाणि न त्वं वेत्थ परन्तप ॥

śrī-bhagavān uvāca
bahūni me vyatītāni
janmāni tava cārjuna
tāny ahaṁ veda sarvāṇi
na tvaṁ vettha parantapa

Sri Bhagavan said –
Arjuna, know for a fact that both you and Me have taken birth many times in the past. The only difference between us is that I remember each of our birth, whereas you don't remember the past.

6

अजोऽपि सन्नव्ययात्मा भूतानामीश्वरोऽपि सन् ।
प्रकृतिं स्वामधिष्ठाय सम्भवाम्यात्ममायया ॥

ajo 'pi sann avyayātmā
bhūtānām īśvaro 'pi san
prakṛtiṁ svām adhiṣṭhāya
sambhavāmy ātma-māyayā

Though I appear in this world in every millennium, understand that I am birth less and that My body is non material and imperishable. Know Me to be the master of all living beings and I appear by the dint of My own energies.

7

यदा यदा हि धर्मस्य ग्लानिर्भवति भारत ।
अभ्युत्थानमधर्मस्य तदात्मानं सृजाम्यहम् ॥

yadā yadā hi dharmasya
glānir bhavati bhārata
abhyutthānam adharmasya
tadātmānaṁ sṛjāmy aham

Whenever and wherever righteousness declines and unrighteousness drastically rises, I appear.

8

परित्राणाय साधूनां विनाशाय च दुष्कृताम् ।
धर्मसंस्थापनार्थाय सम्भवामि युगे युगे ॥

paritrāṇāya sādhūnāṁ
vināśāya ca duṣkṛtām
dharma-saṁsthāpanārthāya
sambhavāmi yuge yuge

In order to protect the saintly people, eliminate the evil ones and reestablish the higher principles, I Myself appear millennium after millennium.

9

जन्म कर्म च मे दिव्यमेवं यो वेत्ति तत्त्वतः ।
त्यक्त्वा देहं पुनर्जन्म नैति मामेति सोऽर्जुन ॥

janma karma ca me divyam
evaṁ yo vetti tattvataḥ
tyaktvā dehaṁ punar janma
naiti mām eti so 'rjuna

My birth and activities are divine. Anyone who understands just this, does not take another birth again but rather attains My eternal abode.

10

वीतरागभयक्रोधा मन्मया मामुपाश्रिताः ।
बहवो ज्ञानतपसा पूता मद्भावमागताः ॥

vīta-rāga-bhaya-krodhā
man-mayā mām upāśritāḥ
bahavo jñāna-tapasā
pūtā mad-bhāvam āgatāḥ

Giving up attachments, fear and anger, being absorbed in Me, while taking full shelter of Me, many people in the past have been purified by the fire of knowledge of Me and attained perfection of love for Me.

11

ये यथा मां प्रपद्यन्ते तांस्तथैव भजाम्यहम् ।
मम वर्त्मानुवर्तन्ते मनुष्याः पार्थ सर्वशः ॥

ye yathā māṁ prapadyante
tāṁs tathaiva bhajāmy aham
mama vartmānuvartante
manuṣyāḥ pārtha sarvaśaḥ

Depending on the way in which people approach Me, I reciprocate accordingly. Everyone ultimately follows My path only.

12

काङ्क्षन्तः कर्मणां सिद्धिं यजन्त इह देवताः ।
क्षिप्रं हि मानुषे लोके सिद्धिर्भवति कर्मजा ॥

kāṅkṣantaḥ karmaṇāṁ siddhiṁ
yajanta iha devatāḥ
kṣipraṁ hi mānuṣe loke
siddhir bhavati karma-jā

Those who seek success in their efforts prefer to approach the demigods through the process of sacrifices. Such people experience quick results from such worship.

13

चातुर्वर्ण्यं मया सृष्टं गुणकर्मविभागशः ।
तस्य कर्तारमपि मां विद्ध्यकर्तारमव्ययम् ॥

cātur-varṇyaṁ mayā sṛṣṭaṁ
guṇa-karma-vibhāgaśaḥ
tasya kartāram api māṁ
viddhy akartāram avyayam

I created the four divisions of human society to be implemented according to people's qualities and activities. Though I am the creator of the system, I am not responsible for the results obtained by it, as I am transcendental to it.

14

न मां कर्माणि लिम्पन्ति न मे कर्मफले स्पृहा ।
इति मां योऽभिजानाति कर्मभिर्न स बध्यते ॥

na māṁ karmāṇi limpanti
na me karma-phale spṛhā
iti māṁ yo 'bhijānāti
karmabhir na sa badhyate

Neither any work in this world affects Me nor am I interested in the results of work. Anyone who understands this truth about Me does not get bound by the reactions of his own actions.

15

एवं ज्ञात्वा कृतं कर्म पूर्वैरपि मुमुक्षुभिः ।
कुरु कर्मैव तस्मात्त्वं पूर्वैः पूर्वतरं कृतम् ॥

evaṁ jñātvā kṛtaṁ karma
pūrvair api mumukṣubhiḥ
kuru karmaiva tasmāt tvaṁ
pūrvaiḥ pūrvataraṁ kṛtam

Liberated souls in the past who knew this, engaged in action and therefore you should also act according to your duties following in their footsteps.

16

किं कर्म किमकर्मेति कवयोऽप्यत्र मोहिताः ।
तत्ते कर्म प्रवक्ष्यामि यज्ज्ञात्वा मोक्ष्यसेऽशुभात् ॥

kiṁ karma kim akarmeti
kavayo 'py atra mohitāḥ
tat te karma pravakṣyāmi
yaj jñātvā mokṣyase 'śubhāt

What is action and what is inaction is a highly confusing subject matter. Even learned people in the past pondered in confusion on this subject. I will now clearly explain the concept of action, which will liberate you from negativity.

17

कर्मणो ह्यपि बोद्धव्यं बोद्धव्यं च विकर्मणः ।
अकर्मणश्च बोद्धव्यं गहना कर्मणो गतिः ॥

karmaṇo hy api boddhavyaṁ
boddhavyaṁ ca vikarmaṇaḥ
akarmaṇaś ca boddhavyaṁ
gahanā karmaṇo gatiḥ

One must endeavor to understand clearly what right action (*karma*) is, what wrong action (*vikarma*) is and what inaction (*akarma*) is. Accurately understanding these concepts is extremely difficult.

18

कर्मण्यकर्म यः पश्येदकर्मणि च कर्म यः ।
स बुद्धिमान्मनुष्येषु स युक्तः कृत्स्नकर्मकृत् ॥

karmaṇy akarma yaḥ paśyed
akarmaṇi ca karma yaḥ
sa buddhimān manuṣyeṣu
sa yuktaḥ kṛtsna-karma-kṛt

A person who is spiritually evolved can perceive inaction in action and action in inaction. Such a discerning person performs all types of actions.

19

यस्य सर्वे समारम्भा: कामसङ्कल्पवर्जिता: ।
ज्ञानाग्निदग्धकर्माणं तमाहु: पण्डितं बुधा: ॥

yasya sarve samārambhāḥ
kāma-saṅkalpa-varjitāḥ
jñānāgni-dagdha-karmāṇaṁ
tam āhuḥ paṇḍitaṁ budhāḥ

Keeping aside desires to enjoy the results of action, the one who performs his actions in knowledge, such a person is considered to be wise. The fire of knowledge burns up the reactions to all his actions.

20

त्यक्त्वा कर्मफलासङ्गं नित्यतृप्तो निराश्रय: ।
कर्मण्यभिप्रवृत्तोऽपि नैव किञ्चित्करोति स: ॥

tyaktvā karma-phalāsaṅgaṁ
nitya-tṛpto nirāśrayaḥ
karmaṇy abhipravṛtto 'pi
naiva kiñcit karoti saḥ

Though externally doing a lot of action, a person who has no attachment to the results of action, who is always satisfied and not dependent on others, is considered to be doing nothing at all.

21

निराशीर्यतचित्तात्मा त्यक्तसर्वपरिग्रहः ।
शारीरं केवलं कर्म कुर्वन्नाप्नोति किल्बिषम् ॥

nirāśīr yata-cittātmā
tyakta-sarva-parigrahaḥ
śārīraṁ kevalaṁ karma
kurvan nāpnoti kilbiṣam

When a person acts with spiritually disciplined intelligence and without a sense of proprietorship, he incurs no reaction for his actions.

22

यदृच्छालाभसन्तुष्टो द्वन्द्वातीतो विमत्सरः ।
समः सिद्धावसिद्धौ च कृत्वापि न निबध्यते ॥

yadṛcchā-lābha-santuṣṭo
dvandvātīto vimatsaraḥ
samaḥ siddhāv asiddhau ca
kṛtvāpi na nibadhyate

A person who is content with what comes of its own accord, who is free from dualities and envy and who is unaffected by success or failure, is not bound by reactions of his actions.

23

गतसङ्गस्य मुक्तस्य ज्ञानावस्थितचेतसः ।
यज्ञायाचरतः कर्म समग्रं प्रविलीयते ॥

gata-saṅgasya muktasya
jñānāvasthita-cetasaḥ
yajñāyācarataḥ karma
samagraṁ pravilīyate

An unattached liberated soul who is absorbed in knowledge and whose every action is a sacrifice, does not accrue reactions for his actions.

24

ब्रह्मार्पणं ब्रह्म हविर्ब्रह्माग्नौ ब्रह्मणा हुतम् ।
ब्रह्मैव तेन गन्तव्यं ब्रह्मकर्मसमाधिना ॥

brahmārpaṇaṁ brahma havir
brahmāgnau brahmaṇā hutam
brahmaiva tena gantavyaṁ
brahma-karma-samādhinā

A person who is fully absorbed in higher activities will attain the spiritual kingdom because his actions are completely spiritual.

25

दैवमेवापरे यज्ञं योगिनः पर्युपासते ।
ब्रह्माग्नावपरे यज्ञं यज्ञेनैवोपजुह्वति ॥

daivam evāpare yajñaṁ
yoginaḥ paryupāsate
brahmāgnāv apare yajñaṁ
yajñenaivopajuhvati

Some yogis prefer to worship the demigods by offering sacrifices to them and yet others prefer to offer themselves in the fire of knowledge.

26

श्रोत्रादीनीन्द्रियाण्यन्ये संयमाग्निषु जुह्वति ।
शब्दादीन्विषयानन्य इन्द्रियाग्निषु जुह्वति ॥

śrotrādīnīndriyāṇy anye
saṁyamāgniṣu juhvati
śabdādīn viṣayān anya
indriyāgniṣu juhvati

The celibate students sacrifice their sense of hearing into the fire of the controlled mind. While the regulated householders sacrifice the sense objects into the fire of the senses.

27

सर्वाणीन्द्रियकर्माणि प्राणकर्माणि चापरे ।
आत्मसंयमयोगाग्नौ जुह्वति ज्ञानदीपिते ॥

sarvāṇīndriya-karmāṇi
prāṇa-karmāṇi cāpare
ātma-saṁyama-yogāgnau
juhvati jñāna-dīpite

The controlled yogis sacrifice their senses and life breath into the fire of the controlled mind.

28

द्रव्ययज्ञास्तपोयज्ञा योगयज्ञास्तथापरे ।
स्वाध्यायज्ञानयज्ञाश्च यतयः संशितव्रताः ॥

dravya-yajñās tapo-yajñā
yoga-yajñās tathāpare
svādhyāya-jñāna-yajñāś ca
yatayaḥ saṁśita-vratāḥ

Yet others perform sacrifices through modes of charity, austerity, eight-fold yogic process and the study of Vedas.

29

अपाने जुह्वति प्राणं प्राणेऽपानं तथापरे ।
प्राणापानगती रुद्ध्वा प्राणायामपरायणाः ।
अपरे नियताहाराः प्राणान्प्राणेषु जुह्वति ॥

apāne juhvati prāṇaṁ
prāṇe 'pānaṁ tathāpare
prāṇāpāna-gatī ruddhvā
prāṇāyāma-parāyaṇāḥ
apare niyatāhārāḥ
prāṇān prāṇeṣu juhvati

Some perform sacrifices through the breathing process by offering the outgoing breath into the incoming and the incoming breath into the outgoing and eventually stop breathing totally. And yet others perform sacrifices by controlling the eating process.

30

सर्वेऽप्येते यज्ञविदो यज्ञक्षपितकल्मषाः ।
यज्ञशिष्टामृतभुजो यान्ति ब्रह्म सनातनम् ॥

sarve 'py ete yajña-vido
yajña-kṣapita-kalmaṣāḥ
yajña-śiṣṭāmṛta-bhujo
yānti brahma sanātanam

Being mindful of the essence of the sacrifices and actually performing them, these personalities purify themselves of any sinful reactions associated with their actions. The result of such sacrificial performance leads them to attain the eternal spiritual abode.

31

नायं लोकोऽस्त्ययज्ञस्य कुतोऽन्य: कुरुसत्तम ॥

nāyaṁ loko 'sty ayajñasya
kuto 'nyaḥ kuru-sattama

Know for sure that anyone who does not perform sacrifices will never be happy either in this life or the next.

32

एवं बहुविधा यज्ञा वितता ब्रह्मणो मुखे ।
कर्मजान्विद्धि तान्सर्वानेवं ज्ञात्वा विमोक्ष्यसे ॥

evaṁ bahu-vidhā yajñā
vitatā brahmaṇo mukhe
karma-jān viddhi tān sarvān
evaṁ jñātvā vimokṣyase

All these sacrifices that are approved by the Vedas stem from different types of works or actions of the body, mind and words. Just knowing them is good enough for liberation.

33

श्रेयान्द्रव्यमयाद्यज्ञाज्ज्ञानयज्ञ: परन्तप ।
सर्वं कर्माखिलं पार्थ ज्ञाने परिसमाप्यते ॥

śreyān dravya-mayād yajñāj
jñāna-yajñaḥ parantapa
sarvaṁ karmākhilaṁ pārtha
jñāne parisamāpyate

Of the plethora of sacrifices possible, the sacrifice based on knowledge is superior to sacrifice based on giving up material possessions. This is because all sacrifices of work culminate in divine knowledge.

34

तद्विद्धि प्रणिपातेन परिप्रश्नेन सेवया ।
उपदेक्ष्यन्ति ते ज्ञानं ज्ञानिनस्तत्त्वदर्शिन: ॥

tad viddhi praṇipātena
paripraśnena sevayā

upadekṣyanti te jñānaṁ
jñāninas tattva-darśinaḥ

The steps to acquire this divine knowledge include approaching a bonafide spiritual master with genuine humility, inquiring submissively from him and rendering service unto him. Self-realized souls can easily impart this knowledge to anyone because they have seen the truth.

35

यज्ज्ञात्वा न पुनर्मोहमेवं यास्यसि पाण्डव ।
येन भूतान्यशेषाणि द्रक्ष्यस्यात्मन्यथो मयि ॥

yaj jñātvā na punar moham
evaṁ yāsyasi pāṇḍava
yena bhūtāny aśeṣāṇi
drakṣyasy ātmany atho mayi

When one acquires real knowledge from a self-realized soul, one will never be bewildered again. By dint of this knowledge one will be able to see clearly that each and every living being is a part of Me and is Mine.

36

अपि चेदसि पापेभ्यः सर्वेभ्यः पापकृत्तमः ।
सर्वं ज्ञानप्लवेनैव वृजिनं सन्तरिष्यसि ॥

api ced asi pāpebhyaḥ
sarvebhyaḥ pāpa-kṛt-tamaḥ
sarvaṁ jñāna-plavenaiva
vṛjinaṁ santariṣyasi

This divine knowledge is like a boat that even the most sinful of the sinners can use to cross over the ocean of miseries.

37

यथैधांसि समिद्धोऽग्निर्भस्मसात्कुरुतेऽर्जुन ।
ज्ञानाग्निः सर्वकर्माणि भस्मसात्कुरुते तथा ॥

yathaidhāṁsi samiddho 'gnir
bhasma-sāt kurute 'rjuna
jñānāgniḥ sarva-karmāṇi
bhasma-sāt kurute tathā

Like fire reduces wood to ashes, this divine knowledge burns away all reactions of actions performed in this world.

38

न हि ज्ञानेन सदृशं पवित्रमिह विद्यते ।
तत्स्वयं योगसंसिद्धः कालेनात्मनि विन्दति ॥

na hi jñānena sadṛśaṁ
pavitram iha vidyate
tat svayaṁ yoga-saṁsiddhaḥ
kālenātmani vindati

This knowledge is the purest thing in this world and is the realized wisdom of mystics and those who are perfect in the practice of yoga.

39

श्रद्धावाँल्लभते ज्ञानं तत्परः संयतेन्द्रियः ।
ज्ञानं लब्ध्वा परां शान्तिमचिरेणाधिगच्छति ॥

śraddhāvāl labhate jñānaṁ
tat-paraḥ saṁyatendriyaḥ
jñānaṁ labdhvā parāṁ śāntim
acireṇādhigacchati

A person who with great faith and controlled senses dedicates himself to acquire this knowledge achieves success in his efforts and as a result attains supreme peace.

40

अज्ञश्चाश्रद्दधानश्च संशयात्मा विनश्यति ।
नायं लोकोऽस्ति न परो न सुखं संशयात्मनः ॥

ajñaś cāśraddadhānaś ca
saṁśayātmā vinaśyati
nāyaṁ loko 'sti na paro
na sukhaṁ saṁśayātmanaḥ

The ignorant, faithless and doubting souls experience happiness or success neither in this world nor in the next and eventually perish.

41

योगसन्न्यस्तकर्माणं ज्ञानसञ्छिन्नसंशयम् ।
आत्मवन्तं न कर्माणि निबध्नन्ति धनञ्जय ॥

yoga-sannyasta-karmāṇaṁ
jñāna-sañchinna-saṁśayam
ātmavantaṁ na karmāṇi
nibadhnanti dhanañjaya

The one who acts while renouncing the results of his action and whose doubts are allayed on the strength of divine knowledge, is considered to be a self-realized soul. Such a person is never bound by the reactions of his work.

42

तस्मादज्ञानसम्भूतं हृत्स्थं ज्ञानासिनात्मनः ।
छित्त्वैनं संशयं योगमातिष्ठोत्तिष्ठ भारत ॥

tasmād ajñāna-sambhūtaṁ
hṛt-sthaṁ jñānāsinātmanaḥ
chittvainaṁ saṁśayaṁ yogam
ātiṣṭhottiṣṭha bhārata

Using the sword of knowledge, slash the doubts that have arisen in your heart out of ignorance. Understanding the science of action, stand up and fight, O descendant of Bharata.

Chapter

05

Karma Sannyasa Yoga

After hearing Krishna's exhaustive explanations, Arjuna still does not have clarity on what he is supposed to do. Krishna has confused him by simultaneously appreciating both: renouncing action to focus on gaining knowledge and working with no attachment to result. He asks which of the two is better?

Krishna replies that both lead to the highest perfection. But of the two, selfless work or working with no attachment to results is better. He who is greedy for the results of his actions gets entangled in reactions of his actions. One who is neither averse to nor desires the results of action is actually considered renounced. Results acquired by following the process of gaining knowledge can also be obtained by the process of detached work.

Krishna warns Arjuna that there are pitfalls in renouncing action without appropriate understanding and practice. On the other hand, when a person in knowledge engages himself in detached work, he very quickly achieves the perfection of his life. He who offers the results of all his activities to God attains lasting peace.

Such a person is never entangled even though he is always working. He understands very well that in all his activities, be it seeing, hearing, touching, eating, breathing, talking, or even blinking the eyes, he does nothing at all. Like a lotus leaf untouched by water, he is never affected by the sins of those actions. Such a *karma yogi* acts with his body, mind, intelligence and senses, only to get purified.

One whose intelligence, mind and faith are fixed on the Lord taking complete shelter of Him, his ignorance is washed away by knowledge. Just like the sun lights up everything, knowledge destroys ignorance and reveals everything. Such a person is on the path to liberation and never takes birth again.

While mentally detached, the soul stays joyfully in the body, the city of nine gates, which are two eyes, two nostrils, two ears, one mouth, the anus and genitals. Whereas the bewildered soul forgetting its own spiritual identity, is conditioned by the three modes of material nature and acts under their influence. The Supreme Lord is thus not responsible for a living being's sinful or pious activities.

A truly knowledgeable person is characterized by humility and sees the same spirit soul in a *brahmana*, a cow, an elephant or a dog. Being impartial, perceiving everyone with an equal vision, he is considered to have conquered the cycle of birth and death.

He neither rejoices nor laments for material gains or losses. He remains undisturbed with a stable intelligence in knowledge of his spiritual identity. Not attracted to external pleasures for sense gratification, he explores joy within. Absorption in the Supreme Lord within brings him great happiness.

Happiness derived by fulfilling sensual desires with sense objects is actually temporary leading to misery; because that happiness has a beginning as well as an end. The wise therefore do not seek such happiness.

Happiest in the world is one who can live by tolerating the urges of the senses and the forces of desires and anger. Those self-realized saintly people, who have full control over their minds being free from anger and material desire, who find satisfaction within, happiness and enlightenment within, and not in matter, such self-realized yogis ultimately attain liberation.

And finally Krishna gives Arjuna a three-legged peace formula—one who remembers that Krishna is the enjoyer of all sacrifices and austerities, Krishna is the absolute controller of all the worlds and Krishna is the dearest well-wishing friend of all living beings, he attains peace.

1

अर्जुन उवाच
सन्न्यासं कर्मणां कृष्ण पुनर्योगं च शंससि ।
यच्छ्रेय एतयोरेकं तन्मे ब्रूहि सुनिश्चितम् ॥

arjuna uvāca
sannyāsaṁ karmaṇāṁ kṛṣṇa
punar yogaṁ ca śaṁsasi
yac chreya etayor ekaṁ
tan me brūhi suniścitam

Arjuna said –

You are confusing me by simultaneously appreciating both; the process of renouncing action to focus on gaining knowledge and also the process of working with no attachment to result. Can you not tell me clearly which of the two is better?

2

श्रीभगवानुवाच
सन्न्यासः कर्मयोगश्च निःश्रेयसकरावुभौ ।
तयोस्तु कर्मसन्न्यासात्कर्मयोगो विशिष्यते ॥

śrī-bhagavān uvāca
sannyāsaḥ karma-yogaś ca
niḥśreyasa-karāv ubhau

tayos tu karma-sannyāsāt
karma-yogo viśiṣyate

Sri Bhagavan said –

The process of renunciation of action to focus on gaining knowledge as well as the process of working with no attachment to results, both lead to the highest perfection. But of the two, selfless work or working with no attachment to results is better.

3

ज्ञेय: स नित्यसन्न्यासी यो न द्वेष्टि न काङ्क्षति ।
निर्द्वन्द्वो हि महाबाहो सुखं बन्धात्प्रमुच्यते ॥

jñeyaḥ sa nitya-sannyāsī
yo na dveṣṭi na kāṅkṣati
nirdvandvo hi mahā-bāho
sukhaṁ bandhāt pramucyate

A detached worker who is neither averse to nor desires the results of action is actually considered renounced. By becoming free from these dualities, he becomes free from material bondage and is considered liberated.

4

सांख्ययोगौ पृथग्बाला: प्रवदन्ति न पण्डिता: ।
एकमप्यास्थित: सम्यगुभयोर्विन्दते फलम् ॥

sāṅkhya-yogau pṛthag bālāḥ
pravadanti na paṇḍitāḥ
ekam apy āsthitaḥ samyag
ubhayor vindate phalam

Only a naïve person would argue that selfless work is different from the process of cultivating knowledge. The intelligent understand that the results of both the paths are exactly the same.

5

यत्सांख्यै: प्राप्यते स्थानं तद्योगैरपि गम्यते ।
एकं सांख्यं च योगं च य: पश्यति स पश्यति ॥

yat sāṅkhyaiḥ prāpyate sthānaṁ
tad yogair api gamyate
ekaṁ sāṅkhyaṁ ca yogaṁ ca
yaḥ paśyati sa paśyati

The one who understands that the results acquired by following the process of gaining knowledge can also be obtained by the process of detached work, is a person who has clear vision.

6

सन्न्यासस्तु महाबाहो दु:खमाप्तुमयोगत: ।
योगयुक्तो मुनिर्ब्रह्म न चिरेणाधिगच्छति ॥

sannyāsas tu mahā-bāho
duḥkham āptum ayogataḥ
yoga-yukto munir brahma
na cireṇādhigacchati

Mere renunciation of action while focusing on gaining knowledge without the practice of detached work is very distressing. On the other hand when a person in knowledge engages himself in detached work, he very quickly achieves the perfection of his life.

7

योगयुक्तो विशुद्धात्मा विजितात्मा जितेन्द्रिय: ।
सर्वभूतात्मभूतात्मा कुर्वन्नपि न लिप्यते ॥

yoga-yukto viśuddhātmā
vijitātmā jitendriyaḥ
sarva-bhūtātma-bhūtātmā
kurvann api na lipyate

A pure soul who is engaged in selfless work with controlled mind and senses is dear to all and everyone is dear to him. Such a person is never entangled even though he is always working.

8 – 9

नैव किञ्चित्करोमीति युक्तो मन्येत तत्त्ववित् ।
पश्यन्स्पृशञ्जिघ्रन्नश्नन्गच्छन्स्वपन्श्वसन् ॥
प्रलपन्विसृजन्गृह्णन्नुन्मिषन्निमिषन्नपि ।
इन्द्रियाणीन्द्रियार्थेषु वर्तन्त इति धारयन् ॥

naiva kiñcit karomīti
yukto manyeta tattva-vit
paśyañ śṛṇvan spṛśañ jighrann
aśnan gacchan svapan śvasan
pralapan visṛjan gṛhṇann
unmiṣan nimiṣann api
indriyāṇīndriyārtheṣu
vartanta iti dhārayan

One who performs detached work based on knowledge, understands very well that in all his activities, be it seeing, hearing, touching, smelling, eating, walking, sleeping, breathing, talking, evacuating, accepting things and even blinking the eyes, he does nothing at all. It is merely the senses that are engaged with their objects, while he remains aloof.

10

ब्रह्मण्याधाय कर्माणि सङ्गं त्यक्त्वा करोति यः ।
लिप्यते न स पापेन पद्मपत्रमिवाम्भसा ॥

brahmaṇy ādhāya karmāṇi
saṅgaṁ tyaktvā karoti yaḥ
lipyate na sa pāpena
padma-patram ivāmbhasā

Like a lotus leaf untouched by water, one who offers all the results of his actions to the Supreme Lord, giving up all traces of attachment, is never affected by the sins of those actions.

11

कायेन मनसा बुद्ध्या केवलैरिन्द्रियैरपि ।
योगिनः कर्म कुर्वन्ति सङ्गं त्यक्त्वात्मशुद्धये ॥

kāyena manasā buddhyā
kevalair indriyair api
yoginaḥ karma kurvanti
saṅgaṁ tyaktvātma-śuddhaye

Although detached, the only reason a *karma yogi* acts with his body, mind, intelligence and senses is to get purified.

12

युक्तः कर्मफलं त्यक्त्वा शान्तिमाप्नोति नैष्ठिकीम् ।
अयुक्तः कामकारेण फले सक्तो निबध्यते ॥

yuktaḥ karma-phalaṁ tyaktvā
śāntim āpnoti naiṣṭhikīm
ayuktaḥ kāma-kāreṇa
phale sakto nibadhyate

The one who offers the results of all their activities to Me attains lasting peace. While a person who is greedy for the results of his actions gets entangled in reactions of his actions.

13

सर्वकर्माणि मनसा सन्न्यस्यास्ते सुखं वशी ।
नवद्वारे पुरे देही नैव कुर्वन्न कारयन् ॥

sarva-karmāṇi manasā
sannyasyāste sukhaṁ vaśī
nava-dvāre pure dehī
naiva kurvan na kārayan

While mentally detached, the soul stays joyfully in the city of nine gates, i.e. the body; doing nothing himself nor being the cause of any work.

14

न कर्तृत्वं न कर्माणि लोकस्य सृजति प्रभुः ।
न कर्मफलसंयोगं स्वभावस्तु प्रवर्तते ॥

na kartṛtvaṁ na karmāṇi
lokasya sṛjati prabhuḥ
na karma-phala-saṁyogaṁ
svabhāvas tu pravartate

In reality the soul does not create activities, nor induces others to act, nor creates the results of actions. All this is carried out by the modes of material nature.

15

नादत्ते कस्यचित्पापं न चैव सुकृतं विभुः ।
अज्ञानेनावृतं ज्ञानं तेन मुह्यन्ति जन्तवः ॥

nādatte kasyacit pāpaṁ
na caiva sukṛtaṁ vibhuḥ
ajñānenāvṛtaṁ jñānaṁ
tena muhyanti jantavaḥ

The Supreme Lord is not responsible for a living being's sinful and pious activities. The bewildered ignorant soul who is conditioned by material nature is responsible for it himself.

16

ज्ञानेन तु तदज्ञानं येषां नाशितमात्मनः ।
तेषामादित्यवज्ज्ञानं प्रकाशयति तत्परम् ॥

jñānena tu tad ajñānaṁ
yeṣāṁ nāśitam ātmanaḥ
teṣām āditya-vaj jñānaṁ
prakāśayati tat param

Just like the sun lights up everything in daytime, similarly knowledge destroys ignorance and reveals everything.

17

तद्बुद्धयस्तदात्मानस्तन्निष्ठास्तत्परायणाः ।
गच्छन्त्यपुनरावृत्तिं ज्ञाननिर्धूतकल्मषाः ॥

tad-buddhayas tad-ātmānas
tan-niṣṭhās tat-parāyaṇāḥ
gacchanty apunar-āvṛttiṁ
jñāna-nirdhūta-kalmaṣāḥ

One whose intelligence, mind and faith are fixed on the Supreme Lord taking complete shelter of Him, and one whose ignorance is washed off by knowledge, such a person is on the path to liberation and never takes birth again.

18

विद्याविनयसम्पन्ने ब्राह्मणे गवि हस्तिनि ।
शुनि चैव श्वपाके च पण्डिता: समदर्शिन: ॥

vidyā-vinaya-sampanne
brāhmaṇe gavi hastini
śuni caiva śva-pāke ca
paṇḍitāḥ sama-darśinaḥ

A truly knowledgeable person is filled with humility and as a result perceives a *brahmana*, a cow, an elephant, a dog and an outcast, all equally.

19

इहैव तैजत: सर्गो येषां साम्ये स्थितं मन: ।
निर्दोषं हि समं ब्रह्म तस्माद्ब्रह्मणि ते स्थिता: ॥

ihaiva tair jitaḥ sargo
yeṣāṁ sāmye sthitaṁ manaḥ
nirdoṣaṁ hi samaṁ brahma
tasmād brahmaṇi te sthitāḥ

Impartial people who mentally perceive everyone with an equal vision are considered to have already conquered the cycle of birth and death. Because they are like the Lord in being impartial, they are considered to have already acquired absolute nature of the Lord.

20

न प्रहृष्येत्प्रियं प्राप्य नोद्विजेत्प्राप्य चाप्रियम् ।
स्थिरबुद्धिरसम्मूढो ब्रह्मविद्ब्रह्मणि स्थितः ॥

na prahṛṣyet priyaṁ prāpya
nodvijet prāpya cāpriyam
sthira-buddhir asammūḍho
brahma-vid brahmaṇi sthitaḥ

A person who has divine knowledge and lives by it, neither rejoices on gaining something favorable nor laments on coming across something unfavorable. He remains unperturbed with a stable intelligence.

21

बाह्यस्पर्शेष्वसक्तात्मा विन्दत्यात्मनि यत्सुखम् ।
स ब्रह्मयोगयुक्तात्मा सुखमक्षयमश्नुते ॥

bāhya-sparśeṣv asaktātmā
vindaty ātmani yat sukham
sa brahma-yoga-yuktātmā
sukham akṣayam aśnute

Such a self-realized person is not attracted to external pleasures but rather explores joy within. Due to his great absorption in the Supreme Lord within, he experiences great happiness.

22

ये हि संस्पर्शजा भोगा दु:खयोनय एव ते ।
आद्यन्तवन्त: कौन्तेय न तेषु रमते बुध: ॥

ye hi saṁsparśajā bhogā
duḥkha-yonaya eva te
ādy-antavantaḥ kaunteya
na teṣu ramate budhaḥ

Pleasures that are born due to contact of senses with sense objects are in reality sources of misery since they have a beginning as well as an end. The wise therefore do not rejoice in them.

23

शक्नोतीहैव यः सोढुं प्राक्शरीरविमोक्षणात् ।
कामक्रोधोद्भवं वेगं स युक्तः स सुखी नरः ॥

śaknotīhaiva yaḥ soḍhuṁ
prāk śarīra-vimokṣaṇāt
kāma-krodhodbhavaṁ vegaṁ
sa yuktaḥ sa sukhī naraḥ

One who can live by tolerating the urges of the senses and the forces of desires and anger is considered to be a happy person in this world.

24

योऽन्तःसुखोऽन्तरारामस्तथान्तर्ज्योतिरेव यः ।
स योगी ब्रह्मनिर्वाणं ब्रह्मभूतोऽधिगच्छति ॥

yo 'ntaḥ-sukho 'ntar-ārāmas
tathāntar-jyotir eva yaḥ
sa yogī brahma-nirvāṇaṁ
brahma-bhūto 'dhigacchati

One who finds satisfaction within, happiness within, enlightenment within, such a yogi is considered to be self-realized and ultimately attains liberation.

25

लभन्ते ब्रह्मनिर्वाणमृषयः क्षीणकल्मषाः ।
छिन्नद्वैधा यतात्मानः सर्वभूतहिते रताः ॥

labhante brahma-nirvāṇam
ṛṣayaḥ kṣīṇa-kalmaṣāḥ
chinna-dvaidhā yatātmānaḥ
sarva-bhūta-hite ratāḥ

Achieving liberation is easily possible for those who are devoid of sins, who are doubtless, who are self-controlled and who are actively engaged in the welfare of all beings.

26

कामक्रोधविमुक्तानां यतीनां यतचेतसाम् ।
अभितो ब्रह्मनिर्वाणं वर्तते विदितात्मनाम् ॥

kāma-krodha-vimuktānāṁ
yatīnāṁ yata-cetasām
abhito brahma-nirvāṇaṁ
vartate viditātmanām

Those self-realized saintly people, who have full control over their minds being free from anger and material desire, will surely attain liberation in the very near future.

27 – 28

स्पर्शान्कृत्वा बहिर्बाह्यांश्चक्षुश्चैवान्तरे भ्रुवोः ।
प्राणापानौ समौ कृत्वा नासाभ्यन्तरचारिणौ ॥
यतेन्द्रियमनोबुद्धिर्मुनिर्मोक्षपरायणः ।
विगतेच्छाभयक्रोधो यः सदा मुक्त एव सः ॥

sparśān kṛtvā bahir bāhyāṁś
cakṣuś caivāntare bhruvoḥ
prāṇāpānau samau kṛtvā
nāsābhyantara-cāriṇau
yatendriya-mano-buddhir
munir mokṣa-parāyaṇaḥ
vigatecchā-bhaya-krodho
yaḥ sadā mukta eva saḥ

While abstaining from sense objects, focusing the vision between the two eyebrows, balancing the incoming and outgoing breaths, while controlling the mind, senses and intelligence, with a desire for liberation, a spiritualist gains freedom from desire, fear and anger. Such a person is already liberated.

29

भोक्तारं यज्ञतपसां सर्वलोकमहेश्वरम् ।
सुहृदं सर्वभूतानां ज्ञात्वा मां शान्तिमृच्छति ॥

bhoktāraṁ yajña-tapasāṁ
sarva-loka-maheśvaram
suhṛdaṁ sarva-bhūtānāṁ
jñātvā māṁ śāntim ṛcchati

A person who knows me to be the enjoyer of the results of all sacrifices and austerities, the absolute controller of all the worlds and the dearest well-wishing friend of all living beings, attains peace.

Chapter

06

Dhyana Yoga

Krishna continues giving his opinion on what true renunciation means. A person who does his assigned duties without any attachment to results, without desire to enjoy, is a true renunciant and not one who quits his work or performance of sacrifices.

Both *sanyasa* and yoga refer to one and the same thing that is linking oneself to the Supreme. By renouncing the desire for self-gratification, one becomes a yogi.

For a beginner on the path of yoga, performing prescribed duties with detachment helps purifies desires. One is elevated on the path of yoga when he has neither attachment to objects of pleasure nor to the work done to achieve them.

With the help of mind control, one can elevate and advance in yoga. The mind can either be a conditioned soul's friend or his enemy. A conquered mind is the best friend and an unconquered mind is the worst enemy.

A person with a conquered mind has in reality attained the Supreme. With realization of knowledge, he is self-satisfied, self-controlled and self-realized. He is completely tranquil amidst happiness and distress, heat and cold, honor and dishonor. He has an equal vision and sees pebbles, stone and gold equally; regards a well-wisher, a friend, an enemy, a sinner and a pious person with an equal vision.

An advanced yogi engages his mind in God while living alone in a secluded place, freeing oneself from desires and possessiveness. He seats himself neither too high nor too low on an area covered with deer skin and a soft cloth placed over *kusa* grass. He sits with his body, neck and head in an erect alignment, and stares steadily at the tip of his nose, avoiding any distractions. With a peaceful fearless mind following the vows of celibacy, he focuses his thoughts on God, considering God the ultimate goal of life.

The prerequisite of becoming such a yogi is regulated living; balanced eating, balanced recreation, balanced working, balanced sleeping and waking. Like the unwavering flame of a lamp in a windless place, a mind in control remains steady in meditation.

This process of yoga requires great determination allowing no deviation. One must abandon all material desires that are churned by the mind and regulate all senses. Gradually one is completely absorbed in a higher consciousness, ceasing all other mental activities. The soul transcends material pleasures of the senses and finds pleasure within. Such a soul is firmly established in the truth that there is no greater gain in this world.

But the unsteady mind tends to wander away. Every time the mind wanders, a yogi pulls it back.

Gradually, the mind becomes peaceful, unaffected by modes of passion; experiencing the highest level of happiness due to constant touch with the Supreme.

Such a genuine yogi sees the Supersoul or the Supreme Lord residing in all living beings and all living beings situated in the Supersoul. Once he understands that God is situated in everyone's heart he engages in devotional service and associates with him under all circumstances.

Now that Krishna has explained the yoga process, Arjuna confesses that this system requires immense steadiness of the mind whereas his mind was restless. Wasn't it a highly impractical process given that the mind was flickering, extremely agitated, very strong and obstinate? Arjuna expresses his inability to follow this path of yoga.

Krishna agrees to Arjuna's argument that controlling the mind is far more difficult than controlling the raging wind. Self-realization is difficult for one whose mind is uncontrolled. But for one who strives to follow the right method and controls his mind by suitable practice and detachment, it is definitely possible. Yoga practice requires mental control.

Now Arjuna is curious as to what happens to an unsuccessful yogi who begins the path of self-realization with faith but somewhere in between strays? Won't this person who deviates from his pursuit of transcendence, lose both material success as well as spiritual goals? Will he not feel like a riven cloud without a foothold in either world?

Krishna assures Arjuna that a person who ventures on this auspicious path will never face destruction, neither in this world nor in the spiritual world. One who sincerely takes up an activity aimed at self-realization and not for material gratification, will never face misfortune.

If one falls soon after taking the spiritual path, he attains the higher planets for enjoyment. After that he is given another opportunity to elevate himself by being reborn either in a pious or rich family.

On the other hand, if a yogi has practiced for a long duration and then deviates from the path, he gets a very rare opportunity of birth in a family of highly evolved transcendentalists. He retains the divine consciousness of his previous birth and resumes his practice from where he had disconnected his endeavor towards spiritual perfection. Due to his evolved consciousness from his previous life, he naturally becomes attracted towards a higher lifestyle. By such practice and restraint of the mind through many lifetimes, slowly and steadily, he washes off all his evil contaminations and finally attains the supreme goal.

Thus Krishna clears Arjuna's doubts about which process is better. He sums it up by saying a yogi is greater than a *tapasvi* performing austerities, superior to a *jnani* or empiricist acquiring knowledge and greater than a *karmi* working with material desires. And amongst yogis, the greatest yogi is one who is intimately connected with God through great faith, worship and devotion.

1

श्रीभगवानुवाच
अनाश्रित: कर्मफलं कार्यं कर्म करोति य: ।
स सन्न्यासी च योगी च न निरग्निर्न चाक्रिय: ॥

śrī-bhagavān uvāca
anāśritaḥ karma-phalaṁ
kāryaṁ karma karoti yaḥ
sa sannyāsī ca yogī ca
na niragnir na cākriyaḥ

Sri Bhagavan said –
A person who does his assigned duties without any attachment to the results that accrue is a true renunciant and not one who quits his work or performance of sacrifices.

2

यं सन्न्यासमिति प्राहुर्योगं तं विद्धि पाण्डव ।
न ह्यसन्न्यस्तसङ्कल्पो योगी भवति कश्चन ॥

yaṁ sannyāsam iti prāhur
yogaṁ taṁ viddhi pāṇḍava
na hy asannyasta-saṅkalpo
yogī bhavati kaścana

Sanyasa or renunciation refers to the process of giving up the results of work. The word yoga refers to the process of detaching oneself from the desires for sense gratification. Thus both *sanyasa* and yoga refer to the same thing and essentially aim at linking oneself to the Supreme.

3

आरुरुक्षोर्मुनेर्योगं कर्म कारणमुच्यते ।
योगारूढस्यतस्यैव शम: कारणमुच्यते ॥

ārurukṣor muner yogaṁ
karma kāraṇam ucyate
yogārūḍhasya tasyaiva
śamaḥ kāraṇam ucyate

For a beginner on the path of yoga, detached work is the means of elevation. But for someone who is already elevated on the path of yoga, giving up work is said to be path of growth.

4

यदा हि नेन्द्रियार्थेषु न कर्मस्वनुषज्जते ।
सर्वसङ्कल्पसन्न्यासी योगारूढस्तदोच्यते ॥

yadā hi nendriyārtheṣu
na karmasv anuṣajjate
sarva-saṅkalpa-sannyāsī
yogārūḍhas tadocyate

A person who has renounced all material motivation is considered to be elevated on the path of yoga when he has neither attachment to objects of pleasure nor to the work done to achieve them.

5

उद्धरेदात्मनात्मानं नात्मानमवसादयेत् ।
आत्मैव ह्यात्मनो बन्धुरात्मैव रिपुरात्मनः ॥

uddhared ātmanātmānaṁ
nātmānam avasādayet
ātmaiva hy ātmano bandhur
ātmaiva ripur ātmanaḥ

One can either elevate oneself with the help of the mind or degrade oneself. The mind can either be a conditioned soul's friend or his enemy.

6

बन्धुरात्मात्मनस्तस्य येनात्मैवात्मना जितः ।
अनात्मनस्तु शत्रुत्वे वर्तेतात्मैव शत्रुवत् ॥

bandhur ātmātmanas tasya
yenātmaivātmanā jitaḥ
anātmanas tu śatrutve
vartetātmaiva śatru-vat

A conquered mind is the best friend and an unconquered mind is the worst enemy.

7

जितात्मनः प्रशान्तस्य परमात्मा समाहितः ।
शीतोष्णसुखदुःखेषु तथा मानापमानयोः ॥

jitātmanaḥ praśāntasya
paramātmā samāhitaḥ
śītoṣṇa-sukha-duḥkheṣu
tathā mānāpamānayoḥ

A person with a conquered mind has in reality attained the Supreme. He is completely tranquil amidst happiness and distress, heat and cold, honor and dishonor.

8

ज्ञानविज्ञानतृप्तात्मा कूटस्थो विजितेन्द्रियः ।
युक्त इत्युच्यते योगी समलोष्ट्राश्मकाञ्चनः ॥

jñāna-vijñāna-tṛptātmā
kūṭa-stho vijitendriyaḥ
yukta ity ucyate yogī
sama-loṣṭrāśma-kāñcanaḥ

A person who has both knowledge and wisdom (which is realization of that knowledge), is self-satisfied, self-controlled and self-realized. Such a person has an equal vision and sees pebbles, stone and gold equally.

9

सुहृन्मित्रार्युदासीनमध्यस्थद्वेष्यबन्धुषु ।
साधुष्वपि च पापेषु समबुद्धिर्विशिष्यते ॥

suhṛn-mitrāry-udāsīna-madhyastha-
dveṣya-bandhuṣu
sādhuṣv api ca pāpeṣu
sama-buddhir viśiṣyate

Even more advanced is a person who regards a well-wisher, a friend, a neutral person, a mediator, an enemy, a relative, a sinner and a pious person with an equal vision.

10

योगी युञ्जीत सततमात्मानं रहसि स्थित: ।
एकाकी यतचित्तात्मा निराशीरपरिग्रह: ॥

yogī yuñjīta satatam
ātmānaṁ rahasi sthitaḥ
ekākī yata-cittātmā
nirāśīr aparigrahaḥ

While living alone in a secluded place, carefully controlling the mind, freeing oneself from desires and feelings of possessiveness, a yogi engages his mind in the Supreme.

11 – 12

शुचौ देशे प्रतिष्ठाप्य स्थिरमासनमात्मन: ।
नात्युच्छ्रितं नातिनीचं चैलाजिनकुशोत्तरम् ॥
तत्रैकाग्रं मन: कृत्वा यतचित्तेन्द्रियक्रिय: ।
उपविश्यासने युञ्ज्याद्योगमात्मविशुद्धये ॥

śucau deśe pratiṣṭhāpya
sthiram āsanam ātmanaḥ

nāty-ucchritaṁ nāti-nīcaṁ
cailājina-kuśottaram
tatraikāgraṁ manaḥ kṛtvā
yata-cittendriya-kriyaḥ
upaviśyāsane yuñjyād
yogam ātma-viśuddhaye

Going to such a sanctified secluded place, he seats himself neither too high nor too low on an area covered with deer skin and a soft cloth placed over kusa grass. Sitting firmly on such a seat, a yogi begins to focus the mind on one single point by controlling his activities, senses and mind with purification of the heart as his goal.

13 – 14

समं कायशिरोग्रीवं धारयन्नचलं स्थिरः ।
सम्प्रेक्ष्य नासिकाग्रं स्वं दिशश्चानवलोकयन् ॥
प्रशान्तात्मा विगतभीर्ब्रह्मचारिव्रते स्थितः ।
मनः संयम्य मच्चित्तो युक्त आसीत मत्परः ॥

samaṁ kāya-śiro-grīvaṁ
dhārayann acalaṁ sthiraḥ
samprekṣya nāsikāgraṁ svaṁ
diśaś cānavalokayan
praśāntātmā vigata-bhīr

brahmacāri-vrate sthitaḥ
manaḥ saṁyamya mac-citto
yukta āsīta mat-paraḥ

Holding the body, neck and head in an erect alignment, a yogi stares steadily at the tip of his nose, thus avoiding straying towards any distractions. With a peaceful fearless mind following the vows of celibacy, he focuses his thoughts on Me, considering Me to be the ultimate goal of life.

15

युञ्जन्नेवं सदात्मानं योगी नियतमानसः ।
शान्तिं निर्वाणपरमां मत्संस्थामधिगच्छति ॥

yuñjann evaṁ sadātmānaṁ
yogī niyata-mānasaḥ
śāntiṁ nirvāṇa-paramāṁ
mat-saṁsthām adhigacchati

By such practice of controlling the body, mind and actions, a yogi attains the kingdom of God.

16

नात्यश्नतस्तु योगोऽस्ति न चैकान्तमनश्नतः ।
न चातिस्वप्नशीलस्य जाग्रतो नैव चार्जुन ॥

nāty-aśnatas tu yogo 'sti
na caikāntam anaśnataḥ
na cāti-svapna-śīlasya
jāgrato naiva cārjuna

A person, who doesn't know the science of balance between eating too much and too little, between sleeping too much and too little, can never become a yogi.

17

युक्ताहारविहारस्य युक्तचेष्टस्य कर्मसु ।
युक्तस्वप्नावबोधस्य योगो भवति दुःखहा ॥

yuktāhāra-vihārasya
yukta-ceṣṭasya karmasu
yukta-svapnāvabodhasya
yogo bhavati duḥkha-hā

Balanced eating, balanced recreation, balanced working, balanced sleeping and waking, along with practice of yoga leads to a misery-free life.

18

यदा विनियतं चित्तमात्मन्येवावतिष्ठते ।
निस्पृहः सर्वकामेभ्यो युक्त इत्युच्यते तदा ॥

yadā viniyataṁ cittam
ātmany evāvatiṣṭhate
nispṛhaḥ sarva-kāmebhyo
yukta ity ucyate tadā

When a yogi disciplines his mental activities to be devoid of material desires and focus on self-realization, he is said to have achieved the perfection in yoga.

19

यथा दीपो निवातस्थो नेङ्गते सोपमा स्मृता ।
योगिनो यतचित्तस्य युञ्जतो योगमात्मनः ॥

yathā dīpo nivāta-stho
neṅgate sopamā smṛtā
yogino yata-cittasya
yuñjato yogam ātmanaḥ

Just like the flame of a lamp in a windless place does not waver, similarly one whose mind is controlled remains steady in his meditation.

~ 20 – 23 ~

यत्रोपरमते चित्तं निरुद्धं योगसेवया ।
यत्र चैवात्मनात्मानं पश्यन्नात्मनि तुष्यति ॥
सुखमात्यन्तिकं यत्तद्बुद्धिग्राह्यमतीन्द्रियम् ।
वेत्ति यत्र न चैवायं स्थितश्चलति तत्त्वतः ॥
यं लब्ध्वा चापरं लाभं मन्यते नाधिकं ततः ।
यस्मिन्स्थितो न दुःखेन गुरुणापि विचाल्यते ॥
तं विद्याद्दुःखसंयोगवियोगं योगसंज्ञितम् ॥

yatroparamate cittaṁ
niruddhaṁ yoga-sevayā
yatra caivātmanātmānaṁ
paśyann ātmani tuṣyati
sukham ātyantikaṁ yat tad
buddhi-grāhyam atīndriyam
vetti yatra na caivāyaṁ
sthitaś calati tattvataḥ
yam labdhva capram labham
manyate nadhikam tatah
yasmin sthito na dukhena
gurunapi vicalyate
taṁ vidyād duḥkha-saṁyoga-viyogaṁ
yoga-saṁjñitam

In the perfectional stage of yoga, the mind is totally restrained from material activities even on a mental level. This stage is characterized by self-realization and self-satisfaction. This is the stage of *samadhi* in which there is freedom from all material miseries arising from material conduct. Such a soul is firmly established in the truth and is convinced that there cannot be a greater gain in this world. Even in the midst of the greatest difficulties in life, such a person remains unperturbed.

24

स निश्चयेन योक्तव्यो योगोऽनिर्विण्णचेतसा ।
सङ्कल्पप्रभवान्कामांस्त्यक्त्वा सर्वानशेषत: ।
मनसैवेन्द्रियग्रामं विनियम्य समन्तत: ॥

sa niścayena yoktavyo
yogo 'nirviṇṇa-cetasā
saṅkalpa-prabhavān kāmāṁs
tyaktvā sarvān aśeṣataḥ
manasaivendriya-grāmaṁ
viniyamya samantataḥ

In order to attain such a state, a person should practice the process of yoga with great determination, allowing no deviation. One must abandon all material desires that are churned by the mind and regulate the senses on all sides.

25

शनैः शनैरुपरमेद्बुद्ध्या धृतिगृहीतया ।
आत्मसंस्थं मनः कृत्वा न किञ्चिदपि चिन्तयेत् ॥

śanaiḥ śanair uparamed
buddhyā dhṛti-gṛhītayā
ātma-saṁsthaṁ manaḥ kṛtvā
na kiñcid api cintayet

Gradually one should be completely absorbed in a higher consciousness with the help of the intelligence powered by complete conviction. Focusing the mind totally on self-realization, all other mental activities should cease.

26

यतो यतो निश्चलति मनश्चञ्चलमस्थिरम् ।
ततस्ततो नियम्यैतदात्मन्येव वशं नयेत् ॥

yato yato niścalati
manaś cañcalam asthiram
tatas tato niyamyaitad
ātmany eva vaśaṁ nayet

The unsteady fickle mind tends to wander away. Every time the mind wanders away, a yogi pulls it back to remain under the control of the self.

27

प्रशान्तमनसं ह्येनं योगिनं सुखमुत्तमम् ।
उपैति शान्तरजसं ब्रह्मभूतमकल्मषम् ॥

praśānta-manasaṁ hy enaṁ
yoginaṁ sukham uttamam
upaiti śānta-rajasaṁ
brahma-bhūtam akalmaṣam

The one whose mind is peaceful, who is unaffected by modes of passion and is free from evil, such a person achieves ultimate happiness in self-realization.

28

युञ्जन्नेवं सदात्मानं योगी विगतकल्मषः ।
सुखेन ब्रह्मसंस्पर्शमत्यन्तं सुखमश्नुते ॥

yuñjann evaṁ sadātmānaṁ
yogī vigata-kalmaṣaḥ
sukhena brahma-saṁsparśam
atyantaṁ sukham aśnute

Thus a yogi who is always engaged in yoga practice, slowly becomes freed from impurities and experiences the highest level of happiness due to his being in constant touch with the Supreme.

29

सर्वभूतस्थमात्मानं सर्वभूतानि चात्मनि ।
ईक्षते योगयुक्तात्मा सर्वत्र समदर्शनः ॥

sarva-bhūta-stham ātmānaṁ
sarva-bhūtāni cātmani
īkṣate yoga-yuktātmā
sarvatra sama-darśanaḥ

Such a genuine yogi sees the Supersoul or the Supreme Lord residing in all living beings and all living beings situated in the Supersoul. Thus he sees the Supreme Lord everywhere.

30

यो मां पश्यति सर्वत्र सर्वं च मयि पश्यति ।
तस्याहं न प्रणश्यामि स च मे न प्रणश्यति ॥

yo māṁ paśyati sarvatra
sarvaṁ ca mayi paśyati
tasyāhaṁ na praṇaśyāmi
sa ca me na praṇaśyati

Whoever sees Me everywhere and everything in Me, such a person is always connected to Me and I am always connected to him.

31

सर्वभूतस्थितं यो मां भजत्येकत्वमास्थित: ।
सर्वथा वर्तमानोऽपि स योगी मयि वर्तते ॥

sarva-bhūta-sthitaṁ yo māṁ
bhajaty ekatvam āsthitaḥ
sarvathā vartamāno 'pi
sa yogī mayi vartate

One who understands that it is Me who is situated in everyone's heart and consequently engages in My devotional service, exists in Me under all circumstances.

32

आत्मौपम्येन सर्वत्र समं पश्यति योऽर्जुन ।
सुखं वा यदि वा दु:खं स योगी परमो मत: ॥

ātmaupamyena sarvatra
samaṁ paśyati yo 'rjuna
sukhaṁ vā yadi vā duḥkhaṁ
sa yogī paramo mataḥ

A yogi who perceives the pains and pleasures of others as if they were his own, is considered the best.

33

अर्जुन उवाच
योऽयं योगस्त्वया प्रोक्तः साम्येन मधुसूदन ।
एतस्याहं न पश्यामि चञ्चलत्वात्स्थितिं स्थिराम् ॥

arjuna uvāca
yo 'yaṁ yogas tvayā proktaḥ
sāmyena madhusūdana
etasyāhaṁ na paśyāmi
cañcalatvāt sthitiṁ sthirām

Arjuna said –
O killer of the Madhu demon, this system of yoga that you have just described that requires steadiness of the mind, appears highly impractical to me since I have a restless mind.

34

चञ्चलं हि मनः कृष्ण प्रमाथि बलवद्दृढम् ।
तस्याहं निग्रहं मन्ये वायोरिव सुदुष्करम् ॥

cañcalaṁ hi manaḥ kṛṣṇa
pramāthi balavad dṛḍham
tasyāhaṁ nigrahaṁ manye
vāyor iva su-duṣkaram

Krishna, the mind is flickering, highly agitated, very strong and highly obstinate. To control it is far more difficult than controlling the raging wind.

35

श्रीभगवानुवाच
असंशयं महाबाहो मनो दुर्निग्रहं चलम् ।
अभ्यासेन तु कौन्तेय वैराग्येण च गृह्यते ॥

śrī-bhagavān uvāca
asaṁśayaṁ mahā-bāho
mano durnigrahaṁ calam
abhyāsena tu kaunteya
vairāgyeṇa ca gṛhyate

Sri Bhagavan said –
No doubt it is difficult to curb the flickering mind, but by suitable practice and detachment, it can be subdued.

36

असंयतात्मना योगो दुष्प्राप इति मे मतिः ।
वश्यात्मना तु यतता शक्योऽवाप्तुमुपायतः ॥

asaṁyatātmanā yogo
duṣprāpa iti me matiḥ

vaśyātmanā tu yatatā
śakyo 'vāptum upāyataḥ

Definitely self-realization is difficult for one whose mind is uncontrolled. But in My opinion, for the one who strives to follow the right method and controls his mind, it is definitely possible.

37

अर्जुन उवाच
अयतिः श्रद्धयोपेतो योगाच्चलितमानसः ।
अप्राप्य योगसंसिद्धिं कां गतिं कृष्ण गच्छति ॥

arjuna uvāca
ayatiḥ śraddhayopeto
yogāc calita-mānasaḥ
aprāpya yoga-saṁsiddhiṁ
kāṁ gatiṁ kṛṣṇa gacchati

Arjuna said –
Krishna please tell me what happens to an unsuccessful yogi who begins the path of self-realization with faith but somewhere in between strays from the path of perfection?

38

कच्चिन्नोभयविभ्रष्टश्छिन्नाभ्रमिव नश्यति ।
अप्रतिष्ठो महाबाहो विमूढो ब्रह्मण: पथि ॥

kaccin nobhaya-vibhraṣṭaś
chinnābhram iva naśyati
apratiṣṭho mahā-bāho
vimūḍho brahmaṇaḥ pathi

Won't this person who deviates from his pursuit of transcendence lose both, material success as well as spiritual goals? Will he not feel like a riven cloud without any footing in either world?

39

एतन्मे संशयं कृष्ण छेत्तुमर्हस्यशेषत: ।
त्वदन्य: संशयस्यास्य छेत्ता न ह्युपपद्यते ॥

etan me saṁśayaṁ kṛṣṇa
chettum arhasy aśeṣataḥ
tvad-anyaḥ saṁśayasyāsya
chettā na hy upapadyate

This is the doubt plaguing my mind now, O Krishna! None other than you is capable of allaying my doubts.

40

श्रीभगवानुवाच
पार्थ नैवेह नामुत्र विनाशस्तस्य विद्यते ।
न हि कल्याणकृत्कश्चिद्दुर्गतिं तात गच्छति ॥

śrī-bhagavān uvāca
pārtha naiveha nāmutra
vināśas tasya vidyate
na hi kalyāṇa-kṛt kaścid
durgatiṁ tāta gacchati

Sri Bhagavan said –
O son of Prtha, a person who ventures on this auspicious path will never face destruction, neither in this world nor in the spiritual world. One who sincerely walks this path will never face misfortune.

41

प्राप्य पुण्यकृतां लोकानुषित्वा शाश्वती: समा: ।
शुचीना श्रीमतां गेहे योगभ्रष्टोऽभिजायते ॥

prāpya puṇya-kṛtāṁ lokān
uṣitvā śāśvatīḥ samāḥ
śucīnāṁ śrīmatāṁ gehe
yoga-bhraṣṭo 'bhijāyate

If one falls from the path of yoga, he attains the higher realms where he enjoys for a prolonged duration of time. He is then reborn either in a family of pious people or in a family of rich aristocracy.

42

अथवा योगिनामेव कुले भवति धीमताम् ।
एतद्धि दुर्लभतरं लोके जन्म यदीदृशम् ॥

atha vā yoginām eva
kule bhavati dhīmatām
etad dhi durlabhataraṁ
loke janma yad īdṛśam

On the other hand, if a yogi has practiced for a long duration and then deviates from the path, he gets a very rare opportunity of birth in a family of highly evolved transcendentalists.

43

तत्र तं बुद्धिसंयोगं लभते पौर्वदेहिकम् ।
यतते च ततो भूयः संसिद्धौ कुरुनन्दन ॥

tatra taṁ buddhi-saṁyogaṁ
labhate paurva-dehikam

yatate ca tato bhūyaḥ
saṁsiddhau kuru-nandana

On taking such a birth, he retains the divine consciousness of his previous birth and continues his practice from where he had disconnected his endeavor towards perfection.

44

पूर्वाभ्यासेन तेनैव ह्रियते ह्यवशोऽपि सः ।
जिज्ञासुरपि योगस्य शब्दब्रह्मातिवर्तते ॥

pūrvābhyāsena tenaiva
hriyate hy avaśo 'pi saḥ
jijñāsur api yogasya
śabda-brahmātivartate

Due to his evolved consciousness in his previous life, without even trying, he naturally becomes drawn towards a higher lifestyle. Such a yogi stands way above the ritualistic adaptation of the scriptures.

45

प्रयत्नाद्यतमानस्तु योगी संशुद्धकिल्बिषः ।
अनेकजन्मसंसिद्धस्ततो याति परां गतिम् ॥

prayatnād yatamānas tu
yogī saṁśuddha-kilbiṣaḥ
aneka-janma-saṁsiddhas
tato yāti parāṁ gatim

Slowly, by rigid practice and restraint of the mind, through many lifetimes, he washes off all his evil contaminations and finally attains the supreme goal.

46

तपस्विभ्योऽधिको योगी ज्ञानिभ्योऽपि मतोऽधिकः ।
कर्मिभ्यश्चाधिको योगी तस्माद्योगी भवार्जुन ॥

tapasvibhyo 'dhiko yogī
jñānibhyo 'pi mato 'dhikaḥ
karmibhyaś cādhiko yogī
tasmād yogī bhavārjuna

A yogi is greater than a *tapasvi* or an ascetic who performs austerities, superior to a *jnani* or empiricist who acquires knowledge and greater than a *karmi* or fruitive worker who works with material desires.

Therefore strive to be a yogi in all circumstances, O Arjuna.

47

योगिनामपि सर्वेषां मद्गतेनान्तरात्मना ।
श्रद्धावान्भजते यो मां स मे युक्ततमो मतः ॥

yogināṁ api sarveṣāṁ
mad-gatenāntar-ātmanā
śraddhāvān bhajate yo māṁ
sa me yuktatamo mataḥ

Of all types of yogis, one who always thinks of Me with great faith and worships Me with devotion, he according to Me is the greatest yogi and is intimately united with Me.

Chapter

07

Jnyana Vijnyana Yoga

Krishna now urges Arjuna to hear carefully as he is about to give Arjuna that complete knowledge and realization knowing which there will be nothing left to know in this world. To strengthen Arjuna's faith, he's going to share with him how Arjuna can understand God in completeness. This is because out of thousands of men, hardly one very rare person truly understands God.

Out of thousands of men, hardly one very rare person knows God in truth.

Krishna explains that he is the source of all material energies, namely, earth, water, fire, air, ether, mind, intellect and the false ego. These eight constitute his inferior energies while the superior energy consists of souls or living beings. Thus everything originates in these two energies and there is nothing else superior to him. He is the source of manifestation as well as destruction of the world. Everything rests on him, like pearls strung on a thread.

Krishna lists 15 places where we can see him and feel his presence. He is the taste of pure water; the radiance of the moon and the sun; the sacred enchantment *Om* in all Vedic texts; the sound in ether; the ability in man. He is the original fragrance of the earth; the heat in fire; the life force of all living beings; the austerity performed by the ascetics. He is the original seed of all beings; the intelligence of the wise and the prowess of the powerful. The strength of the strong that is without desire and attachment. Love that is not contrary to principles of righteousness. He is the cause as well as the essence.

The three material modes of nature, namely goodness, passion and ignorance originate from him. But he remains independent of the modes. The whole world, being under the illusory grip of the three modes of material nature, fails to recognize him. His illusory energy is very difficult to defeat. The only way to overcome this illusory energy is to surrender to him.

Those who do not surrender to him are divided in four categories of people. The grossly foolish attached to the fruits of their work for sense gratification; they have no time to eat or hear about spiritual truths. The lowest of mankind who do not pay heed to their primary duties and the principles of righteousness. The misguided influenced by the illusory energy; they seem to be very scholarly but are limited to knowledge of material world only. And the atheistic demons who have taken shelter of their lower nature.

Then again there are four kinds of pious people who worship and surrender to him; the distressed who come for solutions to their problems; seekers of wealth for satisfying their wants; the inquisitive whose objective is self-realization; and the knowledgeable who have no material desires but surrender out of pure love.

Krishna considers all four to be magnanimous because they have come to him. But the one in knowledge, always connected with him in devotion is most dear to him. After many births, a person in knowledge realizes that Krishna is the cause of everything and then he surrenders to Krishna. Such a great soul is very rare.

There are also some who surrender to *devatas* or demigods and follow rituals to fulfill their desires.

Whoever one may want to worship, in whichever way one may want to worship, Krishna himself propels that faith. Thus inspired, they worship that demigod and obtain the fulfillment of their desires. But in reality it is Krishna and not demigods who have actually arranged for fulfillment of his desires. Those who worship the demigods attain them and those who worship Krishna, attain Krishna.

Because Krishna keeps himself hidden under the veil of his illusory energy, fools never understand that he is unborn and infallible. Ignorant men think that he was previously unmanifested and has now taken a manifested material form. But those who seek freedom from the cycle of birth and death understand him and take shelter of him. They are free from illusions caused by dualities and engage themselves in devotional service with great determination.

Krishna reiterates that those who know him to be the governing principle behind the entire material manifestation, the governing principle behind all the demigods, the governing principle behind all the sacrifices, only they can know him even at the time of death and fix their minds on him.

1

श्रीभगवानुवाच
मय्यासक्तमनाः पार्थ योगं युञ्जन्मदाश्रयः ।
असंशयं समग्रं मां यथा ज्ञास्यसि तच्छृणु ॥

śrī-bhagavān uvāca
mayy āsakta-manāḥ pārtha
yogaṁ yuñjan mad-āśrayaḥ
asaṁśayaṁ samagraṁ māṁ
yathā jñāsyasi tac chṛṇu

Sri Bhagavan said –
With your mind attached to Me and fully conscious of Me, practice the yogic process. Listen as I share with you how this process can help you know Me in completeness without any doubts.

2

ज्ञानं तेऽहं सविज्ञानमिदं वक्ष्याम्यशेषतः ।
यज्ज्ञात्वा नेह भूयोऽन्यज्ज्ञातव्यमवशिष्यते ॥

jñānaṁ te 'haṁ sa-vijñānam
idaṁ vakṣyāmy aśeṣataḥ
yaj jñātvā neha bhūyo 'nyaj
jñātavyam avaśiṣyate

I shall now offer you complete knowledge and realization, knowing which there will be nothing left to know in this world.

3

मनुष्याणां सहस्रेषु कश्चिद्यतति सिद्धये ।
यततामपि सिद्धानां कश्चिन्मां वेत्ति तत्त्वतः ॥

manuṣyāṇāṁ sahasreṣu
kaścid yatati siddhaye
yatatām api siddhānāṁ
kaścin māṁ vetti tattvataḥ

Out of thousands of men, just one strives for perfection. And of those who have achieved perfection, hardly one very rare person knows Me in truth.

4

भूमिरापोऽनलो वायुः खं मनो बुद्धिरेव च ।
अहङ्कार इतीयं मे भिन्ना प्रकृतिरष्टधा ॥

bhūmir āpo 'nalo vāyuḥ
khaṁ mano buddhir eva ca
ahaṅkāra itīyaṁ me
bhinnā prakṛtir aṣṭadhā

Earth, water, fire, air, ether, mind, intellect and the false ego, all these eight together formulate my separated material energies.

5

अपरेयमितस्त्वन्यां प्रकृतिं विद्धि मे पराम् ।
जीवभूतां महाबाहो ययेदं धार्यते जगत् ॥

apareyam itas tv anyāṁ
prakṛtiṁ viddhi me parām
jīva-bhūtāṁ mahā-bāho
yayedaṁ dhāryate jagat

Besides these inferior energies, I have a superior energy that you should know about. The superior energy consists of souls or living beings that utilize the inferior energies.

6

एतद्योनीनि भूतानि सर्वाणीत्युपधारय ।
अहं कृत्स्नस्य जगतः प्रभवः प्रलयस्तथा ॥

etad-yonīni bhūtāni
sarvāṇīty upadhāraya
ahaṁ kṛtsnasya jagataḥ
prabhavaḥ pralayas tathā

All beings have their origin in these two energies and I am the source of manifestation as well as destruction of the world.

7

मत्तः परतरं नान्यत्किञ्चिदस्ति धनञ्जय ।
मयि सर्वमिदं प्रोतं सूत्रे मणिगणा इव ॥

mattaḥ parataraṁ nānyat
kiñcid asti dhanañjaya
mayi sarvam idaṁ protaṁ
sūtre maṇi-gaṇā iva

There is nothing else superior to Me. Everything is dependent on Me, just as much as pearls strung on a thread rest on it.

8

रसोऽहमप्सु कौन्तेय प्रभास्मि शशिसूर्ययो: ।
प्रणव: सर्ववेदेषु शब्द: खे पौरुषं नृषु ॥

raso 'ham apsu kaunteya
prabhāsmi śaśi-sūryayoḥ
praṇavaḥ sarva-vedeṣu
śabdaḥ khe pauruṣaṁ nṛṣu

I am the taste of water; I am the radiance of the moon and the sun; I am the sacred enchantment *Om* in all the Vedic texts; I am the sound in ether; and I am the ability in man.

9

पुण्यो गन्ध: पृथिव्यां च तेजश्चास्मि विभावसौ ।
जीवनं सर्वभूतेषु तपश्चास्मि तपस्विषु ॥

puṇyo gandhaḥ pṛthivyāṁ ca
tejaś cāsmi vibhāvasau
jīvanaṁ sarva-bhūteṣu
tapaś cāsmi tapasviṣu

I am the original fragrance of the earth, I am the heat in fire, I am the life force of all living beings and I am also the austerity performed by the ascetics.

10

बीजं मां सर्वभूतानां विद्धि पार्थ सनातनम् ।
बुद्धिर्बुद्धिमतामस्मि तेजस्तेजस्विनामहम् ॥

bījaṁ māṁ sarva-bhūtānāṁ
viddhi pārtha sanātanam
buddhir buddhimatām asmi
tejas tejasvinām aham

Understand Me to be the original seed of all beings; I am the intelligence of the wise and I am the prowess of the powerful.

11

बलं बलवतां चाहं कामरागविवर्जितम् ।
धर्माविरुद्धो भूतेषु कामोऽस्मि भरतर्षभ ॥

balaṁ balavatāṁ cāhaṁ
kāma-rāga-vivarjitam
dharmāviruddho bhūteṣu
kāmo 'smi bharatarṣabha

I am the strength of the strong that is without desire and attachment. I am love that is not contrary to principles of righteousness.

12

ये चैव सात्त्विका भावा राजसास्तामसाश्च ये।
मत्त एवेति तान्विद्धि न त्वहं तेषु ते मयि ॥

ye caiva sāttvikā bhāvā
rājasās tāmasāś ca ye
matta eveti tān viddhi
na tv ahaṁ teṣu te mayi

The three material modes of nature, namely goodness, passion and ignorance originate from Me. I am independent of the modes. Though they are in Me, I am not in them.

13

त्रिभिर्गुणमयैर्भावैरेभिः सर्वमिदं जगत् ।
मोहितं नाभिजानाति मामेभ्यः परमव्ययम् ॥

tribhir guṇa-mayair bhāvair
ebhiḥ sarvam idaṁ jagat
mohitaṁ nābhijānāti
mām ebhyaḥ param avyayam

Under the illusory grip of the three modes of material nature, the whole world does not recognize Me. I am above the purview of the three modes and am inexhaustible.

14

दैवी ह्येषा गुणमयी मम माया दुरत्यया ।
मामेव ये प्रपद्यन्ते मायामेतां तरन्ति ते ॥

daivī hy eṣā guṇa-mayī
mama māyā duratyayā
mām eva ye prapadyante
māyām etāṁ taranti te

This divine energy consisting of the three modes is My illusory energy and is very difficult to defeat. Only for those who surrender to Me, overcoming this illusory energy becomes easy.

15

न मां दुष्कृतिनो मूढाः प्रपद्यन्ते नराधमाः ।
माययापहृतज्ञाना आसुरं भावमाश्रिताः ॥

na māṁ duṣkṛtino mūḍhāḥ
prapadyante narādhamāḥ
māyayāpahṛta-jñānā
āsuraṁ bhāvam āśritāḥ

The grossly foolish who are attached to the fruits of their work, the lowest of mankind who are socially developed but do not pay heed to principles of righteousness, the misguided who seem to be very learned but whose knowledge is influenced by the illusory energy and the atheistic demons who have taken shelter of the lower nature; these categories of people never surrender to Me.

16

चतुर्विधा भजन्ते मां जनाः सुकृतिनोऽर्जुन ।
आर्तो जिज्ञासुरर्थार्थी ज्ञानी च भरतर्षभ ॥

catur-vidhā bhajante māṁ
janāḥ sukṛtino 'rjuna
ārto jijñāsur arthārthī
jñānī ca bharatarṣabha

There are four kinds of pious people who worship Me; the distressed who come to Me for solutions to their problems, the seekers of wealth who approach me for satisfying their wants, the inquisitive whose objective is self-realization and the knowledgeable who have no material desires but surrender out of pure love.

17

तेषां ज्ञानी नित्ययुक्त एकभक्तिर्विशिष्यते ।
प्रियो हि ज्ञानिनोऽत्यर्थमहं स च मम प्रियः ॥

teṣāṁ jñānī nitya-yukta
eka-bhaktir viśiṣyate
priyo hi jñānino 'tyartham
ahaṁ sa ca mama priyaḥ

Out of these four, the man in knowledge who is always connected with Me in devotion is the best. I am very dear to a person in knowledge and he is also dear to Me.

18

उदाराः सर्व एवैते ज्ञानी त्वात्मैव मे मतम् ।
आस्थितः स हि युक्तात्मा मामेवानुत्तमां गतिम् ॥

udārāḥ sarva evaite
jñānī tv ātmaiva me matam
āsthitaḥ sa hi yuktātmā
mām evānuttamāṁ gatim

All the four are certainly exalted, but the knowledgeable person I consider to be akin to Myself. Constantly engaging in My devotional service, he will surely attain Me, the highest goal.

19

बहूनां जन्मनामन्ते ज्ञानवान्मां प्रपद्यते ।
वासुदेवः सर्वमिति स महात्मा सुदुर्लभः ॥

bahūnāṁ janmanām ante
jñānavān māṁ prapadyate
vāsudevaḥ sarvam iti
sa mahātmā sudurlabhaḥ

After several births, a person in knowledge surrenders unto Me on gaining this realization that I am the cause behind everything. Such a great soul is very rare.

20

कामैस्तैस्तैर्हृतज्ञानाः प्रपद्यन्तेऽन्यदेवताः ।
तं तं नियममास्थाय प्रकृत्या नियताः स्वया ॥

kāmais tais tair hṛta-jñānāḥ
prapadyante 'nya-devatāḥ
taṁ taṁ niyamam āsthāya
prakṛtyā niyatāḥ svayā

Those whose knowledge is covered over by various desires surrender to the *devatas* or demigods and inspired by their own nature follow various rituals.

21

योो यो यां यां तनुं भक्तः श्रद्धयार्चितुमिच्छति ।
तस्य तस्याचलां श्रद्धां तामेव विदधाम्यहम् ॥

yo yo yāṁ yāṁ tanuṁ bhaktaḥ
śraddhayārcitum icchati
tasya tasyācalāṁ śraddhāṁ
tām eva vidadhāmy aham

Whoever they want to worship and in whichever way they want to worship, the faith to steadily worship is given to them by Me.

22

स तया श्रद्धया युक्तस्तस्याराधनमीहते ।
लभते च ततः कामान्मयैव विहितान्हितान् ॥

sa tayā śraddhayā yuktas
tasyārādhanam īhate
labhate ca tataḥ kāmān
mayaiva vihitān hi tān

Inspired by that faith, he worships that demigod and obtains the fulfillment of his desires. But in reality it is Me who has actually arranged for fulfillment of his desires.

23

अन्तवत्तु फलं तेषां तद्भवत्यल्पमेधसाम् ।
देवान्देवयजो यान्ति मद्भक्ता यान्ति मामपि ॥

antavat tu phalaṁ teṣāṁ
tad bhavaty alpa-medhasām
devān deva-yajo yānti
mad-bhaktā yānti mām api

The results obtained by such worship of demigods by these less intelligent men are short-lived. Those who worship the demigods attain them and those who worship Me, attain Me.

24

अव्यक्तं व्यक्तिमापन्नं मन्यन्ते मामबुद्धय: ।
परं भावमजानन्तो ममाव्ययमनुत्तमम् ॥

avyaktaṁ vyaktim āpannaṁ
manyante mām abuddhayaḥ
paraṁ bhāvam ajānanto
mamāvyayam anuttamam

Without knowing My imperishable superior and supreme nature, ignorant men think that I was previously unmanifested and have now taken a manifested material form.

25

नाहं प्रकाशः सर्वस्य योगमायासमावृतः ।
मूढोऽयं नाभिजानाति लोको मामजमव्ययम् ॥

nāhaṁ prakāśaḥ sarvasya
yoga-māyā-samāvṛtaḥ
mūḍho 'yaṁ nābhijānāti
loko mām ajam avyayam

I do not reveal Myself to everyone, but rather keep Myself hidden within a veil of My illusory potency. Thus the fools never understand that I am unborn and infallible.

26

वेदाहं समतीतानि वर्तमानानि चार्जुन ।
भविष्याणि च भूतानि मां तु वेद न कश्चन ॥

vedāhaṁ samatītāni
vartamānāni cārjuna
bhaviṣyāṇi ca bhūtāni
māṁ tu veda na kaścana

I know the past, present and future of all living beings but no one knows Me.

27

इच्छाद्वेषसमुत्थेन द्वन्द्वमोहेन भारत ।
सर्वभूतानि सम्मोहं सर्गे यान्ति परन्तप ॥

icchā-dveṣa-samutthena
dvandva-mohena bhārata
sarva-bhūtāni sammohaṁ
sarge yānti parantapa

Right from the moment they are born, all living entities are cast into delusion by the dualities that arise from desire and hatred.

28

येषां त्वन्तगतं पापं जनानां पुण्यकर्मणाम् ।
ते द्वन्द्वमोहनिर्मुक्ता भजन्ते मां दृढव्रताः ॥

yeṣāṁ tv anta-gataṁ pāpaṁ
janānāṁ puṇya-karmaṇām
te dvandva-moha-nirmuktā
bhajante māṁ dṛḍha-vratāḥ

But those people who have acted piously previously due to which their sinful reactions have been wiped out and are thus free from illusions caused by the dualities, engage themselves in devotional service with great determination.

29

जरामरणमोक्षाय मामाश्रित्य यतन्ति ये ।
ते ब्रह्म तद्विदुः कृत्स्नमध्यात्मं कर्म चाखिलम् ॥

jarā-maraṇa-mokṣāya
mām āśritya yatanti ye
te brahma tad viduḥ kṛtsnam
adhyātmaṁ karma cākhilam

Those who seek freedom from the cycle of birth and death take shelter of Me. Such people are actually divine because they know everything about spiritual activities and material result-oriented activities.

30

साधिभूताधिदैवं मां साधियज्ञं च ये विदुः ।
प्रयाणकालेऽपि च मां ते विदुर्युक्तचेतसः ॥

sādhibhūtādhidaivaṁ māṁ
sādhiyajñaṁ ca ye viduḥ
prayāṇa-kāle 'pi ca māṁ
te vidur yukta-cetasaḥ

Those who know Me to be the governing principle behind the entire material manifestation, the governing principle behind all the demigods, the governing principle behind all the sacrifices, they can know Me even at the time of death and fix their minds on Me.

Chapter

08

Akshara Brahma Yoga

Based on what Krishna just said, Arjuna throws a volley of questions at him to which Krishna replies.

What is the meaning of the word *brahmana*? The imperishable supreme person is called *brahmana*.

What is the meaning of the word *adhyatma*? The eternal living entity is called *adhyatma*.

What does *karma* or fruitive action actually mean? The action that gives rise to material bodies of living beings is called *karma*.

What is the meaning of the word *adibhuta*? The changing temporary material nature is called *adibhuta*.

What is the meaning of the word *adidaiva*? The universal manifestation of the Lord that includes all the demigods is called *adidaiva*.

Who is *adiyajna*? How does he live within the body? Situated as the Supersoul in the heart of every living being, Krishna is called *adiyajna*.

How can a person remember Krishna at the time of death? Krishna answers this question at length.

Whatever one remembers at the time of quitting the body, that final thought determines his next destination. Remembering Krishna while quitting the body will attain him. In order to remember Krishna at the end of life, one must practice remembering him constantly, meditating on him at all times, and surrendering one's mind and intelligence to him.

Once again Krishna reminds Arjuna to remember him and fight.

Krishna, the Supreme person, can be meditated upon as the one who is all-knowledgeable, the oldest, the controller, smaller than the smallest, the maintainer of everything, one who has an inconceivable form, one who is effulgent like the sun and is divine far beyond the material modes.

Renounced sages and Vedic scholars think of Krishna by controlling all senses in a yogic trance and fixing the mind on the heart, the seat of the *Paramatma*. In this yogic trance, if a person thinks of the Supreme Lord while reverberating the sacred syllable *Om* and gives up the body, he attains the highest spiritual destination.

Similarly, the experience of rebirth in this temporary miserable world does not recur for those who constantly think of Krishna, without deviation of mind. Such great souls attain the highest perfection.

Even from the higher planets, including Lord Brahma's planet, one eventually returns to the material world. Only those who attain Krishna's spiritual abode never face rebirth again.

A thousand millenniums or ages form one day of Lord Brahma and the same is the duration of his night. Brahma begins his day by manifesting the universe and at night returns it to its unmanifested state. At the beginning of each day of Brahma, all living beings are born and at the beginning of his night, all are helplessly annihilated.

Higher than this material state, that is alternately manifest and unmanifest, created and destroyed, is an eternal supreme spiritual state that is always unmanifest and does not perish when everything else is annihilated.

This spiritual unmanifested realm is the infallible supreme destination; one never returns from here. This is Krishna's supreme abode which can be attained through the process of undiluted devotion. He is simultaneously present everywhere and everything is present in Him.

Now that Krishna has described the spiritual world, he explains the ideal time for passing away from this world based on which it is determined whether one comes back to this world or not.

The Vedas opine that there are only two ways of passing away from this world, the path of light and the path of darkness. If one who passes away in light, during the day, during the fortnight of the waxing moon or during the six months of the sun's northern sojourn, he attains the Supreme.

If one passes away at night, during the fortnight of the waning moon or during the six months of the sun's southern sojourn, such yogis attain the moon planet only to return after some time.

The one who passes away following the path of light never returns while the one who passes away following the path of darkness definitely returns. A spiritualist fixed in the process of devotion knows both these different paths and is not confused.

Surpassing the results obtained from the Vedas, performance of sacrifices, undertaking of penances, offering of charity and pursuit of pious activities, such a person attains all this but over and above this he ultimately attains the supreme eternal abode.

1

अर्जुन उवाच
किं तद्ब्रह्म किमध्यात्मं किं कर्म पुरुषोत्तम ।
अधिभूतं च किं प्रोक्तमधिदैवं किमुच्यते ॥

arjuna uvāca
kiṁ tad-brahma kim adhyātmaṁ
kiṁ karma puruṣottama
adhibhūtaṁ ca kiṁ proktam
adhidaivaṁ kim ucyate

Arjuna said –
What is the meaning of the word *brahmana*? What is the meaning of the word *adhyatma*? What does *karma* or fruitive action actually mean? What is the meaning of the word *adibhuta*? What is the meaning of the word *adidaiva*?

2

अधियज्ञः कथं कोऽत्र देहेऽस्मिन्मधुसूदन ।
प्रयाणकाले च कथं ज्ञेयोऽसि नियतात्मभिः ॥

adhiyajñaḥ kathaṁ ko 'tra
dehe 'smin madhusūdana
prayāṇa-kāle ca kathaṁ
jñeyo 'si niyatātmabhiḥ

Who is *adiyajna*? How does he live within the body? How can a self-controlled person engaged in Your service know You at the time of death?

~ 3 ~

श्रीभगवानुवाच
अक्षरं ब्रह्म परमं स्वभावोऽध्यात्ममुच्यते ।
भूतभावोद्भवकरो विसर्गः कर्मसंज्ञितः ॥

śrī-bhagavān uvāca
akṣaraṁ brahma paramaṁ
svabhāvo 'dhyātmam ucyate
bhūta-bhāvodbhava-karo
visargaḥ karma-saṁjñitaḥ

Sri Bhagavan said –

The imperishable supreme person is called *brahmana*. The eternal living entity is called *adhyatma*. The action that gives rise to material bodies of living beings is called *karma*.

4

अधिभूतं क्षरो भाव: पुरुषश्चाधिदैवतम् ।
अधियज्ञोऽहमेवात्र देहे देहभृतां वर ॥

adhibhūtaṁ kṣaro bhāvaḥ
puruṣaś cādhidaivatam
adhiyajño 'ham evātra
dehe deha-bhṛtāṁ vara

The changing temporary material nature is called *adibhuta*. The universal manifestation of the Lord that includes all the demigods is called *adidaiva*. Situated as the supersoul in the heart of every living being, I am called *adiyajna*.

5

अन्तकाले च मामेव स्मरन्मुक्त्वा कलेवरम् ।
य: प्रयाति स मद्भावं याति नास्त्यत्र संशय: ॥

anta-kāle ca mām eva
smaran muktvā kalevaram
yaḥ prayāti sa mad-bhāvaṁ
yāti nāsty atra saṁśayaḥ

At the end of life, whoever remembers Me while quitting the body, attains My nature without a doubt.

6

यं यं वापि स्मरन्भावं त्यजत्यन्ते कलेवरम् ।
तं तमेवैति कौन्तेय सदा तद्भावभावित: ॥

yaṁ yaṁ vāpi smaran bhāvaṁ
tyajaty ante kalevaram
taṁ tam evaiti kaunteya
sadā tad-bhāva-bhāvitaḥ

Whatever one remembers at the time of quitting the body, that final thought will determine his next destination.

7

तस्मात्सर्वेषु कालेषु मामनुस्मर युध्य च ।
मय्यर्पितमनोबुद्धिर्मामेवैष्यस्यसंशय: ॥

tasmāt sarveṣu kāleṣu
mām anusmara yudhya ca
mayy arpita-mano buddhir
mām evaiṣyasy asaṁśayaḥ

Therefore at all times, always remember Me and fight. By surrendering your mind and intelligence to Me, you will surely attain Me.

8

अभ्यासयोगयुक्तेन चेतसा नान्यगामिना ।
परमं पुरुषं दिव्यं याति पार्थानुचिन्तयन् ॥

abhyāsa-yoga-yuktena
cetasā nānya-gāminā
paramaṁ puruṣaṁ divyaṁ
yāti pārthānucintayan

One who meditates on the Supreme divine person without any deviation of his mind and intelligence, is sure to attain Him.

9

कविं पुराणमनुशासितार-
मणोरणीयांसमनुस्मरेद्यः ।
सर्वस्य धातारमचिन्त्यरूप-
मादित्यवर्णं तमसः परस्तात् ॥

kaviṁ purāṇam anuśāsitāram
aṇor aṇīyāṁsam anusmared yaḥ
sarvasya dhātāram acintya-rūpam
āditya-varṇaṁ tamasaḥ parastāt

The Supreme person can be meditated upon as the all-knowing person, the oldest person, the controller, smaller than the smallest thing in the world, the maintainer of everything, one who has an inconceivable form, one who is effulgent like the sun and is divine far beyond the lower modes.

10

प्रयाणकाले मनसाचलेन
भक्त्या युक्तो योगबलेन चैव ।
भ्रुवोर्मध्ये प्राणमावेश्य सम्यक्
स तं परं पुरुषमुपैति दिव्यम् ॥

prayāṇa-kāle manasācalena
bhaktyā yukto yoga-balena caiva
bhruvor madhye prāṇam āveśya samyak
sa taṁ paraṁ puruṣam upaiti divyam

A person who at the time of death with the power of yoga and using his undeviated mind, focuses his life airs between his eyebrows while completely meditating on the Supreme Lord, such a person attains the spiritual kingdom.

11

यदक्षरं वेदविदो वदन्ति
विशन्ति यद्यतयो वीतरागाः ।
यदिच्छन्तो ब्रह्मचर्यं चरन्ति
तत्ते पदं सङ्ग्रहेण प्रवक्ष्ये ॥

yad akṣaraṁ veda-vido vadanti
viśanti yad yatayo vīta-rāgāḥ
yad icchanto brahmacaryaṁ caranti
tat te padaṁ saṅgraheṇa pravakṣye

Let me now explain to you about that infallible path about which the knowers of the Vedas speak and which the great renounced sages desire to attain by practicing celibacy.

12

सर्वद्वाराणि संयम्य मनो हृदि निरुध्य च ।
मूर्ध्न्याधायात्मनः प्राणमास्थितो योगधारणाम् ॥

sarva-dvārāṇi saṁyamya
mano hṛdi nirudhya ca
mūrdhny ādhāyātmanaḥ prāṇam
āsthito yoga-dhāraṇām

Controlling all the senses that are called gates, fixing the mind on the heart, which is the seat of the

Paramatma, and transferring the life airs to the top of the head, a person situates himself in yogic trance.

13

ॐ इत्येकाक्षरं ब्रह्म व्याहरन्मामनुस्मरन् ।
यः प्रयाति त्यजन्देहं स याति परमां गतिम् ॥

om̐ ity ekākṣaram̐ brahma
vyāharan mām anusmaran
yaḥ prayāti tyajan deham̐
sa yāti paramām̐ gatim

Being thus situated in yogic trance, if a person thinks of the Supreme Lord while reverberating the sacred syllable *Om* and gives up the body, he attains the highest spiritual destination.

14

अनन्यचेताः सततं यो मां स्मरति नित्यशः ।
तस्याहं सुलभः पार्थ नित्ययुक्तस्य योगिनः ॥

ananya-cetāḥ satatam̐
yo mām̐ smarati nityaśaḥ
tasyāham̐ sulabhaḥ pārtha
nitya-yuktasya yoginaḥ

Without deviation of the mind, one who constantly thinks of Me, for such a person I am easy to obtain due to his constant connection with Me.

15

मामुपेत्य पुनर्जन्म दु:खालयमशाश्वतम् ।
नाप्नुवन्ति महात्मानः संसिद्धिं परमां गताः ॥

mām upetya punar janma
duḥkhālayam aśāśvatam
nāpnuvanti mahātmānaḥ
saṁsiddhiṁ paramāṁ gatāḥ

On achieving Me, the experience of rebirth in this temporary miserable world does not recur since these great souls attain the highest perfection.

16

आब्रह्मभुवनाल्लोकाः पुनरावर्तिनोऽर्जुन ।
मामुपेत्य तु कौन्तेय पुनर्जन्म न विद्यते ॥

ā-brahma-bhuvanāl lokāḥ
punar āvartino 'rjuna

mām upetya tu kaunteya
punar janma na vidyate

From all higher realms including Lord Brahma's planet, one eventually returns to the material world. Only those who attain My abode, such people never face rebirth again.

17

सहस्रयुगपर्यन्तमहर्यद्ब्रह्मणो विदुः ।
रात्रिं युगसहस्रान्तां तेऽहोरात्रविदो जनाः ॥

sahasra-yuga-paryantam
ahar yad brahmaṇo viduḥ
rātriṁ yuga-sahasrāntāṁ
te 'ho-rātra-vido janāḥ

A thousand millenniums or ages by human standards together form one day of Lord Brahma and the same is the duration of his night.

18

अव्यक्ताद्‍ व्यक्तय: सर्वा: प्रभवन्त्यहरागमे ।
रात्र्यागमे प्रलीयन्ते तत्रैवाव्यक्तसंज्ञके ॥

avyaktād vyaktayaḥ sarvāḥ
prabhavanty ahar-āgame
rātry-āgame pralīyante
tatraivāvyakta-saṁjñake

With the beginning of Brahma's day, everything is brought from an unmanifested state to a manifested state. With the beginning of Brahma's night, everything that was manifest is again returned to its unmanifested state.

19

भूतग्राम: स एवायं भूत्वा भूत्वा प्रलीयते ।
रात्र्यागमेऽवश: पार्थ प्रभवत्यहरागमे ॥

bhūta-grāmaḥ sa evāyaṁ
bhūtvā bhūtvā pralīyate
rātry-āgame 'vaśaḥ pārtha
prabhavaty ahar-āgame

At the beginning of each day of Brahma, all living beings are born and at the beginning of his night, all are helplessly annihilated.

20

परस्तस्मात्तु भावोऽन्योऽव्यक्तोऽव्यक्तात्सनातनः ।
यः स सर्वेषु भूतेषु नश्यत्सु न विनश्यति ॥

paras tasmāt tu bhāvo 'nyo
'vyakto 'vyaktāt sanātanaḥ
yaḥ sa sarveṣu bhūteṣu
naśyatsu na vinaśyati

Higher than this material state, that is alternately manifest and unmanifest, is an eternal supreme spiritual state that is always unmanifested and does not perish when everything else is annihilated.

21

अव्यक्तोऽक्षर इत्युक्तस्तमाहुः परमां गतिम् ।
यं प्राप्य न निवर्तन्ते तद्धाम परमं मम ॥

avyakto 'kṣara ity uktas
tam āhuḥ paramāṁ gatim
yaṁ prāpya na nivartante
tad dhāma paramaṁ mama

This spiritual unmanifested realm is considered to be infallible and is the supreme destination; by attaining which one never returns again. This is My supreme abode.

22

पुरुष: स पर: पार्थ भक्त्या लभ्यस्त्वनन्यया ।
यस्यान्त:स्थानि भूतानि येन सर्वमिदं ततम् ॥

puruṣaḥ sa paraḥ pārtha
bhaktyā labhyas tv ananyayā
yasyāntaḥ-sthāni bhūtāni
yena sarvam idaṁ tatam

The supreme greatest person is attained through the process of undiluted devotion. Though He is present in his eternal abode, He is simultaneously present everywhere and everything is present in Him.

23

यत्र काले त्वनावृत्तिमावृत्तिं चैव योगिन: ।
प्रयाता यान्ति तं कालं वक्ष्यामि भरतर्षभ ॥

yatra kāle tv anāvṛttim
āvṛttiṁ caiva yoginaḥ
prayātā yānti taṁ kālaṁ
vakṣyāmi bharatarṣabha

O descendent of Bharata dynasty, I will now explain to you about the ideal times of passing away from this world based on which it is determined whether one comes back to this world or never returns.

24

अग्निर्ज्योतिरहः शुक्लः षण्मासा उत्तरायणम् ।
तत्र प्रयाता गच्छन्ति ब्रह्म ब्रह्मविदो जनाः ॥

agnir jyotir ahaḥ śuklaḥ
ṣaṇ-māsā uttarāyaṇam
tatra prayātā gacchanti
brahma brahma-vido janāḥ

If one who knows the supreme person or *brahmana* passes away during the influence of the fire god, in light, during the day, during the fortnight of the waxing moon or during the six months of the sun's northern sojourn, he attains the Supreme.

25

धूमो रात्रिस्तथा कृष्णः षण्मासा दक्षिणायनम् ।
तत्र चान्द्रमसं ज्योतिर्योगी प्राप्य निवर्तते ॥

dhūmo rātris tathā kṛṣṇaḥ
ṣaṇ-māsā dakṣiṇāyanam
tatra cāndramasaṁ jyotir
yogī prāpya nivartate

If one passes away during smoke, at night, during the fortnight of the waning moon or during the six months of the sun's southern sojourn, such yogis attain the moon planet but once again return after some time.

26

श‍ुक्लकृष्णे गती ह्येते जगतः शाश्वते मते ।
एकया यात्यनावृत्तिमन्ययावर्तते पुनः ॥

śukla-kṛṣṇe gatī hy ete
jagataḥ śāśvate mate
ekayā yāty anāvṛttim
anyayāvartate punaḥ

The Vedas opine that there are only two ways of passing away from this world, the path of light and the path of darkness. The one who passes away following the path of light never returns while the one who passes away following the path of darkness definitely returns.

27

नैते सृती पार्थ जानन्योगी मुह्यति कश्चन ।
तस्मात्सर्वेषु कालेषु योगयुक्तो भवार्जुन ॥

naite sṛtī pārtha jānan
yogī muhyati kaścana
tasmāt sarveṣu kāleṣu
yoga-yukto bhavārjuna

A spiritualist who knows both these different paths is not confused. Therefore at all times one must be fixed in the process of devotion, Arjuna.

28

वेदेषु यज्ञेषु तपःसु चैव
दानेषु यत्पुण्यफलं प्रदिष्टम् ।
अत्येति तत्सर्वमिदं विदित्वा
योगी परं स्थानमुपैति चाद्यम् ॥

vedeṣu yajñeṣu tapaḥsu caiva
dāneṣu yat puṇya-phalaṁ pradiṣṭam
atyeti tat sarvam idaṁ viditvā
yogī paraṁ sthānam upaiti cādyam

Surpassing the results obtained from study of the Vedas, performance of sacrifices, undertaking of penances, offering of charity and the pursuit of pious activities, a person who engages himself in the process of devotional service attains all this but over and above this he ultimately attains the supreme eternal abode.

Chapter

09

Raja Vidya Rajaguhya Yoga

Having answered Arjuna's questions to his satisfaction, Krishna then proceeds to share this most confidential 'king of knowledge' with Arjuna. This knowledge is timeless; the topmost purifying agent; the highest form of religion that is buried in the middle of Bhagavad Gita. It is the king of all secrets that he wants to share with Arjuna because Arjuna is qualified to hear having a heart free of envy. With the help of this knowledge, Arjuna would be safeguarded from the miseries of this world.

Krishna states a few simple facts about himself. That he is the creator and maintainer of all living beings, yet he is not a part of this material world. Just like the powerful wind that blows everywhere is always situated in the sky, similarly all beings rest in him always. He is not bound to his creation; he is unattached and indifferent. At the end of every millennium, all material manifestations are annihilated and in the beginning of the millennium, they are again recreated by Krishna's energies and will.

Not having any knowledge about Krishna's divine nature, faithless and foolish men ridicule him when they see him in human form. By taking shelter of the deluding demoniac atheistic nature, they are bound to return to the path of repeated birth and death in the material existence. But those who take shelter of Krishna understand him to be the origin of everything and remain absorbed in him. These great souls worship him with determination.

There are yet others who worship Krishna as non-different from themselves. And some who worship demigods through Vedic study and sacrifices, seeking heavenly realms. After they get purified of sinful reactions, they attain the heavenly abode of Indra where they enjoy for a prolonged duration of time. Such people are eventually worshiping Krishna not directly but indirectly.

As they enjoy the heavenly delights, at some point, the quantum of their pious credits gets exhausted. Then they are thrown back to this mortal planet once again. Thus those who seek the path of mundane pleasures by following the ritualistic path prescribed by the Vedas end up only being trapped in the cycle of repeated birth and death.

Krishna stresses the point that those who worship any other demigod with great faith, in reality end up worshiping Krishna only since Krishna is the real enjoyer and master of all sacrifices. They are unaware of this truth about his divine nature and fall down.

There are still others who worship him by worshipping the universal form. To them, who concentrate on worshipping Krishna directly with an undeviated mind, he himself supplies what they lack and maintain what they have.

The worshippers of the demigods go to the demigods. The worshippers of the ancestors go to the ancestors. The worshippers of the ghosts go to the ghosts. And worshippers of Krishna go to Krishna.

Everything rests in Krishna as he is the rituals, the sacrifices, the oblations to the ancestors, the remedial herb, the divine chants, the clarified butter used in sacrifices, the sacrificial fire itself and also the act of offering.

He is the father, mother, supporter and the grandfather of this world; the goal of knowledge; the purifier; the sacred syllable *Om*; also the Rig, Sama and Yajur Vedas. He is the destination, the maintainer, the master, the witness, the abode, the shelter, the best friend, the creator, the destroyer, the basis of everything, the storehouse of everything and he is the imperishable seed.

He is ready to accept simple offerings of a leaf, a flower, a fruit, a little water, if offered with devotion, and a pure consciousness. Any activity, whether it is eating, or austerities, or giving, should be done as a conscious offering to him. Such offerings liberate one from the shackles of auspicious and inauspicious results of work. Being detached from the results of work, a person with mind firmly set on Krishna, attains Krishna.

Krishna is equal towards all living beings. Neither hateful nor partial to anyone. Even if one makes mistakes or performs wrong actions in devotional service, Krishna still considers him a saint because of his strong resolve to serve him. Very soon such a person will become highly righteous and attain eternal peace.

Krishna urges Arjuna to declare it to the world that Krishna's devotee will never perish because immaterial of birth or qualifications, taking Krishna's shelter guarantees the supreme destination.

And then Krishna speaks what is considered the topmost verse of Bhagavad Gita. He urges Arjuna to engage his mind in thinking of Krishna, in being his devotee, in worshipping him, making him the center of life; then he can surely reach Krishna.

1

श्रीभगवानुवाच
इदं तु ते गुह्यतमं प्रवक्ष्याम्यनसूयवे ।
ज्ञानं विज्ञानसहितं यज्ज्ञात्वा मोक्ष्यसेऽशुभात् ॥

śrī-bhagavān uvāca
idaṁ tu te guhyatamaṁ
pravakṣyāmy anasūyave
jñānaṁ vijñāna-sahitaṁ
yaj jñātvā mokṣyase 'śubhāt

Sri Bhagavan said –
I will share this most confidential knowledge with you, combined with realized wisdom since you have no envy in your heart. This knowledge will help you remain unaffected by the inauspiciousness of this world.

2

राजविद्या राजगुह्यं पवित्रमिदमुत्तमम् ।
प्रत्यक्षावगमं धर्म्यं सुसुखं कर्तुमव्ययम् ॥

rāja-vidyā rāja-guhyaṁ
pavitram idam uttamam
pratyakṣāvagamaṁ dharmyaṁ
su-sukhaṁ kartum avyayam

This is the king of all knowledge and the king of all secrets. This knowledge is the topmost purifying agent. It can be understood by direct perception and is the highest form of religion. This knowledge is timeless and makes the practitioner happy.

3

अश्रद्दधानाः पुरुषा धर्मस्यास्य परन्तप ।
अप्राप्य मां निवर्तन्ते मृत्युसंसारवर्त्मनि ॥

aśraddadhānāḥ puruṣā
dharmasyāsya parantapa
aprāpya māṁ nivartante
mṛtyu-saṁsāra-vartmani

Those people who are faithless towards the process of devotion do not attain Me and therefore are bound to return to the path of repeated birth and death in the material existence.

4

मया ततमिदं सर्वं जगदव्यक्तमूर्तिना ।
मत्स्थानि सर्वभूतानि न चाहं तेष्ववस्थित: ॥

mayā tatam idaṁ sarvaṁ
jagad avyakta-mūrtinā
mat-sthāni sarva-bhūtāni
na cāhaṁ teṣv avasthitaḥ

I pervade the entire creation in My unmanifested cosmic form. Thus all beings are in Me but I am not in them.

5

न च मत्स्थानि भूतानि पश्य मे योगमैश्वरम् ।
भूतभृन्न च भूतस्थो ममात्मा भूतभावन: ॥

na ca mat-sthāni bhūtāni
paśya me yogam aiśvaram
bhūta-bhṛn na ca bhūta-stho
mamātmā bhūta-bhāvanaḥ

Everything that is created is not situated in Me. Do not be bewildered by the contradiction; this is simply My mystic opulence in action. Though I am the maintainer of all living beings and though I am all pervading, I am yet not a part of this material world as I am the source of all creation.

6

यथाकाशस्थितो नित्यं वायुः सर्वत्रगो महान् ।
तथा सर्वाणि भूतानि मत्स्थानीत्युपधारय ॥

yathākāśa-sthito nityaṁ
vāyuḥ sarvatra-go mahān
tathā sarvāṇi bhūtāni
mat-sthānīty upadhāraya

Just like the powerful wind that blows everywhere is always situated in the sky, similarly all beings rest in me always.

7

सर्वभूतानि कौन्तेय प्रकृतिं यान्ति मामिकाम् ।
कल्पक्षये पुनस्तानि कल्पादौ विसृजाम्यहम् ॥

sarva-bhūtāni kaunteya
prakṛtiṁ yānti māmikām
kalpa-kṣaye punas tāni
kalpādau visṛjāmy aham

At the end of every millennium, all material manifestations enter into Me and in the beginning of the millennium, they are again recreated by my energies.

8

प्रकृतिं स्वामवष्टभ्य विसृजामि पुनः पुनः ।
भूतग्राममिमं कृत्स्नमवशं प्रकृतेर्वशात् ॥

prakṛtiṁ svām avaṣṭabhya
visṛjāmi punaḥ punaḥ
bhūta-grāmam imaṁ kṛtsnam
avaśaṁ prakṛter vaśāt

By My will, the material manifestation is created again and again. These beings are sent forth in accordance with their natures.

9

न च मां तानि कर्माणि निबध्नन्ति धनञ्जय ।
उदासीनवदासीनमसक्तं तेषु कर्मसु ॥

na ca māṁ tāni karmāṇi
nibadhnanti dhanañjaya
udāsīnavad āsīnam
asaktaṁ teṣu karmasu

All this work of creation does not bind Me since I am not attached to them and remain indifferent.

10

मयाध्यक्षेण प्रकृतिः सूयते सचराचरम् ।
हेतुनानेन कौन्तेय जगद्विपरिवर्तते ॥

mayādhyakṣeṇa prakṛtiḥ
sūyate sa-carācaram
hetunānena kaunteya
jagad viparivartate

Material nature works under My superintendence bringing about the production of both moving and non-moving beings.

11

अवजानन्ति मां मूढा मानुषीं तनुमाश्रितम् ।
परं भावमजानन्तो मम भूतमहेश्वरम् ॥

avajānanti māṁ mūḍhā
mānuṣīṁ tanum āśritam
paraṁ bhāvam ajānanto
mama bhūta-maheśvaram

Foolish men ridicule Me when I assume a human form, without having any knowledge about My divine nature being the Supreme proprietor of everything.

12

मोघाशा मोघकर्माणो मोघज्ञाना विचेतसः ।
राक्षसीमासुरीं चैव प्रकृतिं मोहिनीं श्रिताः ॥

moghāśā mogha-karmāṇo
mogha-jñānā vicetasaḥ
rākṣasīm āsurīṁ caiva
prakṛtiṁ mohinīṁ śritāḥ

For those who take shelter of the deluding demoniac atheistic nature, their hopes are futile, their actions are futile and their knowledge is futile.

13

महात्मानस्तु मां पार्थ दैवीं प्रकृतिमाश्रिताः ।
भजन्त्यनन्यमनसो ज्ञात्वा भूतादिमव्ययम् ॥

mahātmānas tu māṁ pārtha
daivīṁ prakṛtim āśritāḥ
bhajanty ananya-manaso
jñātvā bhūtādim avyayam

But those great souls who take shelter of the divine nature, they are fully absorbed in undeviated devotional service unto Me knowing Me to be imperishable and the origin of everything.

14

सततं कीर्तयन्तो मां यतन्तश्च दृढव्रताः ।
नमस्यन्तश्च मां भक्त्या नित्ययुक्ता उपासते ॥

satataṁ kīrtayanto māṁ
yatantaś ca dṛḍha-vratāḥ
namasyantaś ca māṁ bhaktyā
nitya-yuktā upāsate

Incessantly chanting My names, striving intensely with great determination, while offering their respects to Me, such great souls perennially worship Me with great devotion.

15

ज्ञानयज्ञेन चाप्यन्ये यजन्तो मामुपासते ।
एकत्वेन पृथक्त्वेन बहुधा विश्वतोमुखम् ॥

jñāna-yajñena cāpy anye
yajanto mām upāsate
ekatvena pṛthaktvena
bahudhā viśvato-mukham

There are others who through the process of knowledge worship Me as non-different from themselves. There are yet others who worship Me by worshiping various demigods through the medium of sacrifices. There are still others who worship Me by worshipping the universal form.

16

अहं क्रतुरहं यज्ञः स्वधाहमहमौषधम् ।
मन्त्रोऽहमहमेवाज्यमहमग्निरहं हुतम् ॥

ahaṁ kratur ahaṁ yajñaḥ
svadhāham aham auṣadham
mantro 'ham aham evājyam
aham agnir ahaṁ hutam

I am the rituals, I am the sacrifices, I am the oblations to the ancestors, I am the remedial herb, I am the divine chants, I am the clarified butter used in sacrifices, I am the sacrificial fire itself and I am also the act of offering.

17

पिताहमस्य जगतो माता धाता पितामहः ।
वेद्यं पवित्रम् ॐकार ऋक् साम यजुरेव च ॥

pitāham asya jagato
mātā dhātā pitāmahaḥ
vedyaṁ pavitram oṁkāra
ṛk sāma yajur eva ca

I am the father, mother, supporter and the grandfather of this world. I am the goal of knowledge, I am the purifier, I am the sacred syllable *Om*, I am also the Rig, Sama and Yajur Vedas.

18

गतिर्भर्ता प्रभुः साक्षी निवासः शरणं सुहृत् ।
प्रभवः प्रलयः स्थानं निधानं बीजमव्ययम् ॥

gatir bhartā prabhuḥ sākṣī
nivāsaḥ śaraṇaṁ suhṛt
prabhavaḥ pralayaḥ sthānaṁ
nidhānaṁ bījam avyayam

I am the destination, the maintainer, the master, the witness, the abode, the shelter, the best friend, the creator, the destroyer, the basis of everything, the storehouse of everything and I am the imperishable seed.

19

तपाम्यहमहं वर्षं निगृह्णाम्युत्सृजामि च ।
अमृतं चैव मृत्युश्च सदसच्चाहमर्जुन ॥

tapāmy aham ahaṁ varṣaṁ
nigṛhṇāmy utsṛjāmi ca
amṛtaṁ caiva mṛtyuś ca
sad asac cāham arjuna

I radiate heat, I send or withhold rains, I am the nectar of immortality, I am also death; both matter and spirit exist in Me.

20

त्रैविद्या मां सोमपा: पूतपापा
यज्ञैरिष्ट्वा स्वर्गतिं प्रार्थयन्ते ।
ते पुण्यमासाद्य सुरेन्द्रलोक-
मश्नन्ति दिव्यान्दिवि देवभोगान् ॥

trai-vidyā māṁ soma-pāḥ pūta-pāpā
yajñair iṣṭvā svar-gatiṁ prārthayante
te puṇyam āsādya surendra-lokam
aśnanti divyān divi deva-bhogān

Persons seeking the heavenly realms, adopt the process of study of the three Vedas and consumption of Soma juice. Such people worship Me indirectly. Purified of sinful reactions by following this process, they attain the heavenly abode of Indra where they enjoy for a prolonged duration of time.

21

ते तं भुक्त्वा स्वर्गलोकं विशालं
क्षीणे पुण्ये मर्त्यलोकं विशन्ति ।
एवं त्रयीधर्ममनुप्रपन्ना
गतागतं कामकामा लभन्ते ॥

te taṁ bhuktvā svarga-lokaṁ viśālaṁ
kṣīṇe puṇye martya-lokaṁ viśanti

evaṁ trayī-dharmam anuprapannā
gatāgataṁ kāma-kāmā labhante

As they enjoy the heavenly delights, at a certain point during their residence there, the quantum of their pious credits gets exhausted. Then they are thrown back to this mortal planet once again. Thus those who seek the path of mundane pleasures by following the ritualistic path prescribed by the three Vedas end up only being trapped in the cycle of repeated birth and death.

22

अनन्याश्चिन्तयन्तो मां ये जनाः पर्युपासते ।
तेषां नित्याभियुक्तानां योगक्षेमं वहाम्यहम् ॥

ananyāś cintayanto māṁ
ye janāḥ paryupāsate
teṣāṁ nityābhiyuktānāṁ
yoga-kṣemaṁ vahāmy aham

For those who concentrate their attention on worshipping Me with an undeviated mind, I supply what they lack and maintain what they have.

23

येऽप्यन्यदेवताभक्ता यजन्ते श्रद्धयान्विताः ।
तेऽपि मामेव कौन्तेय यजन्त्यविधिपूर्वकम् ॥

ye 'py anya-devatā-bhaktā
yajante śraddhayānvitāḥ
te 'pi mām eva kaunteya
yajanty avidhi-pūrvakam

Even those who worship any other demigod with great faith, in reality worship Me only although they do it in the wrong manner.

24

अहं हि सर्वयज्ञानां भोक्ता च प्रभुरेव च ।
न तु मामभिजानन्ति तत्त्वेनातश्च्यवन्ति ते ॥

ahaṁ hi sarva-yajñānāṁ
bhoktā ca prabhur eva ca
na tu mām abhijānanti
tattvenātaś cyavanti te

I am the real enjoyer and master of all sacrifices. Those who do not know this truth in essence about my divine nature, fall down.

25

यान्ति देवव्रता देवान्पितृन्यान्ति पितृव्रता: ।
भूतानि यान्ति भूतेज्या यान्ति मद्याजिनोऽपि माम् ॥

yānti deva-vratā devān
pitṝn yānti pitṛ-vratāḥ
bhūtāni yānti bhūtejyā
yānti mad-yājino 'pi mām

The worshippers of the demigods go to the demigods. The worshippers of the ancestors go to the ancestors. The worshippers of the ghosts go to the ghosts. Those who are My worshippers come to Me.

26

पत्रं पुष्पं फलं तोयं यो मे भक्त्या प्रयच्छति ।
तदहं भक्त्युपहृतमश्नामि प्रयतात्मन: ॥

patraṁ puṣpaṁ phalaṁ toyaṁ
yo me bhaktyā prayacchati
tad ahaṁ bhakty-upahṛtam
aśnāmi prayatātmanaḥ

A leaf, a flower, a fruit, a little water, if offered to Me with devotion, I accept such offerings that are offered with great devotion and a pure consciousness.

27

यत्करोषि यदश्नासि यज्जुहोषि ददासि यत् ।
यत्तपस्यसि कौन्तेय तत्कुरुष्व मदर्पणम् ॥

yat karoṣi yad aśnāsi
yaj juhoṣi dadāsi yat
yat tapasyasi kaunteya
tat kuruṣva mad arpaṇam

Anything you do, anything you eat, anything you give away, any austerity you undergo, do everything as an offering to Me.

28

शुभाशुभफलैरेवं मोक्ष्यसे कर्मबन्धनैः ।
सन्न्यासयोगयुक्तात्मा विमुक्तो मामुपैष्यसि ॥

śubhāśubha-phalair evaṁ
mokṣyase karma-bandhanaiḥ
sannyāsa-yoga-yuktātmā
vimukto mām upaiṣyasi

This will liberate you from the shackles of auspicious and inauspicious results of work. Being detached from the results of work, a person whose mind is firmly set in Me, comes to Me.

29

समोऽहं सर्वभूतेषु न मे द्वेष्योऽस्ति न प्रियः ।
ये भजन्ति तु मां भक्त्या मयि ते तेषु चाप्यहम् ॥

samo 'haṁ sarva-bhūteṣu
na me dveṣyo 'sti na priyaḥ
ye bhajanti tu māṁ bhaktyā
mayi te teṣu cāpy aham

I am equally disposed towards all living beings. Neither am I hateful towards anyone nor am I dear to anyone. For those who worship Me with devotion are in Me and I am in them.

30

अपि चेत्सुदुराचारो भजते मामनन्यभाक् ।
साधुरेव स मन्तव्यः सम्यग्व्यवसितो हि सः ॥

api cet su-durācāro
bhajate mām ananya-bhāk
sādhur eva sa mantavyaḥ
samyag vyavasito hi saḥ

Even if someone is badly behaved and performs wrong actions, but engages himself in devotional service, such a person is to be considered a saint because of his strong resolve to serve Me.

31

क्षिप्रं भवति धर्मात्मा शश्वच्छान्तिं निगच्छति ।
कौन्तेय प्रतिजानीहि न मे भक्तः प्रणश्यति ॥

kṣipraṁ bhavati dharmātmā
śaśvac-chāntiṁ nigacchati
kaunteya pratijānīhi
na me bhaktaḥ praṇaśyati

Very soon such a person will become highly righteous and attain eternal peace. O son of Kunti, I urge you to declare it to the world that My devotee will never perish.

32

मां हि पार्थ व्यपाश्रित्य येऽपि स्युः पापयोनयः ।
स्त्रियो वैश्यास्तथा शूद्रास्तेऽपि यान्ति परां गतिम् ॥

māṁ hi pārtha vyapāśritya
ye 'pi syuḥ pāpa-yonayaḥ
striyo vaiśyās tathā śūdrās
te 'pi yānti parāṁ gatim

Anyone taking shelter of Me, immaterial of their birth or qualifications, attains the supreme destination.

33

किं पुनर्ब्राह्मणाः पुण्या भक्ता राजर्षयस्तथा ।
अनित्यमसुखं लोकमिमं प्राप्य भजस्व माम् ॥

kiṁ punar brāhmaṇāḥ puṇyā
bhaktā rājarṣayas tathā
anityam asukhaṁ lokam
imaṁ prāpya bhajasva mām

That being the case, then what to speak of righteous *brahmanas*, devotees and saintly kings. Having come to this temporary world devoid of happiness, engage yourself in loving service to Me.

34

मन्मना भव मद्भक्तो मद्याजी मां नमस्कुरु ।
मामेवैष्यसि युक्त्वैवमात्मानं मत्परायणः ॥

man-manā bhava mad-bhakto
mad-yājī māṁ namaskuru
mām evaiṣyasi yuktvaivam
ātmānaṁ mat-parāyaṇaḥ

Absorb your mind in Me. Become My devotee! Worship me. Pay respects to Me. One who is so much absorbed in Me and devoted to Me, will surely come to Me.

Chapter 10

Vibhuti Yoga

After having explained to Arjuna to fix his mind on him, Krishna, being Arjuna's well-wisher and dear friend, gives him the topmost advice for his welfare.

Krishna announces that neither the demigods nor great sages can understand his origins; that he is unborn, has no beginning and is the controller of the world. One who understands this, such an undeluded person is at once freed of all sinful reactions. One who learns of his opulence, he will have no doubt but to engage himself in his devotional service.

Krishna is the origin of all qualities; intelligence, knowledge, freedom from illusion, forgiveness, truthfulness, self-control, mind control, happiness, distress, existence, non-existence, fear, fearlessness, non-violence, equanimity, satisfaction, austerity, charity, fame and infamy. He traces the line of descent; the seven ancient sages, the four Kumaras and the Manus from whom all living beings descended, are born from his mind.

Krishna summarizes the entire Bhagavad Gita in four verses of this chapter. He is the source of everything and everything emanates from him. The intelligent who understand this surrender to him, worship him and dedicate their life to him. They derive great satisfaction and pleasure in discussing his glories amongst themselves, thus enlightening each other. In reciprocation of their love and devotion, Krishna showers special grace on them. He dispels the darkness of ignorance from within their hearts by the shining lamp of knowledge. He gives them the wisdom by which they can come to him.

It is Arjna's turn to speak now. He accepts all that Krishna has said as total truth. He accepts Krishna as the supreme *Brahmana*, the supreme abode, the supreme purifier; the eternal divine personality, the original deity, the unborn and the greatest. Arjuna also gives Vedic references for his acceptance. All these attributes of Krishna have been confirmed by powerful sages like the divine Narada, Asita, Devala and Vyasa. And now Krishna had confirmed it first-hand.

He is eager to hear further details about Krishna's divine manifestations through which he permeates and influences all of creation. He enquires how he should meditate on Krishna, in which variegated ways should he think of Krishna.

Krishna agrees to reveal prominent aspects of divine opulence. He reveals that he is the Supersoul seated in the heart of every living being. Of the *Adityas*, he is Vishnu. Of the lights, he is the radiant sun. Of the stars, he is the moon. Of the Vedas, he is Sama Veda. Of the demigods, he is Indra. Of the senses, he is the mind. Of the living beings, he is the consciousness. Of the Rudras, he is Shankara. Of great sages, he is Brighu. Of incantations, he is the single divine syllable Om. Of sacrifices, he is *japa yajna* or chanting of the holy names. Of immovable things, he is the Himalayan mountain. Of trees, he is the Banyan tree. Of godly sages, he is Narada.

Of cows, he is the Surabhi cow. Of multi-hooded snakes, he is Ananta. Of law keepers, he is Yama, the God of death. Of animals, he is the lion. Of birds, he is Garuda. Of experts in weapons, he is Rama. Of fishes, he is the shark. Of flowing rivers, he is the Ganga. Of letters, he is the first letter A. He is the endless time. Of creators, he is Brahma. He is death, the destroyer of everything.

Of the descendants of Vrsni, he is Vaasudeva. Of the Pandavas, he is Arjuna. Of the sages, he is Vyasa. He is the seed of all creations. Nothing moving or non-moving can exist without him.

In short, whatever and wherever there is opulence, beauty, splendor, it is a spark of him. It is enough to understand that he pervades through and sustains the entire creation by just a single portion of himself.

1

श्रीभगवानुवाच
भूय एव महाबाहो शृणु मे परमं वचः ।
यत्तेऽहं प्रीयमाणाय वक्ष्यामि हितकाम्यया ॥

śrī-bhagavān uvāca
bhūya eva mahā-bāho
śṛṇu me paramaṁ vacaḥ
yat te 'haṁ prīyamāṇāya
vakṣyāmi hita-kāmyayā

Sri Bhagavan said –
O Arjuna, listen attentively to the topmost advice which I am about to share with you, desiring your welfare, since you are My dear friend.

2

न मे विदुः सुरगणाः प्रभवं न महर्षयः ।
अहमादिर्हि देवानां महर्षीणां च सर्वशः ॥

na me viduḥ sura-gaṇāḥ
prabhavaṁ na maharṣayaḥ
aham ādir hi devānāṁ
maharṣīṇāṁ ca sarvaśaḥ

Neither the host of demigods can understand my origins nor can the great sages. But I am the origin of all the demigods and the sages.

3

यो मामजमनादिं च वेत्ति लोकमहेश्वरम् ।
असम्मूढः स मर्त्येषु सर्वपापैः प्रमुच्यते ॥

yo mām ajam anādiṁ ca
vetti loka-maheśvaram
asammūḍhaḥ sa martyeṣu
sarva-pāpaiḥ pramucyate

One who understands that I am unborn, I have no beginning and that I am the controller of the world, such an undeluded person is at once freed of all sinful reactions.

4 – 5

बुद्धिर्ज्ञानमसम्मोहः क्षमा सत्यं दमः शमः ।
सुखं दुःखं भवोऽभावो भयं चाभयमेव च ॥
अहिंसा समता तुष्टिस्तपो दानं यशोऽयशः ।
भवन्ति भावा भूतानां मत्त एव पृथग्विधाः ॥

buddhir jñānam asammohaḥ
kṣamā satyaṁ damaḥ śamaḥ
sukhaṁ duḥkhaṁ bhavo 'bhāvo
bhayaṁ cābhayam eva ca
ahiṁsā samatā tuṣṭis
tapo dānaṁ yaśo 'yaśaḥ
bhavanti bhāvā bhūtānāṁ
matta eva pṛthag-vidhāḥ

Intelligence, knowledge, freedom from illusion, forgiveness, truthfulness, self-control, mind control, happiness, distress, existence, non-existence, fear, fearlessness, non-violence, equanimity, satisfaction, austerity, charity, fame and infamy; these qualities in living beings arise from Me only.

6

महर्षय: सप्त पूर्वे चत्वारो मनवस्तथा ।
मद्भावा मानसा जाता येषां लोक इमा: प्रजा: ॥

maharṣayaḥ sapta pūrve
catvāro manavas tathā
mad-bhāvā mānasā jātā
yeṣāṁ loka imāḥ prajāḥ

The seven ancient sages, the four Kumaras and the Manus from whom all living beings descended, are all born from My mind.

7

एतां विभूतिं योगं च मम यो वेत्ति तत्त्वतः ।
सोऽविकल्पेन योगेन युज्यते नात्र संशयः ॥

etāṁ vibhūtiṁ yogaṁ ca
mama yo vetti tattvataḥ
so 'vikalpena yogena
yujyate nātra saṁśayaḥ

Anyone who knows these opulence of Mine in essence, undoubtedly engages himself in My devotional service.

8

अहं सर्वस्य प्रभवो मत्तः सर्वं प्रवर्तते ।
इति मत्वा भजन्ते मां बुधा भावसमन्विताः ॥

ahaṁ sarvasya prabhavo
mattaḥ sarvaṁ pravartate
iti matvā bhajante māṁ
budhā bhāva-samanvitāḥ

I am the source of everything and everything emanates from Me. The intelligent who understand this absorb themselves in serving Me and worshipping Me with all their hearts.

9

मच्चित्ता मद्गतप्राणा बोधयन्तः परस्परम् ।
कथयन्तश्च मां नित्यं तुष्यन्ति च रमन्ति च ॥

mac-cittā mad-gata-prāṇā
bodhayantaḥ parasparam
kathayantaś ca māṁ nityaṁ
tuṣyanti ca ramanti ca

With their thoughts dwelling on Me, their lives fully dedicated to Me, they gain great satisfaction and pleasure in discussing My glories amongst themselves, thus enlightening each other.

10

तेषां सततयुक्तानां भजतां प्रीतिपूर्वकम् ।
ददामि बुद्धियोगं तं येन मामुपयान्ति ते ॥

teṣāṁ satata-yuktānāṁ
bhajatāṁ prīti-pūrvakam

dadāmi buddhi-yogaṁ taṁ
yena mām upayānti te

Those who keep themselves incessantly engaged in worshipping Me with love and devotion, I offer them the wisdom using which they can come to Me.

11

तेषामेवानुकम्पार्थमहमज्ञानजं तमः ।
नाशयाम्यात्मभावस्थो ज्ञानदीपेन भास्वता ॥

teṣām evānukampārtham
aham ajñāna-jaṁ tamaḥ
nāśayāmy ātma-bhāva-stho
jñāna-dīpena bhāsvatā

To bestow special grace on such people, I dispel the darkness of ignorance from within their hearts by the shining lamp of knowledge.

12 – 13

अर्जुन उवाच
परं ब्रह्म परं धाम पवित्रं परमं भवान् ।
पुरुषं शाश्वतं दिव्यमादिदेवमजं विभुम् ॥
आहुस्त्वामृषय: सर्वे देवर्षिर्नारदस्तथा ।
असितो देवलो व्यास: स्वयं चैव ब्रवीषि मे ॥

arjuna uvāca
paraṁ brahma paraṁ dhāma
pavitraṁ paramaṁ bhavān
puruṣaṁ śāśvataṁ divyam
ādi-devam ajaṁ vibhum
āhus tvām ṛṣayaḥ sarve
devarṣir nāradas tathā
asito devalo vyāsaḥ
svayaṁ caiva bravīṣi me

Arjuna said –

You are the supreme *Brahmana*, the supreme abode, the supreme purifier; You are the eternal divine personality, the original deity, the unborn and the greatest. All these attributes have been confirmed about You by powerful sages like the divine Narada, Asita, Devala and Vyasa. And now You Yourself have proclaimed it to me.

14

सर्वमेतदृतं मन्ये यन्मां वदसि केशव ।
न हि ते भगवन्व्यक्तिं विदुर्देवा न दानवा: ॥

sarvam etad ṛtaṁ manye
yan māṁ vadasi keśava
na hi te bhagavan vyaktiṁ
vidur devā na dānavāḥ

Everything You have spoken thus far, I totally accept it as the truth, Krishna. It is certainly not possible for neither the demigods nor the demons to understand Your divine manifestation.

15

स्वयमेवात्मनात्मानं वेत्थ त्वं पुरुषोत्तम ।
भूतभावन भूतेश देवदेव जगत्पते ॥

svayam evātmanātmānaṁ
vettha tvaṁ puruṣottama
bhūta-bhāvana bhūteśa
deva-deva jagat-pate

O Supreme Lord, O origin of everything, O Lord of all beings, O Lord of the demigods, O Lord of the universe, only You can know Yourself through Your internal energies.

16

वक्तुमर्हस्यशेषेण दिव्या ह्यात्मविभूतयः ।
याभिर्विभूतिभिर्लोकानिमांस्त्वं व्याप्य तिष्ठसि ॥

vaktum arhasy aśeṣeṇa
divyā hy ātma-vibhūtayaḥ
yābhir vibhūtibhir lokān
imāṁs tvaṁ vyāpya tiṣṭhasi

Kindly tell me in great details about Your divine manifestations through which You permeate and influence all of creation.

17

कथं विद्यामहं योगिंस्त्वां सदा परिचिन्तयन् ।
केषु केषु च भावेषु चिन्त्योऽसि भगवन्मया ॥

kathaṁ vidyām ahaṁ yogiṁs
tvāṁ sadā paricintayan
keṣu keṣu ca bhāveṣu
cintyo 'si bhagavan mayā

O Supreme Mystic, how am I to know You, how am I to meditate on You; in which variegated ways should I think of You?

18

विस्तरेणात्मनो योगं विभूतिं च जनार्दन ।
भूयः कथय तृप्तिर्हि शृण्वतो नास्ति मेऽमृतम् ॥

vistareṇātmano yogaṁ
vibhūtiṁ ca janārdana
bhūyaḥ kathaya tṛptir hi
śṛṇvato nāsti me 'mṛtam

Kindly tell me yet again about Your mystic opulence in great details. I never feel satiated as much as when I hear Your nectarine words.

19

हन्त ते कथयिष्यामि दिव्या ह्यात्मविभूतयः ।
प्राधान्यतः कुरुश्रेष्ठ नास्त्यन्तो विस्तरस्य मे ॥

śrī-bhagavān uvāca
hanta te kathayiṣyāmi
divyā hy ātma-vibhūtayaḥ
prādhānyataḥ kuru-śreṣṭha
nāsty anto vistarasya me

Sri Bhagavan said –
Yes, I will share with you only the prominent aspects of My divine opulence since there is no end to My opulence.

20

अहमात्मा गुडाकेश सर्वभूताशयस्थितः ।
अहमादिश्च मध्यं च भूतानामन्त एव च ॥

aham ātmā guḍākeśa
sarva-bhūtāśaya-sthitaḥ
aham ādiś ca madhyaṁ ca
bhūtānām anta eva ca

I am the Supersoul seated in the heart of every living being. I am the beginning, the middle and the end of all living beings.

21

आदित्यानामहं विष्णुर्ज्योतिषां रविरंशुमान ।
मरीचिर्मरुतामस्मि नक्षत्राणामहं शशी ॥

ādityānām ahaṁ viṣṇur
jyotiṣāṁ ravir aṁśumān
marīcir marutām asmi
nakṣatrāṇām ahaṁ śaśī

Of the Adityas, I am Vishnu. Of the lights, I am the radiant sun. Of the Maruts, I am Marichi. Of the stars, I am the moon.

22

वेदानां सामवेदोऽस्मि देवानामस्मि वासवः ।
इन्द्रियाणां मनश्चास्मि भूतानामस्मि चेतना ॥

vedānāṁ sāma-vedo 'smi
devānām asmi vāsavaḥ
indriyāṇāṁ manaś cāsmi
bhūtānām asmi cetanā

Of the Vedas, I am Sama Veda. Of the demigods, I am Vaasavah or Indra. Of the senses, I am the mind. Of the living beings, I am the consciousness.

23

रुद्राणां शङ्करश्चास्मि वित्तेशो यक्षरक्षसाम् ।
वसूनां पावकश्चास्मि मेरुः शिखरिणामहम् ॥

rudrāṇāṁ śaṅkaraś cāsmi
vitteśo yakṣa-rakṣasām
vasūnāṁ pāvakaś cāsmi
meruḥ śikhariṇām aham

Of the Rudras, I am Shankara. Of the Yakshas, I am Vittasah or Kuvera. Of the Vasus, I am Agni or the fire god. Of mountains, I am Meru.

24

पुरोधसां च मुख्यं मां विद्धि पार्थ बृहस्पतिम् ।
सेनानीनामहं स्कन्दः सरसामस्मि सागरः ॥

purodhasāṁ ca mukhyaṁ māṁ
viddhi pārtha bṛhaspatim
senānīnām ahaṁ skandaḥ
sarasām asmi sāgaraḥ

Of priests, I am the chief priest Brihaspati. Of military chiefs, I am Skanda or Karttikeya. Of water bodies, I am the ocean.

25

महर्षीणां भृगुरहं गिरामस्म्येकमक्षरम् ।
यज्ञानां जपयज्ञोऽस्मि स्थावराणां हिमालयः ॥

maharṣīṇāṁ bhṛgur ahaṁ
girām asmy ekam akṣaram
yajñānāṁ japa-yajño 'smi
sthāvarāṇāṁ himālayaḥ

Of great sages, I am Brighu. Of incantations, I am the single divine syllable Om. Of sacrifices, I am *japa yajna* or chanting of the holy names. Of immovable things, I am the Himalayan mountain.

26

अश्वत्थ: सर्ववृक्षाणां देवर्षीणां च नारद: ।
गन्धर्वाणां चित्ररथ: सिद्धानां कपिलो मुनि: ॥

aśvatthaḥ sarva-vṛkṣāṇāṁ
devarṣīṇāṁ ca nāradaḥ
gandharvāṇāṁ citrarathaḥ
siddhānāṁ kapilo muniḥ

Of trees, I am the Ashwatha or the Banyan tree. Of godly sages, I am Narada. Of Gandharvas, I am Chitraratha. Of siddhas or perfected beings, I am sage Kapila.

27

उच्चै:श्रवसमश्वानां विद्धि माममृतोद्भवम् ।
ऐरावतं गजेन्द्राणां नराणां च नराधिपम् ॥

uccaiḥśravasam aśvānāṁ
viddhi mām amṛtodbhavam
airāvataṁ gajendrāṇāṁ
narāṇāṁ ca narādhipam

Of horses, I am Ucchaishrava that was born from the churning of the milk ocean. Of kingly elephants, I am Airavata. Of men, I am the king.

28

आयुधानामहं वज्रं धेनूनामस्मि कामधुक् ।
प्रजनश्चास्मि कन्दर्पः सर्पाणामस्मि वासुकिः ॥

āyudhānām ahaṁ vajraṁ
dhenūnām asmi kāmadhuk
prajanaś cāsmi kandarpaḥ
sarpāṇām asmi vāsukiḥ

Of weapons, I am the thunderbolt. Of cows, I am the Surabhi cow. Of progenitors, I am Kandarpa or the God of love. Of serpents, I am Vasuki.

29

अनन्तश्चास्मि नागानां वरुणो यादसामहम् ।
पितॄणामर्यमा चास्मि यमः संयमतामहम् ॥

anantaś cāsmi nāgānāṁ
varuṇo yādasām aham
pitṝṇām aryamā cāsmi
yamaḥ saṁyamatām aham

Of multi-hooded snakes, I am Ananta. Of aquatics, I am Varuna or the ocean god. Of ancestors, I am Aryama. Of law keepers, I am Yama, the God of death.

30

प्रह्लादश्चास्मि दैत्यानां कालः कलयतामहम् ।
मृगाणां च मृगेन्द्रोऽहं वैनतेयश्च पक्षिणाम् ॥

prahlādaś cāsmi daityānāṁ
kālaḥ kalayatām aham
mṛgāṇāṁ ca mṛgendro 'haṁ
vainateyaś ca pakṣiṇām

Of *daityas* or demons, I am Prahlada. Of subduers, I am time. Of animals, I am the lion. Of birds, I am Garuda.

31

पवनः पवतामस्मि रामः शस्त्रभृतामहम् ।
झषाणां मकरश्चास्मि स्रोतसामस्मि जाह्नवी ॥

pavanaḥ pavatām asmi
rāmaḥ śastra-bhṛtām aham
jhaṣāṇāṁ makaraś cāsmi
srotasām asmi jāhnavī

Of purifiers, I am the wind. Of experts in weapons, I am Rama. Of fishes, I am the shark. Of flowing rivers, I am the Ganga.

32

सर्गाणामादिरन्तश्च मध्यं चैवाहमर्जुन ।
अध्यात्मविद्या विद्यानां वादः प्रवदतामहम् ॥

sargāṇām ādir antaś ca
madhyaṁ caivāham arjuna
adhyātma-vidyā vidyānāṁ
vādaḥ pravadatām aham

Of creations, I am the beginning, the end and also the middle. Of knowledge, I am the spiritual science of the self. Of logicians, I am the concluding truth.

33

अक्षराणामकारोऽस्मि द्वन्द्वः सामासिकस्य च ।
अहमेवाक्षयः कालो धाताहं विश्वतोमुखः ॥

akṣarāṇām akāro 'smi
dvandvaḥ sāmāsikasya ca
aham evākṣayaḥ kālo
dhātāhaṁ viśvato-mukhaḥ

Of letters, I am the first letter A. Of compound words, I am the dual compound. Among the destroyers, I am the endless time. Of creators, I am Brahma.

34

मृत्युः सर्वहरश्चाहमुद्भवश्च भविष्यताम् ।
कीर्तिः श्रीर्वाक्च नारीणां स्मृतिर्मेधा धृतिः क्षमा ॥

mṛtyuḥ sarva-haraś cāham
udbhavaś ca bhaviṣyatām
kīrtiḥ śrīr vāk ca nārīṇāṁ
smṛtir medhā dhṛtiḥ kṣamā

I am death, the destroyer of everything. I am the source of all future manifestations. Among women, I am fame, prosperity, good speech, memory, intellect, determination and forgiveness.

35

बृहत्साम तथा साम्नां गायत्री छन्दसामहम् ।
मासानां मार्गशीर्षोऽहमृतूनां कुसुमाकरः ॥

bṛhat-sāma tathā sāmnāṁ
gāyatrī chandasām aham
māsānāṁ mārga-śīrṣo 'ham
ṛtūnāṁ kusumākaraḥ

Of hymns in the Sama Veda, I am the Brhat Sama. Of all poetry, I am the Gayatri. Of months, I am Margasirsha or the months of November-December. Of seasons, I am the flowering spring.

36

द्यूतं छलयतामस्मि तेजस्तेजस्विनामहम् ।
जयोऽस्मि व्यवसायोऽस्मि सत्त्वं सत्त्ववतामहम् ॥

dyūtaṁ chalayatām asmi
tejas tejasvinām aham
jayo 'smi vyavasāyo 'smi
sattvaṁ sattvavatām aham

Of all cheaters, I am gambling. Of the influencers, I am the influence. I am victory and I am adventure. Of the strong, I am the strength.

37

वृष्णीनां वासुदेवोऽस्मि पाण्डवानां धनञ्जयः ।
मुनीनामप्यहं व्यासः कवीनामुशना कविः ॥

vṛṣṇīnāṁ vāsudevo 'smi
pāṇḍavānāṁ dhanañjayaḥ
munīnām apy ahaṁ vyāsaḥ
kavīnām uśanā kaviḥ

Of the descendants of Vrsni, I am Vaasudeva. Of the Pandavas, I am Arjuna. Of the sages, I am Vyasa. Of great poets, I am Ushana.

38

दण्डो दमयता मस्मि नीतिरस्मि जिगीषताम् ।
मौनं चैवास्मि गुह्यानां ज्ञानं ज्ञानवतामहम् ॥

daṇḍo damayatām asmi
nītir asmi jigīṣatām
maunaṁ caivāsmi guhyānāṁ
jñānaṁ jñānavatām aham

Of the means suppressing wrong, I am punishment. Of those seeking victory, I am morality. Of secrets, I am silence. Of the wise, I am wisdom.

39

यच्चापि सर्वभूतानां बीजं तदहमर्जुन ।
न तदस्ति विना यत्स्यान्मया भूतं चराचरम् ॥

yac cāpi sarva-bhūtānāṁ
bījaṁ tad aham arjuna
na tad asti vinā yat syān
mayā bhūtaṁ carācaram

I am the seed of all creations. Nothing moving or non-moving can exist without Me.

40

नान्तोऽस्ति मम दिव्यानां विभूतीनां परन्तप ।
एष तूद्देशतः प्रोक्तो विभूतेर्विस्तरो मया ॥

nānto 'sti mama divyānāṁ
vibhūtīnāṁ parantapa
eṣa tūddeśataḥ prokto
vibhūter vistaro mayā

There is no end to My divine opulence. What I have spoken to you, Arjuna, is just a hint of my infinite opulence.

41

यद्यद्विभूतिमत्सत्त्वं श्रीमदूर्जितमेव वा ।
तत्तदेवावगच्छ त्वं मम तेजोंऽशसम्भवम् ॥

yad yad vibhūtimat sattvaṁ
śrīmad ūrjitam eva vā
tat tad evāvagaccha tvaṁ
mama tejo'ṁśa-sambhavam

Whatever and wherever you see opulent, beautiful and glorious manifestations of creation, you should understand those to be just a spark of my splendor.

42

अथवा बहुनैतेन किं ज्ञातेन तवार्जुन ।
विष्टभ्याहमिदं कृत्स्नमेकांशेन स्थितो जगत् ॥

atha vā bahunaitena
kiṁ jñātena tavārjuna
viṣṭabhyāham idaṁ kṛtsnam
ekāṁśena sthito jagat

There is no real need to understand extensive details of this knowledge if you understand that I pervade through and sustain the entire creation by just a single portion of Myself.

Chapter

11

Vishvarupa Darshan Yoga

After hearing Krishna speak the most confidential knowledge, Arjuna's illusions are dissipated. He understands Krishna's majestic greatness in totality. Although Krishna is standing before him in his original form, he is curious to see that form of Krishna by which he pervades the entire universal creation.

Krishna is happy to fulfill Arjuna's desire. He describes what Arjuna can expect to see in his universal form—marvelous things that he has never seen before, various manifestations of the Adityas, Vasus, Rudras and every other demigod; not only the present but also the past and the future; everything moving and non-moving at one place.

To see this, Krishna grants Arjuna special divine vision. And then Krishna, the greatest mystic, displays his universal form to Arjuna.

Arjuna is astonished to see a multitude of eyes, mouths, faces in that form. Multitude of eyes, mouths, faces are visible in that form. He sees all demigods, living beings, Lord Brahma seated on the lotus flower, as well as all the sages and divine serpents.

Numerous wonderful visions, celestial ornaments, upraised weapons, divine garlands and garments bedeck that universal form. The brilliance of that universal form of the Supreme Lord is akin to millions of suns rising at once in the sky. Completely baffled and mystified, Arjuna's hair stands on its ends.

Arjuna bows down his head and folds his hands in complete awe and reverence. Words of glory pour out from his mouth.

His awe changes to fear when he sees the future too. He sees all sons of Dhritarashtra along with accompanying kings, as well as Bhishma, Drona and Karna including their chief army personnel, helplessly rushing into Krishna's terrible open mouths like rivers gushing into the ocean; or moths rushing into a blazing fire for their own destruction. Some of them are trapped between his teeth with their heads being crushed. Krishna is consuming people from all directions through his flaming mouths and licking their blood in fury. Arjuna is totally bewildered and asks Krishna, who are you? What is your mission?

Krishna affirms that he is time, the greatest destructive force in this word. His mission is to terminate one and all. Whether Arjuna fights the war or not, Krishna will vanquish all soldiers on both sides, apart from the Pandavas. Therefore it made sense for Arjuna to wake up and align himself with Krishna's plan. If he fights knowing that the enemies including Drona, Bhishma, Jayadratha, Karna have already been vanquished by Krishna, then Arjuna has the opportunity to be his instrument in this fight and get all the credit.

After hearing Krishna, the fearful Arjuna

repeatedly offers his respects and speaks to Krishna in a faltering voice; hearing your name brings great joy to the world. You are the unlimited shelter of the universe; the invisible cause behind all causes, the ultimate abode of the world, the all-knowing and the ultimate object of knowledge. You are all-pervading. You are air, fire, water and the moon. You are the first created living being, Brahma. I offer my respects to You from the front, from behind, from all sides. You are the God of limitless strength.

Arjuna further regrets that in ignorance, he considered Krishna as an ordinary friend. Asking for forgiveness, he explains he did it out of affection and foolishness. Just as a father tolerates bad manners of his son, as a friend tolerates the disrespectfulness of a friend or a spouse tolerates the familiarity of the partner; similarly Arjuna requests Krishna to tolerate the mistakes he committed in his dealings with Krishna. He is simultaneously gladdened as well as disturbed by the vision of this universal form. He begs Krishna to again reveal his original form, his four-handed form holding the club, disc, conch and lotus flower in each hand.

Krishna informs that Arjuna alone was shown the greatest universal form within this material existence. Neither by study of the Vedas nor by performance of sacrifices, charitable work, accumulation of pious deeds or intense austerities can one see this form. Before Arjuna no one ever has seen this original, limitless, brilliantly radiant form.

And then Krishna relieves Arjuna of the fear and bewilderment that has enveloped him on seeing this ghastly form. He shows his four-armed form before finally returning back to his original two-handed form. Arjuna is immediately peaceful at the original two-handed form of Krishna.

Again Krishna explains that his two-handed form is actually very rare to see. Even the greatest of demigods are hankering to get an opportunity to see this form. Only by pure devotional service can one enter into the secrets of understanding him completely and getting a chance to see him as he stands before Arjuna.

Krishna concludes by summarizing who can come to him; one who knows him to be the Supreme person and engages in his devotional service, free from contamination of result-oriented work and cultivation of speculative knowledge, who remains affectionate to all living beings and makes him the goal of his life, such a person certainly comes to him.

1

अर्जुन उवाच
मदनुग्रहाय परमं गुह्यमध्यात्मसंज्ञितम् ।
यत्त्वयोक्तं वचस्तेन मोहोऽयं विगतो मम ॥

arjuna uvāca
mad-anugrahāya paramaṁ
guhyam adhyātma-saṁjñitam
yat tvayoktaṁ vacas tena
moho 'yaṁ vigato mama

Arjuna said –
Hearing Your instructions on the most confidential knowledge, my illusion has now dissipated.

2

भवाप्ययौ हि भूतानां श्रुतौ विस्तरशो मया ।
त्वत्तः कमलपत्राक्ष माहात्म्यमपि चाव्ययम् ॥

bhavāpyayau hi bhūtānāṁ
śrutau vistaraśo mayā
tvattaḥ kamala-patrākṣa
māhātmyam api cāvyayam

I have heard in detail about the creation and dissolution of every living being along with Your inestimable greatness.

3

एवमेतद्यथात्थ त्वमात्मानं परमेश्वर ।
द्रष्टुमिच्छामि ते रूपमैश्वरं पुरुषोत्तम ॥

evam etad yathāttha tvam
ātmānaṁ parameśvara
draṣṭum icchāmi te rūpam
aiśvaraṁ puruṣottama

Even though I have heard about Your greatness and I accept it thoroughly, I still wish to see that form of Yours by which You pervade the entire universal creation. Though I see You stationed before me on this chariot in Your original form, I still wish to see You in the form that You have described to me.

4

मन्यसे यदि तच्छक्यं मया द्रष्टुमिति प्रभो ।
योगेश्वर ततो मे त्वं दर्शयात्मानमव्ययम् ॥

manyase yadi tac chakyaṁ
mayā draṣṭum iti prabho
yogeśvara tato me tvaṁ
darśayātmānam avyayam

Although I am requesting You, only if You feel I am qualified enough to behold that mystical form of Yours, kindly show it to me.

5

श्रीभगवानुवाच
पश्य मे पार्थ रूपाणि शतशोऽथ सहस्रशः ।
नानाविधानि दिव्यानि नानावर्णाकृतीनि च ॥

śrī-bhagavān uvāca
paśya me pārtha rūpāṇi
śataśo 'tha sahasraśaḥ
nānā-vidhāni divyāni
nānā-varṇākṛtīni ca

Sri Bhagavan said –

Arjuna, get ready to witness millions of My variegated, wonderful and multifarious forms of excellence that I have spoken to you about.

6

पश्यादित्यान्वसून्रुद्रानश्विनौ मरुतस्तथा ।
बहून्यदृष्टपूर्वाणि पश्याश्चर्याणि भारत ॥

paśyādityān vasūn rudrān
aśvinau marutas tathā
bahūny adṛṣṭa-pūrvāṇi
paśyāścaryāṇi bhārata

Look at the various manifestations of the Adityas, Vasus, Rudras and every other demigod. You can perceive marvelous things that have never been seen before.

7

इहैकस्थं जगत्कृत्स्नं पश्याद्य सचराचरम् ।
मम देहे गुडाकेश यच्चान्यद्द्रष्टुमिच्छसि ॥

ihaika-sthaṁ jagat kṛtsnaṁ
paśyādya sa-carācaram
mama dehe guḍākeśa
yac cānyad draṣṭum icchasi

Everything you may ever wish to see can be seen in this special form of Mine. This universal form can not only show you the present but also the past and the future. You will find everything moving and non-moving at one place.

8

न तु मां शक्यसे द्रष्टुमनेनैव स्वचक्षुषा ।
दिव्यं ददामि ते चक्षुः पश्य मे योगमैश्वरम् ॥

na tu māṁ śakyase draṣṭum
anenaiva sva-cakṣuṣā
divyaṁ dadāmi te cakṣuḥ
paśya me yogam aiśvaram

Your regular vision will not be sufficient to perceive this universal form. I will grant you special divine vision to see the form that I am about to manifest. Behold My mystic grandeaur!

9

सञ्जय उवाच
एवमुक्त्वा ततो राजन्महायोगेश्वरो हरिः ।
दर्शयामास पार्थाय परमं रूपमैश्वरम् ॥

sañjaya uvāca
evam uktvā tato rājan
mahā-yogeśvaro hariḥ

darśayām āsa pārthāya
paramaṁ rūpam aiśvaram

Sanjaya said –
The Supreme Lord who is the greatest mystic displayed his universal form to Arjuna.

10 – 11

अनेकवक्त्रनयनमनेकाद्भुतदर्शनम् ।
अनेकदिव्याभरणं दिव्यानेकोद्यतायुधम् ॥
दिव्यमाल्याम्बरधरं दिव्यगन्धानुलेपनम् ।
सर्वाश्चर्यमयं देवमनन्तं विश्वतोमुखम् ॥

aneka-vaktra-nayanam
anekādbhuta-darśanam
aneka-divyābharaṇaṁ
divyānekodyatāyudham
divya-mālyāmbara-dharaṁ
divya-gandhānulepanam
sarvāścarya-mayaṁ devam
anantaṁ viśvato-mukham

Multitude of eyes, mouths, faces were visible in that form. Numerous wonderful visions, celestial ornaments, upraised weapons, divine garlands and garments bedecked that universal form. A plethora of divine scents was smeared over that divine form. Filled with wonderment, unlimited radiance and with faces turned in every possible direction, the all-expanding universal form was now visible to Arjuna.

12

दिवि सूर्यसहस्रस्य भवेद्युगपदुत्थिता ।
यदि भा: सदृशी सा स्याद्भासस्तस्य महात्मन: ॥

divi sūrya-sahasrasya
bhaved yugapad utthitā
yadi bhāḥ sadṛśī sā syād
bhāsas tasya mahātmanaḥ

The brilliance of that universal form of the Supreme Lord was akin to millions of suns rising at once in the sky.

13

तत्रैकस्थं जगत्कृत्स्नं प्रविभक्तमनेकधा ।
अपश्यद्देवदेवस्य शरीरे पाण्डवस्तदा ॥

tatraikasthaṁ jagat kṛtsnaṁ
pravibhaktam anekadhā

apaśyad deva-devasya
śarīre pāṇḍavas tadā

Arjuna could easily understand that the universal form exhibited the entire diversity of creation in one place although it is actually divided.

14

ततः स विस्मयाविष्टो हृष्टरोमा धनञ्जयः ।
प्रणम्य शिरसा देवं कृताञ्जलिरभाषत ॥

tataḥ sa vismayāviṣṭo
hṛṣṭa-romā dhanañjayaḥ
praṇamya śirasā devaṁ
kṛtāñjalir abhāṣata

Completely baffled and mystified, Arjuna's hair stood on its ends. Bowing down his head with hands folded in respect, Arjuna spoke.

15

अर्जुन उवाच
पश्यामि देवांस्तव देव देहे
सर्वांस्तथा भूतविशेषसङ्घान् ।
ब्रह्माणमीशं कमलासनस्थ-
मृषींश्च सर्वानुरगांश्च दिव्यान् ॥

arjuna uvāca
paśyāmi devāṁs tava deva dehe
sarvāṁs tathā bhūta-viśeṣa-saṅghān
brahmāṇam īśaṁ kamalāsana-stham
ṛṣīṁś ca sarvān uragāṁś ca divyān

Arjuna said –
O my Lord, I can see in Your body, all the demigods and all varieties of living beings. I can see Lord Brahma seated on the lotus flower, Lord Shiva, as well as all the sages and divine serpents.

16

अनेकबाहूदरवक्त्रनेत्रं
पश्यामि त्वां सर्वतोऽनन्तरूपम् ।
नान्तं न मध्यं न पुनस्तवादिं
पश्यामि विश्वेश्वर विश्वरूप ॥

aneka-bāhūdara-vaktra-netraṁ
paśyāmi tvāṁ sarvato 'nanta-rūpam

nāntaṁ na madhyaṁ na punas tavādiṁ
paśyāmi viśveśvara viśva-rūpa

I can perceive in Your limitless form multitudes of arms, mouths, eyes and bellies expanded in every direction. I am unable to fathom the end, middle or beginning of this universal form.

17

किरीटिनं गदिनं चक्रिणं च
तेजोराशिं सर्वतो दीप्तिमन्तम् ।
पश्यामि त्वां दुर्निरीक्ष्यं समन्ता-
द्दीप्तानलार्कद्युतिमप्रमेयम् ॥

kirīṭinaṁ gadinaṁ cakriṇaṁ ca
tejo-rāśiṁ sarvato dīptimantam
paśyāmi tvāṁ durnirīkṣyaṁ samantād
dīptānalārka-dyutim aprameyam

The brilliant effulgence emitting from Your form is blinding like the blazing sun, thus making it difficult for us to see You. Though it's extremely difficult to perceive You completely, I can behold Your crowns, clubs and discs.

18

त्वमक्षरं परमं वेदितव्यं
त्वमस्य विश्वस्य परं निधानम्।
त्वमव्ययः शाश्वतधर्मगोप्ता
सनातनस्त्वं पुरुषो मतो मे ॥

tvam akṣaraṁ paramaṁ veditavyaṁ
tvam asya viśvasya paraṁ nidhānam
tvam avyayaḥ śāśvata-dharma-goptā
sanātanas tvaṁ puruṣo mato me

You are the eternal, oldest, unchanging, inexhaustible, ultimate object of knowledge and the conclusive abode of the whole universe. You are known as the ultimate maintainer and defender of the eternal principles of religion.

19

अनादिमध्यान्तमनन्तवीर्य–
मनन्तबाहुं शशिसूर्यनेत्रम्।
पश्यामि त्वां दीप्तहुताशवक्त्रं
स्वतेजसा विश्वमिदं तपन्तम् ॥

anādi-madhyāntam ananta-vīryam
ananta-bāhuṁ śaśi-sūrya-netram

paśyāmi tvāṁ dīpta-hutāśa-vaktraṁ
sva-tejasā viśvam idaṁ tapantam

With no beginning, middle or end, Your glory is boundless. With numerous arms, having the sun and moon as Your eyes and mouth emitting blazing fire, You are scorching the entire universe.

20

द्यावापृथिव्योरिदमन्तरं हि
व्याप्तं त्वयैकेन दिशश्च सर्वाः ।
दृष्ट्वाद्भुतं रूपमुग्रं तवेदं
लोकत्रयं प्रव्यथितं महात्मन् ॥

dyāv āpṛthivyor idam antaraṁ hi
vyāptaṁ tvayaikena diśaś ca sarvāḥ
dṛṣṭvādbhutaṁ rūpam ugraṁ tavedaṁ
loka-trayaṁ pravyathitaṁ mahātman

Seeing this all-pervading, breathtaking and terrible form, the three worlds shudder in great fear.

21

अमी हि त्वां सुरसङ्घा विशन्ति
केचिद्भीताः प्राञ्जलयो गृणन्ति ।
स्वस्तीत्युक्त्वा महर्षिसिद्धसङ्घाः
स्तुवन्ति त्वां स्तुतिभिः पुष्कलाभिः ॥

amī hi tvāṁ sura-saṅghā viśanti
kecid bhītāḥ prāñjalayo gṛṇanti
svastīty uktvā maharṣi-siddha-saṅghāḥ
stuvanti tvāṁ stutibhiḥ puṣkalābhiḥ

A host of demigods are taking shelter of You and entering into Your form. With fear in their eyes, some of them are offering prayers with folded palms, besieging Your protection. The sages on the other hand are crying out Vedic hymns while trying to pacify You.

22

रुद्रादित्या वसवो ये च साध्या
विश्वेऽश्विनौ मरुतश्चोष्मपाश्च ।
गन्धर्वयक्षासुरसिद्धसङ्घा
वीक्षन्ते त्वां विस्मिताश्चैव सर्वे ॥

rudrādityā vasavo ye ca sādhyā
viśve 'śvinau marutaś coṣmapāś ca

gandharva-yakṣāsura-siddha-saṅghā
vīkṣante tvāṁ vismitāś caiva sarve

The Rudras, Adityas, Vasus, Sadhyas, Vishvadevas, the two Ashvini kumaras, the Maruts, the ancestors, the Gandharvas, the Yakshas, the Asuras and the Siddhas are all completely awestruck.

23

रूपं महत्ते बहुवक्त्रनेत्रं
महाबाहो बहुबाहूरुपादम् ।
बहूदरं बहुदंष्ट्राकरालं
दृष्ट्वा लोकाः प्रव्यथितास्तथाहम् ॥

rūpaṁ mahat te bahu-vaktra-netraṁ
mahā-bāho bahu-bāhūru-pādam
bahūdaraṁ bahu-daṁṣṭrā-karālaṁ
dṛṣṭvā lokāḥ pravyathitās tathāham

Seeing this terrible form with its numerous faces, mouths, ghastly teeth, eyes, ears, arms, bellies, thighs and feet, all the world including me is highly disturbed and shivering in fear.

24

नभ:स्पृशं दीप्तमनेकवर्णं
व्यात्ताननं दीप्तविशालनेत्रम् ।
दृष्ट्वा हि त्वां प्रव्यथितान्तरात्मा
धृतिं न विन्दामि शमं च विष्णो ॥

nabhaḥ spṛśaṁ dīptam aneka-varṇaṁ
vyāttānanaṁ dīpta-viśāla-netram
dṛṣṭvā hi tvāṁ pravyathitāntar-ātmā
dhṛtiṁ na vindāmi śamaṁ ca viṣṇo

On beholding Your form that touches the sky, with many brilliant colors, wide open mouths and glowering eyes, my mind is totally bewildered. This fear has caused me to lose my equilibrium and steadiness of mind.

25

दंष्ट्राकरालानि च ते मुखानि
दृष्ट्वैव कालानलसन्निभानि ।
दिशो न जाने न लभे च शर्म
प्रसीद देवेश जगन्निवास ॥

daṁṣṭrā-karālāni ca te mukhāni
dṛṣṭvaiva kālānala-sannibhāni

diśo na jāne na labhe ca śarma
prasīda deveśa jagan-nivāsa

O Lord of the demigods, O shelter of the three worlds, kindly be considerate to me. I am unable to retain my balance seeing Your ghastly death like faces and terrible teeth. Fear pervades me in every direction and I am totally baffled.

26 – 27

अमी च त्वां धृतराष्ट्रस्य पुत्राः
सर्वे सहैवावनिपालसङ्घैः ।
भीष्मो द्रोणः सूतपुत्रस्तथासौ
सहास्मदीयैरपि योधमुख्यैः ॥
वक्त्राणि ते त्वरमाणा विशन्ति
दंष्ट्राकरालानि भयानकानि ।
केचिद्विलग्ना दशनान्तरेषु
सन्दृश्यन्ते चूर्णितैरुत्तमाङ्गैः ॥

amī ca tvāṁ dhṛtarāṣṭrasya putrāḥ
sarve sahaivāvani-pāla-saṅghaiḥ
bhīṣmo droṇaḥ sūta-putras tathāsau
sahāsmadīyair api yodha-mukhyaiḥ
vaktrāṇi te tvaramāṇā viśanti
daṁṣṭrā-karālāni bhayānakāni

kecid vilagnā daśanāntareṣu
sandṛśyante cūrṇitair uttamāṅgaiḥ

I can see all sons of Dhritarashtra along with accompanying kings, as well as Bhishma, Drona and Karna including their chief army personnel, helplessly rushing into Your terrible open mouths. Some of them I see trapped between Your teeth with their heads being crushed.

28

यथा नदीनां बहवोऽम्बुवेगा:
समुद्रमेवाभिमुखा द्रवन्ति।
तथा तवामी नरलोकवीरा
विशन्ति वक्त्राण्यभिविज्वलन्ति ॥

yathā nadīnāṁ bahavo 'mbu-vegāḥ
samudram evābhimukhā dravanti
tathā tavāmī nara-loka-vīrā
viśanti vaktrāṇy abhivijvalanti

These warriors entering into Your mouth resemble rivers gushing into the ocean.

29

यथा प्रदीप्तं ज्वलनं पतङ्गा
विशन्ति नाशाय समृद्धवेगाः ।
तथैव नाशाय विशन्ति लोका-
स्तवापि वक्त्राणि समृद्धवेगाः ॥

yathā pradīptaṁ jvalanaṁ pataṅgā
viśanti nāśāya samṛddha-vegāḥ
tathaiva nāśāya viśanti lokās
tavāpi vaktrāṇi samṛddha-vegāḥ

All these people are rushing into Your mouth just as moths rush into a blazing fire for their own destruction.

30

लेलिह्यसे ग्रसमानः समन्ता-
ल्लोकान्समग्रान्वदनैर्ज्वलद्भिः।
तेजोभिरापूर्य जगत्समग्रं
भासस्तवोग्राः प्रतपन्ति विष्णो ॥

lelihyase grasamānaḥ samantāl
lokān samagrān vadanair jvaladbhiḥ
tejobhir āpūrya jagat samagraṁ
bhāsas tavogrāḥ pratapanti viṣṇo

O Lord Vishnu, I can see You consuming people from all directions through Your flaming mouths and licking their blood in fury. Your brilliance envelopes the whole universe with its effulgent scorching rays.

31

आख्याहि मे को भवानुग्ररूपो
नमोऽस्तु ते देववर प्रसीद ।
विज्ञातुमिच्छामि भवन्तमाद्यं
न हि प्रजानामि तव प्रवृत्तिम् ॥

ākhyāhi me ko bhavān ugra-rūpo
namo 'stu te deva-vara prasīda
vijñātum icchāmi bhavantam ādyaṁ
na hi prajānāmi tava pravṛttim

O Lord, with such a fierce countenance, who are You? I offer my respects to You. O God of Gods, the original personality, be merciful to me and reveal Yourself to me. Please tell me what Your mission is?

32

श्रीभगवानुवाच
कालोऽस्मि लोकक्षयकृत्प्रवृद्धो
लोकान्समाहर्तुमिह प्रवृत्तः ।
ऋतेऽपि त्वां न भविष्यन्ति सर्वे
येऽवस्थिताः प्रत्यनीकेषु योधाः ॥

śrī-bhagavān uvāca
kālo 'smi loka-kṣaya-kṛt pravṛddho
lokān samāhartum iha pravṛttaḥ
ṛte 'pi tvāṁ na bhaviṣyanti sarve
ye 'vasthitāḥ pratyanīkeṣu yodhāḥ

Sri Bhagavan said –
Time, I am the greatest destructive force in this world and who is here to terminate one and all. Even if you don't fight in this war, apart from you Pandavas, all soldiers on both the sides will be vanquished by Me.

33

तस्मात्त्वमुत्तिष्ठ यशो लभस्व
जित्वा शत्रून्भुङ्क्ष्व राज्यं समृद्धम् ।
मयैवैते निहताः पूर्वमेव
निमित्तमात्रं भव सव्यसाचिन् ॥

tasmāt tvam uttiṣṭha yaśo labhasva
jitvā śatrūn bhuṅkṣva rājyaṁ samṛddham

mayaivaite nihatāḥ pūrvam eva
nimitta-mātraṁ bhava savya-sācin

Therefore wake up and claim your glory! Vanquish your enemies and enjoy a prosperous kingdom. If you fight understanding that your enemies have already been vanquished by Me, then you can be My instrument in this fight and get all the credit.

34

द्रोणं च भीष्मं च जयद्रथं च
कर्णं तथान्यानपि योधवीरान् ।
मया हतांस्त्वं जहि मा व्यथिष्ठा
युध्यस्व जेतासि रणे सपत्नान् ॥

droṇaṁ ca bhīṣmaṁ ca jayadrathaṁ ca
karṇaṁ tathānyān api yodha-vīrān
mayā hatāṁs tvaṁ jahi mā vyathiṣṭhā
yudhyasva jetāsi raṇe sapatnān

Drona, Bhishma, Jayadratha, Karna and other ace fighters have already been terminated by Me. Kill them without fear! Just by attempting to fight, surely you shall conquer the enemy in this war.

35

सञ्जय उवाच
एतच्छ्रुत्वा वचनं केशवस्य
कृताञ्जलिर्वेपमानः किरीटी ।
नमस्कृत्वा भूय एवाह कृष्णं
सगद्गदं भीतभीतः प्रणम्य ॥

sañjaya uvāca
etac chrutvā vacanaṁ keśavasya
kṛtāñjalir vepamānaḥ kirītī
namaskṛtvā bhūya evāha kṛṣṇaṁ
sagadgadaṁ bhīta-bhītaḥ praṇamya

Sanjaya said –
Hearing the words of Krishna, the fearful Arjuna repeatedly offered his respects with folded palms. He then spoke to Krishna in a faltering voice.

36

अर्जुन उवाच
स्थाने हृषीकेश तव प्रकीर्त्या
जगत्प्रहृष्यत्यनुरज्यते च ।
रक्षांसि भीतानि दिशो द्रवन्ति
सर्वे नमस्यन्ति च सिद्धसङ्घाः ॥

arjuna uvāca
sthāne hṛṣīkeśa tava prakīrtyā

jagat prahṛṣyaty anurajyate ca
rakṣāṁsi bhītāni diśo dravanti
sarve namasyanti ca siddha-saṅghāḥ

Arjuna said –
Hearing Your name brings great joy to the world and attracts everyone towards You. Though great souls take shelter of You, those with demoniac mindset flee away from You out of fear.

37

कस्माच्च ते न नमेरन्महात्मन्
गरीयसे ब्रह्मणोऽप्यादिकर्त्रे ।
अनन्त देवेश जगन्निवास
त्वमक्षरं सदसत्तत्परं यत् ॥

kasmāc ca te na nameran mahātman
garīyase brahmaṇo 'py ādi-kartre
ananta deveśa jagan-nivāsa
tvam akṣaraṁ sad-asat tat paraṁ yat

Since You are the original creator of this universe, why should everyone not offer their respects to You? You are the unlimited shelter of the universe; the invisible cause behind all causes, You are beyond this world.

38

त्वमादिदेवः पुरुषः पुराण-
स्त्वमस्य विश्वस्य परं निधानम् ।
वेत्तासि वेद्यं च परं च धाम
त्वया ततं विश्वमनन्तरूप ॥

tvam ādi-devaḥ puruṣaḥ purāṇas
tvam asya viśvasya paraṁ nidhānam
vettāsi vedyaṁ ca paraṁ ca dhāma
tvayā tataṁ viśvam ananta-rūpa

You are the primal person, the ultimate abode of the world, the all-knowing and the ultimate object of knowledge. You are the supreme shelter and beyond material modes.

39

वायुर्यमोऽग्निर्वरुणः शशाङ्कः
प्रजापतिस्त्वं प्रपितामहश्च ।
नमो नमस्तेऽस्तु सहस्रकृत्वः
पुनश्च भूयोऽपि नमो नमस्ते ॥

vāyur yamo ‘gnir varuṇaḥ śaśāṅkaḥ
prajāpatis tvaṁ prapitāmahaś ca
namo namas te ‘stu sahasra-kṛtvaḥ
punaś ca bhūyo ‘pi namo namas te

You are all-pervading. You are air, fire, water and the moon. You are the first created living being, Brahma. I offer my respects to You a million times over and over again.

40

नमः पुरस्तादथ पृष्ठतस्ते
नमोऽस्तु ते सर्वत एव सर्व ।
अनन्तवीर्यामितविक्रमस्त्वं
सर्वं समाप्नोषि ततोऽसि सर्वः ॥

namaḥ purastād atha pṛṣṭhatas te
namo 'stu te sarvata eva sarva
ananta-vīryāmita-vikramas tvaṁ
sarvaṁ samāpnoṣi tato 'si sarvaḥ

I offer my respects to You from the front. I offer my respects to You from behind. I offer my respects to You from all sides. You are the God of limitless strength. You are all-pervading! You are simply everything!

41 – 42

सखेति मत्वा प्रसभं यदुक्तं
हे कृष्ण हे यादव हे सखेति ।
अजानता महिमानं तवेदं
मया प्रमादात्प्रणयेन वापि ॥
यच्चावहासार्थमसत्कृतोऽसि
विहारशय्यासनभोजनेषु ।
एकोऽथ वाप्यच्युत तत्समक्षं
तत्क्षामये त्वामहमप्रमेयम् ॥

sakheti matvā prasabhaṁ yad uktaṁ
he kṛṣṇa he yādava he sakheti
ajānatā mahimānaṁ tavedaṁ
mayā pramādāt praṇayena vāpi
yac cāvahāsārtham asat-kṛto 'si
vihāra-śayyāsana-bhojaneṣu
eko 'tha vāpy acyuta tat-samakṣaṁ
tat kṣāmaye tvām aham aprameyam

Considering You as my ordinary friend, I have carelessly addressed You by various names, Krishna, Yadava and my friend. I did all that out of ignorance, not knowing Your greatness. Please forgive my audacity and consider it done out of affection or foolishness. I may have disrespected You by joking as we spent relaxed times together, while lying down, sitting or eating, either when we were alone or sometimes even in front of our friends. O infallible one, please forgive all my misconduct.

43

पितासि लोकस्य चराचरस्य
त्वमस्य पूज्यश्च गुरुर्गरीयान् ।
न त्वत्समोऽस्त्यभ्यधिकः कुतोऽन्यो
लोकत्रयेऽप्यप्रतिमप्रभाव ॥

pitāsi lokasya carācarasya
tvam asya pūjyaś ca gurur garīyān
na tvat-samo 'sty abhyadhikaḥ kuto 'nyo
loka-traye 'py apratima-prabhāva

You are the father of every moving and stationary being of the entire cosmic universe. You are the worshippable master, the teacher of the scriptures and no one is more venerable than You. How is it possible for anyone to be greater than You within the three worlds?

44

तस्मात्प्रणम्य प्रणिधाय कायं
प्रसादये त्वामहमीशमीड्यम् ।
पितेव पुत्रस्य सखेव सख्युः
प्रियः प्रियायार्हसि देव सोढुम् ॥

tasmāt praṇamya praṇidhāya kāyaṁ
prasādaye tvām aham īśam īḍyam
piteva putrasya sakheva sakhyuḥ
priyaḥ priyāyārhasi deva soḍhum

You are the supreme worshippable object of every living entity. As I offer my respects to You, I besiege Your grace. Just as a father tolerates the bad mannerisms of his son, as a friend tolerates the disrespectfulness of a friend or a spouse tolerates the familiarity of the partner; similarly kindly tolerate the mistakes I may have committed in my dealings with You.

45

अदृष्टपूर्वं हृषितोऽस्मि दृष्ट्वा
भयेन च प्रव्यथितं मनो मे ।
तदेव मे दर्शय देव रूपं
प्रसीद देवेश जगन्निवास ॥

adṛṣṭa-pūrvaṁ hṛṣito 'smi dṛṣṭvā
bhayena ca pravyathitaṁ mano me
tad eva me darśaya deva rūpaṁ
prasīda deveśa jagan-nivāsa

Vision of this universal form that I have never seen before has simultaneously gladdened me as well as disturbed me. I beg You to throw some grace upon me and once again reveal Your form as the Personality of Godhead.

46

किरीटिनं गदिनं चक्रहस्त-
मिच्छामि त्वां द्रष्टुमहं तथैव ।
तेनैव रूपेण चतुर्भुजेन
सहस्रबाहो भव विश्वमूर्ते ॥

kirīṭinaṁ gadinaṁ cakra-hastam
icchāmi tvāṁ draṣṭum ahaṁ tathaiva
tenaiva rūpeṇa catur-bhujena
sahasra-bāho bhava viśva-mūrte

O Universal form! O thousand handed Lord! I now wish to see Your four-handed form holding the club, disc, conch and lotus flower in each hand. I eagerly long to see that form of Yours.

47

श्रीभगवानुवाच
मया प्रसन्नेन तवार्जुनेदं
रूपं परं दर्शितमात्मयोगात् ।
तेजोमयं विश्वमनन्तमाद्यं
यन्मे त्वदन्येन न दृष्टपूर्वम् ॥

śrī-bhagavān uvāca
mayā prasannena tavārjunedaṁ
rūpaṁ paraṁ darśitam ātma-yogāt
tejomayaṁ viśvam anantam ādyaṁ
yan me tvad-anyena na dṛṣṭa-pūrvam

Sri Bhagavan said –

My dear Arjuna, by the dint of My internal energy, I have happily shown you the greatest universal form within this material existence. Never before has this original, limitless, brilliantly radiant form been seen.

48

न वेदयज्ञाध्ययनैर्न दानै-
र्न च क्रियाभिर्न तपोभिरुग्रैः ।
एवंरूपः शक्य अहं नृलोके
द्रष्टुं त्वदन्येन कुरुप्रवीर ॥

na veda-yajñādhyayanair na dānair
na ca kriyābhir na tapobhir ugraiḥ
evaṁ rūpaḥ śakya ahaṁ nṛ-loke
draṣṭuṁ tvad-anyena kuru-pravīra

No one before you has seen this universal form of Mine. One cannot perceive Me in this form by mere study of the Vedas or by performance of sacrifices or by charitable work or by accumulation of pious deeds or by intense austerities.

49

मा ते व्यथा मा च विमूढभावो
दृष्ट्वा रूपं घोरमीदृङ्ममेदम् ।
व्यपेतभीः प्रीतमनाः पुनस्त्वं
तदेव मे रूपमिदं प्रपश्य ॥

mā te vyathā mā ca vimūḍha-bhāvo
dṛṣṭvā rūpaṁ ghoram īdṛṅ mamedam

vyapetabhīḥ prīta-manāḥ punas tvaṁ
tad eva me rūpam idaṁ prapaśya

I am now going to relieve you of the fear and bewilderment that has enveloped you on seeing this ghastly form of Mine. Let My devotee be free from all agitation. Now with a peaceful mind, you can behold the form that you desire to see.

50

सञ्जय उवाच
इत्यर्जुनं वासुदेवस्तथोक्त्वा
स्वकं रूपं दर्शयामास भूयः ।
आश्वासयामास च भीतमेनं
भूत्वा पुनः सौम्यवपुर्महात्मा ॥

sañjaya uvāca
ity arjunaṁ vāsudevas tathoktvā
svakaṁ rūpaṁ darśayām āsa bhūyaḥ
āśvāsayām āsa ca bhītam enaṁ
bhūtvā punaḥ saumya-vapur mahatma

Sanjaya said –
Thereupon, Krishna encouraged the fearful Arjuna by showing His four-armed form and finally returning back to his original two-handed form.

51

अर्जुन उवाच
दृष्ट्वेदं मानुषं रूपं तव सौम्यं जनार्दन ।
इदानीमस्मि संवृत्तः सचेताः प्रकृतिं गतः ॥

arjuna uvāca
dṛṣṭvedaṁ mānuṣaṁ rūpaṁ
tava saumyaṁ janārdana
idānīm asmi saṁvṛttaḥ
sa-cetāḥ prakṛtiṁ gataḥ

As soon as Arjuna glanced at the original two-handed form of Krishna, he said, "O Janardhana, this human like form of Yours is most beautiful. Now my mind is calm and I am in a peaceful state.

52

श्रीभगवानुवाच
सुदुर्दर्शमिदं रूपं दृष्टवानसि यन्मम ।
देवा अप्यस्य रूपस्य नित्यं दर्शनकाङ्क्षिणः ॥

śrī-bhagavān uvāca
sudurdarśam idaṁ rūpaṁ
dṛṣṭavān asi yan mama
devā apy asya rūpasya
nityaṁ darśana-kāṅkṣiṇaḥ

Sri Bhagavan said –

My dear Arjuna, the form that you are presently seeing is actually very rare to see. Even the greatest of demigods are hankering to get an opportunity to see this form which is so dear to you.

53

नाहं वेदैर्न तपसा न दानेन न चेज्यया ।
शक्य एवंविधो द्रष्टुं दृष्टवानसि मां यथा ॥

nāhaṁ vedair na tapasā
na dānena na cejyayā
śakya evaṁ-vidho draṣṭuṁ
dṛṣṭavān asi māṁ yathā

The form that you behold now with your divine eyes can never be comprehended by mere study of Vedas or by undertaking severe austerities or by performance of charitable acts or even by worship. These are not the means to see Me as I am.

54

भक्त्या त्वनन्यया शक्य अहमेवंविधोऽर्जुन ।
ज्ञातुं द्रष्टुं च तत्त्वेन प्रवेष्टुं च परन्तप ॥

bhaktyā tv ananyayā śakya
aham evaṁ-vidho 'rjuna
jñātuṁ draṣṭuṁ ca tattvena
praveṣṭuṁ ca parantapa

Only by devotional service that is uncontaminated with result-oriented work or cultivation of speculative knowledge, can one understand Me properly. Only by performance of such devotional service can one enter into the secrets of understanding Me completely and getting a chance to see Me as I stand before you.

55

मत्कर्मकृन्मत्परमो मद्भक्तः सङ्गवर्जितः ।
निर्वैरः सर्वभूतेषु यः स मामेति पाण्डव ॥

mat-karma-kṛn mat-paramo
mad-bhaktaḥ saṅga-varjitaḥ
nirvairaḥ sarva-bhūteṣu
yaḥ sa mām eti pāṇḍava

Knowing Me to be the Supreme person, if anyone engages in My devotional service, free from contamination of result-oriented work and cultivation of speculative knowledge, who remains affectionate to all living beings and makes Me the goal of his life, such a person certainly comes to Me.

Chapter

12

Bhakti Yoga

Arjuna still has some questions to ask so that there is no doubt whatsoever about what he needs to understand. He enquires from Krishna which form of worship is considered as most desirable, worship of his personal form or worship of impersonal unmanifest form? Krishna replies he prefers those whose minds are fixed on him and worship him with great faith; he considers them to be the most perfect.

Even those who worship the impersonal form that is imperishable, unmanifest, all-pervading, unchangeable, and with complete self-control, having an impartial nature towards everyone and engaging oneself in welfare activities, also attain him.

However on the path of impersonal worship, advancement is very tiresome as the discipline required on this path is very difficult. But those who worship him constantly, dedicating all their activities unto him, meditating on him, having fixed their minds upon him, Krishna personally delivers such people from the ocean of birth and death.

Having given his personal opinion on what is better, Krishna then describes to Arjuna the progressive stages on the path of devotion. Topmost is one who can fix his mind upon Krishna while engaging all the intelligence in him; he was sure to live with him. If one cannot fix the mind on him completely without deviation, then it is advisable to practice the principles of regulated devotional service and slowly develop the desire to attain him. If one cannot even practice the principles of regulated devotional service then he can work for Krishna and by working for Krishna slowly he will come to the stage of perfection. If he cannot even do that, then perform detached work, giving up the attachment to the results of actions. If one is unable to do detached work, then take up the process of meditation. If not meditation then at least gain knowledge. But better than knowledge is meditation and better than meditation is detaching oneself from results of actions. Such detachment will bring peace of mind.

Krishna also enumerates the qualities he finds dear in a devotee; one who is not envious of anyone, who is a kind friend to all, who is devoid of false ego, who is stable in the midst of both happiness and distress, who is tolerant, who is always content, who is self-controlled, who is engaged in devotional service with determination and whose intelligence and mind are constantly fixed on him. One who is not dependent on the results of ordinary course of activities, and free from desires and anxiety, such a person he considers a dear devotee. One who neither rejoices nor mourns, neither hankers nor laments, who is detached from auspicious and inauspicious, such a person is his dear devotee. One who sees equality between friends and enemies, in honor and dishonor, in happiness and distress, fame and infamy; one who keeps himself away from degrading company, who is gravely silent, who is satisfied with anything that comes his way, who is unattached to any place, such a person is his dear devotee.

All those who follow this immortal path of devotion and engage themselves with faith, making Krishna their ultimate destination, are very, very dear to him.

1

अर्जुन उवाच
एवं सततयुक्ता ये भक्तास्त्वां पर्युपासते ।
ये चाप्यक्षरमव्यक्तं तेषां के योगवित्तमाः ॥

arjuna uvāca
evaṁ satata-yuktā ye
bhaktās tvāṁ paryupāsate
ye cāpy akṣaram avyaktaṁ
teṣāṁ ke yoga-vittamāḥ

Arjuna said –
Which form of worship is considered as most perfect, worship of Your personal form through the medium of devotional service or worship of Your impersonal imperishable unmanifest nature?

2

श्रीभगवानुवाच
मय्यावेश्य मनो ये मां नित्ययुक्ता उपासते ।
श्रद्धया परयोपेतास्ते मे युक्ततमा मताः ॥

śrī-bhagavān uvāca
mayy āveśya mano ye māṁ
nitya-yuktā upāsate

śraddhayā parayopetās
te me yuktatamā matāḥ

Sri Bhagavan said –
Those whose minds are fixed on Me and worship Me with great faith are considered by Me to be most perfect.

3 – 4

ये त्वक्षरमनिर्देश्यमव्यक्तं पर्युपासते ।
सर्वत्रगमचिन्त्यं च कूटस्थमचलं ध्रुवम् ॥
सन्नियम्येन्द्रियग्रामं सर्वत्र समबुद्धयः ।
ते प्राप्नुवन्ति मामेव सर्वभूतहिते रताः ॥

ye tv akṣaram anirdeśyam
avyaktaṁ paryupāsate
sarvatra-gam acintyaṁ ca
kūṭastham acalaṁ dhruvam
sanniyamyendriya-grāmaṁ
sarvatra sama-buddhayaḥ
te prāpnuvanti mām eva
sarva-bhūta-hite ratāḥ

Even those who worship the imperishable, inexplicable, unmanifest, all-pervading, unchangeable, immovable, impersonal nature with complete self-control, having an impartial nature towards everyone and engaging oneself in welfare activities, also attain me.

5

क्लेशोऽधिकतरस्तेषामव्यक्तासक्तचेतसाम् ।
अव्यक्ता हि गतिर्दुःखं देहवद्भिरवाप्यते ॥

kleśo 'dhikataras teṣām
avyaktāsakta-cetasām
avyaktā hi gatir duḥkhaṁ
dehavadbhir avāpyate

But for those who follow the path of impersonal worship, advancement is very tiresome as the discipline required on this path is very difficult.

6 – 7

ये तु सर्वाणि कर्माणि मयि सन्न्यस्य मत्पराः ।
अनन्येनैव योगेन मां ध्यायन्त उपासते ॥
तेषामहं समुद्धर्ता मृत्युसंसारसागरात् ।
भवामि न चिरात्पार्थ मय्यावेशितचेतसाम् ॥

ye tu sarvāṇi karmāṇi
mayi sannyasya mat-parāḥ

ananyenaiva yogena
māṁ dhyāyanta upāsate
teṣām ahaṁ samuddhartā
mṛtyu-saṁsāra-sāgarāt
bhavāmi na cirāt pārtha
mayy āveśita-cetasām

Those who worship Me without deviation, dedicating all their activities unto Me, constantly meditating on Me, having fixed their minds upon Me, I personally deliver such people from the ocean of birth and death.

8

मय्येव मन आधत्स्व मयि बुद्धिं निवेशय ।
निवसिष्यसि मय्येव अत ऊर्ध्वं न संशय: ॥

mayy eva mana ādhatsva
mayi buddhiṁ niveśaya
nivasiṣyasi mayy eva
ata ūrdhvaṁ na saṁśayaḥ

Fix your mind upon Me while engaging all your intelligence in Me. If you do this, then without a doubt you will live with Me.

9

अथ चित्तं समाधातुं न शक्नोषि मयि स्थिरम् ।
अभ्यासयोगेन ततो मामिच्छाप्तुं धनञ्जय ॥

atha cittaṁ samādhātuṁ
na śaknoṣi mayi sthiram
abhyāsa-yogena tato
mām icchāptuṁ dhanañjaya

If you cannot fix your mind on Me completely without deviation, then practice following the principles of regulated devotional service and slowly develop the desire to attain Me.

10

अभ्यासेऽप्यसमर्थोऽसि मत्कर्मपरमो भव ।
मदर्थमपि कर्माणि कुर्वन्सिद्धिमवाप्स्यसि ॥

abhyāse 'py asamartho 'si
mat-karma-paramo bhava
mad-artham api karmāṇi
kurvan siddhim avāpsyasi

If you cannot even practice the principles of regulated devotional service then work for Me and by working for Me slowly you will come to the stage of perfection.

11

अथैतदप्यशक्तोऽसि कर्तुं मद्योगमाश्रितः ।
सर्वकर्मफलत्यागं ततः कुरु यतात्मवान् ॥

athaitad apy aśakto 'si
kartuṁ mad-yogam āśritaḥ
sarva-karma-phala-tyāgaṁ
tataḥ kuru yatātmavān

If you cannot even work for Me, then perform detached work, giving up the attachment to the results of actions.

12

श्रेयो हि ज्ञानमभ्यासाज्ज्ञानाद्ध्यानं विशिष्यते ।
ध्यानात्कर्मफलत्यागस्त्यागाच्छान्तिरनन्तरम्॥

śreyo hi jñānam abhyāsāj
jñānād dhyānaṁ viśiṣyate
dhyānāt karma-phala-tyāgas
tyāgāc chāntir anantaram

Better than incomplete practice of continuous remembrance of Me (abhyasat) is realized knowledge of the self (jnana). Better than incomplete realization of atma is meditation on the self (dhyana). Better than unsuccessful meditation on the self is renunciation of results of work (*karma phala tyaga*). By giving up the results of one's work, one attains purification of mind (*santih*). Then with a pure mind, one can perform meditation on the self. Then one can realize the self. As a result, one gains knowledge of the Supreme self. Then one takes to pure *bhakti*.

13 – 14

अद्वेष्टा सर्वभूतानां मैत्रः करुण एव च ।
निर्ममो निरहङ्कारः समदुःखसुखः क्षमी ॥
सन्तुष्टः सततं योगी यतात्मा दृढनिश्चयः ।
मय्यर्पितमनोबुद्धिर्यो मद्भक्तः स मे प्रियः ॥

adveṣṭā sarva-bhūtānāṁ
maitraḥ karuṇa eva ca
nirmamo nirahaṅkāraḥ
sama-duḥkha-sukhaḥ kṣamī
santuṣṭaḥ satataṁ yogī
yatātmā dṛḍha-niścayaḥ
mayy-arpita-mano-buddhir
yo mad-bhaktaḥ sa me priyaḥ

My devotee who is very dear to Me is one who is not envious of anyone, who is a kind friend to all, who doesn't claim proprietorship, who is devoid of false ego, who is stable in the midst of both happiness and distress, who is tolerant, who is always content, who is self-controlled, who is engaged in devotional service with determination and whose intelligence and mind are constantly fixed on Me.

15

यस्मान्नोद्विजते लोको लोकान्नोद्विजते च यः ।
हर्षामर्षभयोद्वेगैर्मुक्तो यः स च मे प्रियः ॥

yasmān nodvijate loko
lokān nodvijate ca yaḥ
harṣāmarṣa-bhayodvegair
mukto yaḥ sa ca me priyaḥ

One who never disturbs anyone and one who is never disturbed by anyone; one who is equanimous in the midst of happiness and distress, fear and anxiety, is very dear to Me.

16

अनपेक्षः शुचिर्दक्ष उदासीनो गतव्यथः ।
सर्वारम्भपरित्यागी यो मद्भक्तः स मे प्रियः ॥

anapekṣaḥ śucir dakṣa
udāsīno gata-vyathaḥ
sarvārambha-parityāgī
yo mad-bhaktaḥ sa me priyaḥ

One who is not dependent on the results of ordinary course of activities, one who is pure, expert, impartial and free from desires and anxiety, such a person is My devotee and is very dear to Me.

17

यो न हृष्यति न द्वेष्टि न शोचति न काङ्क्षति ।
शुभाशुभपरित्यागी भक्तिमान्यः स मे प्रियः ॥

yo na hṛṣyati na dveṣṭi
na śocati na kāṅkṣati
śubhāśubha-parityāgī
bhaktimān yaḥ sa me priyaḥ

One who neither rejoices nor mourns, neither hankers nor laments, who is detached from auspicious and inauspicious, such a person is My devotee and is very dear to Me.

18 – 19

समः शत्रौ च मित्रे च तथा मानापमानयोः ।
शीतोष्णसुखदुःखेषु समः सङ्गविवर्जितः ॥
तुल्यनिन्दास्तुतिर्मौनी सन्तुष्टो येन केनचित् ।
अनिकेतः स्थिरमतिर्भक्तिमान्मे प्रियो नरः ॥

samaḥ śatrau ca mitre ca
tathā mānāpamānayoḥ
śītoṣṇa-sukha-duḥkheṣu
samaḥ saṅga-vivarjitaḥ
tulya-nindā-stutir maunī
santuṣṭo yena kenacit
aniketaḥ sthira-matir
bhaktimān me priyo naraḥ

One who sees equality between friends and enemies, in honor and dishonor, in happiness and distress, fame and infamy; one who keeps himself away from degrading company, who is gravely silent, who is unafftected by criticism and praise, who is satisfied with anything that comes his way, who is unattached to any place, who is fixed in knowledge and who is engaged in devotional service; such a person is My devotee and is very dear to Me.

20

ये तु धर्मामृतमिदं यथोक्तं पर्युपासते ।
श्रद्दधाना मत्परमा भक्तास्तेऽतीव मे प्रियाः ॥

ye tu dharmāmṛtam idaṁ
yathoktaṁ paryupāsate
śraddadhānā mat-paramā
bhaktās te 'tīva me priyāḥ

All those who follow this immortal path of devotion and entirely engage themselves with faith, making Me their ultimate destination, are very, very dear to Me.

Chapter 13

Ksetra Ksetrajna Vibhaga Yoga

Arjuna fires more questions at Krishna to understand better the confidential knowledge he has just heard. He asks Krishna six questions. What is material nature, the enjoyer, the field, the knower of the field, knowledge and the object of knowledge?

Krishna replies, not necessarily in sequence. The physical body is the field of action. The one who knows this body is called the knower of the field. There are two knowers; one who knows his own body is a knower no doubt but Krishna who knows and resides in all bodies is the knower over and above the first knower. This complete knowledge including knowledge of both, the field (body) and the knower of the field (soul and the Supersoul) is complete knowledge and has been logically described by exalted sages in many Vedic texts especially the Vedanta Sutras.

The field of activities, i.e. the body as well as its interactions, comprises the five material elements, the ego, the intelligence, the mind, the ten senses, the five sense objects, desire, hatred, pleasure, pain, the complete whole, the consciousness and the conviction.

Knowledge lies in developing the following qualities. Humility, unpretentiousness, non-violence, tolerance, simplicity, serving the spiritual master, cleanliness, persistence, self-control, abstaining from sense objects, absence of egotism, wisdom to see the pain behind the cycle of birth, death, old age and disease, dispassion, freedom from entanglement with mundane affairs, mental equanimity in the midst of pleasant and unpleasant events, continuous and unwavering devotion to Krishna, desiring to live in secluded places, disinclined towards socializing, prioritizing the pursuit for self-realization and philosophical search for the absolute truth. All this is knowledge, everything else is simply ignorance.

Next Krishna explains the object of knowledge, a prerequisite to attain eternal life. The first object of knowledge that is to be known is the spirit soul, which is without a beginning and subordinate to Krishna himself. The second object of knowledge is the Supersoul that pervades everywhere and in everything.

The Supersoul is the creator of the senses and yet he is without senses. He is beyond the modes of nature and yet the master of the modes of nature. He exists outside as well as inside, in the hearts of all beings. He is subtle and beyond the perception of material senses. As the source of light in luminous objects, he mitigates darkness of ignorance by illuminating one's intelligence. He is knowledge, the object of knowledge as well as the goal of knowledge. Those who understand this about the field (body), knowledge and the object of knowledge can attain love for Krishna.

Material nature is the basis of all material cause and effects. Situated in material nature, the living being or the enjoyer is influenced by the three modes due to which he is caught in repeated births, either good or bad, thereby enjoying or suffering. However, the living entity is not the only enjoyer. There is another enjoyer, the Supersoul, all in one; the witness, the sanctioner, the maintainer, the protector and the proprietor. One who understands this concept of material nature, the living being and his interaction with the three modes, will no doubt be liberated from repeated births.

Some seek the Supersoul within through the eight-fold yoga process, some follow the *sankhya* or the analytical study process and yet others follow the path of *karma* yoga or the detached action process. Apart from these three ways, one can worship the Lord after hearing about him from others. Irrespective of knowledge, choosing to hear from authoritative sources with faith and without material desires, eventually helps one transcend the repetition of birth and death.

Birth and death are nothing but connection and disconnection between the knower and the field.

Real vision is seeing the Supersoul accompanying the individual soul in all bodies and understanding that unlike the body, the soul and the Supersoul are indestructible. Getting this clarity stops one from degrading his consciousness through sense gratification.

A sensible person understands that all activities are performed not by the body, not by the spirit soul but by material nature and the creator of the body. He does not see external differences of material bodies, but he sees the same expanded spiritual spark everywhere. The soul is eternal and beyond the modes of nature. Even when residing inside a material body, the soul remains untainted and does no action. The sky though all-pervading, does not mix with anything else; similarly the spirit soul though situated within the material body, does not mix with the body. Just like the sun illuminates the entire universe by its radiance, the soul illuminates the entire body by the medium of consciousness.

Krishna assures Arjuna that one who can differentiate the body from the knower of the body and understand the process of liberation from bondage of material nature, he surely attains the supreme goal.

1

अर्जुन उवाच
प्रकृतिं पुरुषं चैव क्षेत्रं क्षेत्रज्ञमेव च ।
एतद्वेदितुमिच्छामि ज्ञानं ज्ञेयं च केशव ॥

arjuna uvāca
prakṛtiṁ puruṣaṁ caiva
kṣetraṁ kṣetra-jñam eva ca
etad veditum icchāmi
jñānaṁ jñeyaṁ ca keśava

Arjuna said –
I am desirous of knowing about material nature, the enjoyer, the field, the knower of the field, the process of knowledge and the object of knowledge.

2

श्रीभगवानुवाच
इदं शरीरं कौन्तेय क्षेत्रमित्यभिधीयते ।
एतद्यो वेत्ति तं प्राहुः क्षेत्रज्ञ इति तद्विदः ॥

śrī-bhagavān uvāca
idaṁ śarīraṁ kaunteya
kṣetram ity abhidhīyate
etad yo vetti taṁ prāhuḥ
kṣetra-jñaḥ iti tad-vidaḥ

Sri Bhagavan said –
The body is considered to be the field of action. The one who knows this body is called the knower of the field.

3

क्षेत्रज्ञं चापिमां विद्धि सर्वक्षेत्रेषु भारत ।
क्षेत्रक्षेत्रज्ञयोर्ज्ञानं यत्तज्ज्ञानं मतं मम ॥

kṣetra-jñaṁ cāpi māṁ viddhi
sarva-kṣetreṣu bhārata
kṣetra-kṣetrajñayor jñānaṁ
yat taj jñānaṁ mataṁ mama

Everyone is the knower of his own body. But I am the knower of all bodies since I reside in all bodies. Complete knowledge in My opinion comprises knowledge of both the field (body) and the knower of the field (soul and the Supersoul).

4

तत्क्षेत्रं यच्च यादृक्च यद्विकारि यतश्च यत् ।
स च यो यत्प्रभावश्च तत्समासेन मे शृणु ॥

tat kṣetraṁ yac ca yādṛk ca
yad vikāri yataś ca yat
sa ca yo yat prabhāvaś ca
tat samāsena me śṛṇu

Now listen as I explain about the field, what constitutes it, what changes takes place in it, how it originated, who is the knower of the field and also how much the knower influences the field.

5

ऋषिभिर्बहुधा गीतं छन्दोभिर्विविधैः पृथक् ।
ब्रह्मसूत्रपदैश्चैव हेतुमद्भिर्विनिश्चितैः ॥

ṛṣibhir bahudhā gītaṁ
chandobhir vividhaih pṛthak
brahma-sūtra-padaiś caiva
hetumadbhir viniścitaiḥ

This knowledge about the field of activities and of the knower of the field that I am going to share with you now has been described elaborately by exalted sages in many Vedic texts especially the Vedanta Sutras with all logic.

6 – 7

महाभूतान्यहङ्कारो बुद्धिरव्यक्तमेव च ।
इन्द्रियाणि दशैकं च पञ्च चेन्द्रियगोचराः ॥
इच्छा द्वेषः सुखं दुःखं सङ्घातश्चेतना धृतिः ।
एतत्क्षेत्रं समासेन सविकारमुदाहृतम् ॥

mahā-bhūtāny ahaṅkāro
buddhir avyaktam eva ca
indriyāṇi daśaikaṁ ca
pañca cendriya-gocarāḥ
icchā dveṣaḥ sukhaṁ duḥkhaṁ
saṅghātaś cetanā dhṛtiḥ
etat kṣetraṁ samāsena
sa-vikāram udāhṛtam

The field of activities or the body and its interactions is constituted of the five material elements, the ego, the intelligence, the ten senses, the mind, the five sense objects, desire, hatred, pleasure, pain, the complete whole, the consciousness and the conviction.

~ 8 – 12 ~

अमानित्वमदम्भित्वमहिंसा क्षान्तिरार्जवम् ।
आचार्योपासनं शौचं स्थैर्यमात्मविनिग्रहः ॥
इन्द्रियार्थेषु वैराग्यमनहङ्कार एव च ।
जन्ममृत्युजराव्याधिदुःखदोषानुदर्शनम् ॥
असक्तिरनभिष्वङ्गः पुत्रदारगृहादिषु ।
नित्यं च समचित्तत्वमिष्टानिष्टोपपत्तिषु ॥
मयि चानन्ययोगेन भक्तिरव्यभिचारिणी ।
विविक्तदेशसेवित्वमरतिर्जनसंसदि ॥
अध्यात्मज्ञाननित्यत्वं तत्त्वज्ञानार्थदर्शनम् ।
एतज्ज्ञानमिति प्रोक्तमज्ञानं यदतोऽन्यथा ॥

amānitvam adambhitvam
ahiṁsā kṣāntir ārjavam
ācāryopāsanaṁ śaucaṁ
sthairyam ātma-vinigrahaḥ
indriyārtheṣu vairāgyam
anahaṅkāra eva ca
janma-mṛtyu-jarā-vyādhi
duḥkha-doṣānudarśanam
asaktir anabhiṣvaṅgaḥ
putra-dāra-gṛhādiṣu
nityaṁ ca sama-cittatvam
iṣṭāniṣṭopapattiṣu
mayi cānanya-yogena
bhaktir avyabhicāriṇī
vivikta-deśa-sevitvam

aratir jana-saṁsadi
adhyātma-jñāna-nityatvaṁ
tattva-jñānārtha-darśanam
etaj jñānam iti proktam
ajñānaṁ yad ato 'nyathā

Knowledge according to Me is the following twenty items. Humility, unpretentiousness, non-violence, tolerance, simplicity, serving the spiritual master, cleanliness, persistence, self-control, abstention from sense objects, absence of egotism, wisdom to see the pain behind the cycle of birth, death, old age and disease, dispassion, freedom from entanglement with mundane affairs, mental equanimity in the midst of pleasant and unpleasant events, continuous and unwavering devotion to Me, desiring to live in secluded places, disinclined towards socializing, prioritizing the pursuit for self-realization and philosophical search for the Absolute Truth. All this is knowledge, everything else is simply ignorance.

13

ज्ञेयं यत्तत्प्रवक्ष्यामि यज्ज्ञात्वामृतमश्नुते ।
अनादिमत्परं ब्रह्म न सत्तन्नासदुच्यते ॥

jñeyaṁ yat tat pravakṣyāmi
yaj jñātvāmṛtam aśnute
anādi mat-paraṁ brahma
na sat tan nāsad ucyate

Now I will explain about the object of knowledge. Anyone who truly knows the object of knowledge surely attains eternal life. The first object of knowledge is the spirit soul, which is beginning-less and subordinate to Me. It is unaffected by the cause and effect of the material world.

14

सर्वतः पाणिपादं तत्सर्वतोऽक्षिशिरोमुखम् ।
सर्वतः श्रुतिमल्लोके सर्वमावृत्य तिष्ठति ॥

sarvataḥ pāṇi-pādaṁ tat
sarvato 'kṣi-śiro-mukham
sarvataḥ śrutimal loke
sarvam āvṛtya tiṣṭhati

The second object of knowledge is the Supersoul whose hands, legs, eyes, faces and ears are pervading everywhere and in everything.

15

सर्वेन्द्रियगुणाभासं सर्वेन्द्रियविवर्जितम् ।
असक्तं सर्वभृच्चैव निर्गुणं गुणभोक्तृ च ॥

sarvendriya-guṇābhāsaṁ
sarvendriya-vivarjitam
asaktaṁ sarva-bhṛc caiva
nirguṇaṁ guṇa-bhoktṛ ca

The Supersoul is the creator of the senses and yet He is without senses. The Supersoul is detached though He is the maintainer of all living beings. He is beyond the modes of nature and yet he is the master of the modes of nature.

16

बहिरन्तश्च भूतानामचरं चरमेव च ।
सूक्ष्मत्वात्तदविज्ञेयं दूरस्थं चान्तिके च तत् ॥

bahir antaś ca bhūtānām
acaraṁ caram eva ca

sūkṣmatvāt tad avijñeyaṁ
dūra-sthaṁ cāntike ca tat

The Supersoul exists outside as well as inside of all beings. He moves and yet remains still. He is far and yet very near. He is so subtle that he is incomprehensible for material senses to perceive.

17

अविभक्तं च भूतेषु विभक्तमिव च स्थितम् ।
भूतभर्तृ च तज्ज्ञेयं ग्रसिष्णु प्रभविष्णु च ॥

avibhaktaṁ ca bhūteṣu
vibhaktam iva ca sthitam
bhūta-bhartṛ ca taj jñeyaṁ
grasiṣṇu prabhaviṣṇu ca

The Supersoul though appears to be divided amongst all beings, in reality He is never divided. Rather He is situated as one. He is the maintainer, creator and destroyer of every being.

18

ज्योतिषामपि तज्ज्योतिस्तमसः परमुच्यते ।
ज्ञानं ज्ञेयं ज्ञानगम्यं हृदि सर्वस्य विष्ठितम् ॥

jyotiṣām api taj jyotis
tamasaḥ param ucyate
jñānaṁ jñeyaṁ jñāna-gamyaṁ
hṛdi sarvasya viṣṭhitam

The Supersoul is the source of light in luminous objects. He mitigates darkness of ignorance with the light of knowledge by illuminating one's intelligence. He is knowledge, the object of knowledge as well as the goal of knowledge. He is seated in everyone's heart.

19

इति क्षेत्रं तथा ज्ञानं ज्ञेयं चोक्तं समासतः ।
मद्भक्त एतद्विज्ञाय मद्भावायोपपद्यते ॥

iti kṣetraṁ tathā jñānaṁ
jñeyaṁ coktuṁ samāsataḥ
mad-bhakta etad vijñāya
mad-bhāvāyopapadyate

Only My devotee can understand everything that I have spoken about the field (body), knowledge and the object of knowledge. The one who understands this thoroughly attains love for Me.

20

प्रकृतिं पुरुषं चैव विद्ध्यनादी उभावपि ।
विकारांश्च गुणांश्चैव विद्धि प्रकृतिसम्भवान् ॥

prakṛtiṁ puruṣaṁ caiva
viddhyanādī ubhāv api
vikārāṁś ca guṇāṁś caiva
viddhi prakṛti-sambhavān

Both material nature and the enjoyer are known to be beginning-less. Material nature gives birth to the transformations that occur in this world as well as to the three modes.

21

कार्यकारणकर्तृत्वे हेतुः प्रकृतिरुच्यते ।
पुरुषः सुखदुःखानां भोक्तृत्वे हेतुरुच्यते ॥

kārya-kāraṇa-kartṛtve
hetuḥ prakṛtir ucyate
puruṣaḥ sukha-duḥkhānāṁ
bhoktṛtve hetur ucyate

Material nature is the agent of transformation that brings about all material cause and effects. Whereas the enjoyer or the living being is the cause of numerous sufferings and enjoyments in this world.

22

पुरुषः प्रकृतिस्थो हि भुङ्क्ते प्रकृतिजान्गुणान् ।
कारणं गुणसङ्गोऽस्य सदसद्योनिजन्मसु ॥

puruṣaḥ prakṛti-stho hi
bhuṅkte prakṛti-jān guṇān
kāraṇaṁ guṇa-saṅgo'sya
sad-asad-yoni-janmasu

The living being or the enjoyer is situated in material nature and lives a life influenced by the three modes. Due to his association with the three modes, he takes either good or bad births.

23

उपद्रष्टानुमन्ता च भर्ता भोक्ता महेश्वरः ।
परमात्मेति चाप्युक्तो देहेऽस्मिन्पुरुषः परः ॥

upadraṣṭānumantā ca
bhartā bhoktā maheśvaraḥ—
paramātmeti cāpy ukto
dehe'smin puruṣaḥ paraḥ

There is another enjoyer seated within every field or body. He is called the divine enjoyer. He is called the Supersoul, who is the witness or overseer, the sanctioner or permitter, the maintainer, the protector and the proprietor.

24

य एवं वेत्ति पुरुषं प्रकृतिं च गुणैः सह ।
सर्वथा वर्तमानोऽपि न स भूयोऽभिजायते ॥

ya evaṁ vetti puruṣaṁ
prakṛtiṁ ca guṇaiḥ saha
sarvathā vartamāno'pi
na sa bhūyo 'bhijāyate

Anyone who completely understands this concept of material nature, the living being and his interaction with the three modes, is sure to attain perfection of life and never take birth again regardless of his current situation in life.

25

ध्यानेनात्मनि पश्यन्ति केचिदात्मानमात्मना ।
अन्ये साङ्ख्येन योगेन कर्मयोगेन चापरे ॥

dhyānenātmani paśyanti
kecid ātmānam ātmanā

anye sāṅkhyena yogena
karma-yogena cāpare

There are many ways of attaining the perfection of life or attaining the Supersoul. Some seek the Supersoul within through the eight-fold yoga process, some follow the *sankhya* or the analytical study process and yet others follow the path of *karma* yoga or the detached action process.

26

अन्ये त्वेवमजानन्तः श्रुत्वान्येभ्य उपासते ।
तेऽपि चातितरन्त्येव मृत्युं श्रुतिपरायणाः ॥

anye tv evam ajānantaḥ
śrutvānyebhya upāsate
te'pi cātitaranty eva
mṛtyuṁ śruti-parāyaṇāḥ

Those who cannot follow these processes can begin to worship the Lord after hearing about Him from others. Such people may not be knowledgeable themselves, but since they choose to hear from authoritative sources with faith and without material desires, they also eventually transcend the repetition of birth and death.

27

यावत्सञ्जायते किञ्चित्सत्त्वं स्थावरजङ्गमम्।
क्षेत्रक्षेत्रज्ञसंयोगात्तद्विद्धि भरतर्षभ ॥

yāvat sanjayate kiṅcit
sattvaṁ sthāvara-jaṅgamam
kṣetra-kṣetrajña-saṁyogāt
tad viddhi bharatarṣabha

Anything that is born in this world is simply a combination of the field of activities or material body and the knower of the field or the soul. Birth is connection between the knower and the field. Death is disconnection between the knower and the field.

28

समं सर्वेषु भूतेषु तिष्ठन्तं परमेश्वरम् ।
विनश्यत्स्वविनश्यन्तं यः पश्यति स पश्यति ॥

samaṁ sarveṣu bhūteṣu
tiṣṭhantaṁ parameśvaram
vinaśyatsv avinaśyantaṁ
yaḥ paśyati sa paśyati

Real vision is seeing the Supersoul accompanying the living being or the individual soul in all bodies. It is also in clearly understanding that neither the soul nor the Supersoul is destroyed when the external body is destroyed.

29

समं पश्यन्हि सर्वत्र समवस्थितमीश्वरम् ।
न हिनस्त्यात्मनात्मानं ततो याति परां गतिम् ॥

samaṁ paśyan hi sarvatra
samavasthitam īśvaram
na hinasty ātmanātmānaṁ
tato yāti parāṁ gatim

A person who has this real vision clearly sees the Supersoul pervading everywhere in every living being. Such a person acts with discrimination and does not allow himself to degrade in his consciousness. Rather he steadily approaches the supreme destination.

30

प्रकृत्यैव च कर्माणि क्रियमाणानि सर्वशः ।
यः पश्यति तथात्मानमकर्तारं स पश्यति ॥

prakṛtyaiva ca karmāṇi
kriyamāṇāni sarvaśaḥ

yaḥ paśyati tathātmānam
akartāraṁ sa paśyati

A person who understands that all the activities that are performed by the body, in reality is carried out by material nature, the creator of the body, and not the spirit soul, actually sees with clarity.

31

यदा भूतपृथग्भावमेकस्थमनुपश्यति ।
तत एव च विस्तारं ब्रह्म सम्पद्यते तदा ॥

yadā bhūta-pṛthag-bhāvam
eka-stham anupaśyati
tata eva ca vistāraṁ
brahma sampadyate tadā

A sensible person does not see differences due to external material bodies, but rather sees that the same spiritual spark is expanded everywhere; such a person attains liberation.

32

अनादित्वान्निर्गुणत्वात्परमात्मायमव्ययः ।
शरीरस्थोऽपि कौन्तेय न करोति न लिप्यते ॥

anāditvān nirguṇatvāt
paramātmāyam avyayaḥ
śarīra-stho 'pi kaunteya
na karoti na lipyate

The living being or spirit soul is eternal, beginningless and beyond the modes of nature. Even when residing inside a material body, the soul remains untainted and does no action.

33

यथा सर्वगतं सौक्ष्म्यादाकाशं नोपलिप्यते ।
सर्वत्रावस्थितो देहे तथात्मा नोपलिप्यते ॥

yathā sarva-gataṁ saukṣmyād
ākāśaṁ nopalipyate
sarvatrāvasthito dehe
tathātmā nopalipyate

Just like the sky though all-pervading, does not mix with anything else, similarly the spirit soul though situated within the material body, does not mix with the body.

34

यथा प्रकाशयत्येक: कृत्स्नं लोकमिमं रवि: ।
क्षेत्रं क्षेत्री तथा कृत्स्नं प्रकाशयति भारत ॥

yathā prakāśayaty ekaḥ
kṛtsnaṁ lokam imaṁ raviḥ
kṣetraṁ kṣetrī tathā kṛtsnaṁ
prakāśayati bhārata

Just like the sun illuminates the entire universe by its radiance, similarly the soul or the living being illuminates the entire body by the medium of consciousness.

35

क्षेत्रक्षेत्रज्ञयोरेवमन्तरं ज्ञानचक्षुषा ।
भूतप्रकृतिमोक्षं च ये विदुर्यान्ति ते परम् ॥

kṣetra-kṣetrajñayor evam
antaraṁ jñāna-cakṣuṣā
bhūta-prakṛti-mokṣaṁ ca
ye vidur yānti te param

Any person who can clearly see the difference between the body and the knower of the body and in addition can understand the process of liberation from the bondage of the material nature, surely attains the supreme goal.

Chapter

14

Guna Traya Vibhaga Yoga

After giving so much knowledge, Krishna says that he has yet to give the highest form of knowledge which has helped the greatest of sages attain supreme perfection of their lives and achieve transcendental nature like that of Krishna. He is neither reborn at the time of creation nor disturbed at the time of dissolution.

Material nature is the womb for all living beings to be born and Krishna is their source, the seed giving father. The material nature includes the three modes, namely the mode of goodness, passion and ignorance. As soon as the transcendental spirit soul comes in contact with this material nature it gets bound, controlled and conditioned by these modes.

The *sattva guna* or mode of goodness is the purest. A person influenced by the mode of goodness is enlightened and stays away from sinful actions. This attachment to happiness of goodness and knowledge tends to make this person proud of his superiority. The result of work in goodness is pure. The mode of passion is characterized by an overwhelming flow of desires, hankering for material pleasures and things and attachment to what one already has. Mode of passion people are very attached to result-oriented action. The result of work done in passion leads to misery. The mode of ignorance is characterized by insanity, laziness and excessive sleep. The result of work done in ignorance leads to foolishness.

The mode of goodness binds one to happiness, the mode of passion binds one to activity and the mode of ignorance binds one to delusion. The three modes of nature dominate a person's life alternately. Sometimes mode of goodness manifesting as knowledge is dominant, sometimes mode of passion through greed is dominant and sometimes mode of ignorance, visible by mistakes, madness and illusions, is dominant.

At death, mode of goodness people go upwards to the higher planets where great sages live. Mode of passion people continue to live on the same earthly plane with humans absorbed in selfish activities. Mode of ignorance people go downwards to the hellish planets in animalistic civilizations.

Krishna reveals that although all actions are under the influence of the three modes of nature, he himself is beyond their influence and in fact controlling them; a soul who knows these two things is released from the influence of the three modes and attains his divine spiritual nature.

Arjuna asks Krishna the symptoms of a person who has overcome the influence of the three modes of nature. How is his behavior? And how does he actually manage to overcome the influence of the three modes?

Krishna's answer is this. A person who has overcome the influence of the three modes of nature manifests some symptoms; he neither dislikes nor hankers for the illuminating knowledge of goodness, the attachment to action of passion and the delusion of ignorance. He is indifferent and undisturbed by any reaction knowing well the modus operandi of the three modes of nature. He regards happiness and sorrow equally, blame and praise equally, honor and dishonor equally, friend and foe equally. He is self-satisfied, steadfast and renounced. He sees a chunk of earth, a stone and a piece of gold with an equal vision.

As to how can one overcome the influence of the three modes of nature, it is not at all difficult for one who is engaged in serving Krishna with constant loving devotion. Such a person is at once promoted to blissful liberation or *brahmana* platform of realization.

1

श्रीभगवानुवाच
परं भूयः प्रवक्ष्यामि ज्ञानानां ज्ञानमुत्तमम् ।
यज्ज्ञात्वा मुनयः सर्वे परां सिद्धिमितो गताः ॥

śrī-bhagavān uvāca
paraṁ bhūyaḥ pravakṣyāmi
jñānānāṁ jñānam uttamam
yaj jñātvā munayaḥ sarve
parāṁ siddhim ito gatāḥ

Sri Bhagavan said –
Though I have already shared with you so much knowledge, I will now impart the highest and the best form of knowledge that has enabled all the great sages to attain supreme perfection of their lives.

2

इदं ज्ञानमुपाश्रित्य मम साधर्म्यमागताः ।
सर्गेऽपि नोपजायन्ते प्रलये न व्यथन्ति च ॥

idaṁ jñānam upāśritya
mama sādharmyam āgatāḥ
sarge'pi nopajāyante
pralaye na vyathanti ca

Shelter of this knowledge enables one to attain My nature. One armed with this knowledge is neither reborn at the time of creation nor is disturbed at the time of dissolution.

3

मम योनिर्महद्ब्रह्म तस्मिन्गर्भं दधाम्यहम् ।
सम्भवः सर्वभूतानां ततो भवति भारत ॥

mama yonir mahad-brahma
tasmin garbhaṁ dadhāmy aham
sambhavaḥ sarva-bhūtānāṁ
tato bhavati bhārata

I impregnate the material nature, which becomes the womb for all living beings to be born.

4

सर्वयोनिषु कौन्तेय मूर्तयः सम्भवन्ति याः ।
तासां ब्रह्म महद्योनिरहं बीजप्रदः पिता ॥

sarva-yoniṣu kaunteya
mūrtayaḥ sambhavanti yāḥ
tāsāṁ brahma mahad yonir
ahaṁ bīja-pradaḥ pitā

All forms of living beings are born from the womb of material nature and I am their seed giving father.

5

सत्त्वं रजस्तम इति गुणाः प्रकृतिसम्भवाः ।
निबध्नन्ति महाबाहो देहे देहिनमव्ययम् ॥

sattvaṁ rajas tama iti
guṇāḥ prakṛti-sambhavāḥ
nibadhnanti mahā-bāho
dehe dehinam avyayam

The material nature is fundametally constituted from the three modes, namely the mode of goodness, passion and ignorance. As soon as the spirit soul or living being comes in contact with this material nature it gets bound and intensely conditioned by these modes.

6

तत्र सत्त्वं निर्मलत्वात्प्रकाशकमनामयम् ।
सुखसङ्गेन बध्नाति ज्ञानसङ्गेन चानघ ॥

tatra sattvaṁ nirmalatvāt
prakāśakam anāmayam

sukha-saṅgena badhnāti
jñāna-saṅgena cānagha

Of the three modes of nature, the *sattva guna* or mode of goodness is the purest. A person influenced by the mode of goodness is enlightened and stays away from sinful actions. Mode of goodness people are unfortunately very attached to experiences of happiness and gaining knowledge that tend to make them proud of their superiority.

7

रजो रागात्मकं विद्धि तृष्णासङ्गसमुद्भवम् ।
तन्निबध्नाति कौन्तेय कर्मसङ्गेन देहिनम् ॥

rajo rāgātmakaṁ viddhi
tṛṣṇā-saṅga-samudbhavam
tan nibadhnāti kaunteya
karma-saṅgena dehinam

The mode of passion is characterized by an overwhelming flow of desires, hankering for what one does not have and attachment for what one already has. Mode of passion people are very attached to result-oriented action.

8

तमस्त्वज्ञानजं विद्धि मोहनं सर्वदेहिनाम् ।
प्रमादालस्यनिद्राभिस्तन्निबध्नाति भारत ॥

tamas tv ajñāna-jaṁ viddhi
mohanaṁ sarva-dehinām
pramādālasya-nidrābhis
tan nibadhnāti bhārata

The mode of ignorance is characterized by insanity, laziness and sleep. Mode of ignorance people are always in a high degree of delusion due to lack of knowledge.

9

सत्त्वं सुखे सञ्जयति रजः कर्मणि भारत ।
ज्ञानमावृत्य तु तमः प्रमादे सञ्जयत्युत ॥

sattvaṁ sukhe sañjayati
rajaḥ karmaṇi bhārata
jñānam āvṛtya tu tamaḥ
pramāde sañjayaty uta

The mode of goodness binds one to happiness, the mode of passion binds one to result-oriented actions and the mode of ignorance binds one to delusion.

10

रजस्तमश्चाभिभूय सत्त्वं भवति भारत ।
रजः सत्त्वं तमश्चैव तमः सत्त्वं रजस्तथा ॥

rajas tamaś cābhibhūya
sattvaṁ bhavati bhārata
rajaḥ sattvaṁ tamaś caiva
tamaḥ sattvaṁ rajas tathā

The three modes of nature dominate a person's life alternately. Sometimes mode of goodness is dominant, sometimes mode of passion is dominant and sometimes mode of ignorance is dominant.

11

सर्वद्वारेषु देहेऽस्मिन्प्रकाश उपजायते ।
ज्ञानं यदा तदा विद्याद्विवृद्धं सत्त्वमित्युत ॥

sarva-dvāreṣu dehe'smin
prakāśa upajāyate
jñānaṁ yadā tadā vidyād
vivṛddhaṁ sattvam ity uta

To know which mode is dominant in a person, one should watch its manifestation. When every inch of a person is dominated by discriminating knowledge then it is understood that the mode of goodness is prominent.

12

लोभः प्रवृत्तिरारम्भः कर्मणामशमः स्पृहा ।
रजस्येतानि जायन्ते विवृद्धे भरतर्षभ ॥

lobhaḥ pravṛttir ārambhaḥ
karmaṇām aśamaḥ spṛhā
rajasy etāni jāyante
vivṛddhe bharatarṣabha

When there is an exhibition of overwhelming greed, great attachment, ambitious activity and restless hankering, then it is understood that the mode of passion is dominant.

13

अप्रकाशोऽप्रवृत्तिश्च प्रमादो मोह एव च ।
तमस्येतानि जायन्ते विवृद्धे कुरुनन्दन ॥

aprakāśo 'pravṛttiś ca
pramādo moha eva ca
tamasy etāni jāyante
vivṛddhe kuru-nandana

When there is exhibition of darkness, laziness, bewilderment and delusion, then it is understood that the mode of ignorance is dominant.

14

यदा सत्त्वे प्रवृद्धे तु प्रलयं याति देहभृत् ।
तदोत्तमविदां लोकानमलान्प्रतिपद्यते ॥

yadā sattve pravṛddhe tu
pralayaṁ yāti deha-bhṛt
tadottama-vidāṁ lokān
amalān pratipadyate

When a person dominated by mode of goodness dies, he reaches the higher planets where great sages reside.

15

रजसि प्रलयं गत्वा कर्मसङ्गिषु जायते ।
तथा प्रलीनस्तमसि मूढयोनिषु जायते ॥

rajasi pralayaṁ gatvā
karma-saṅgiṣu jāyate
tathā pralīnas tamasi
mūḍha-yoniṣu jāyate

When a person dominated by the mode of passion dies, he takes rebirth amongst humans who are absorbed in selfish engagements. When a person dominated by the mode of ignorance dies, he takes birth in an animalistic civilization.

16

कर्मणः सुकृतस्याहुः सात्त्विकं निर्मलं फलम् ।
रजसस्तु फलं दुःखमज्ञानं तमसः फलम् ॥

karmaṇaḥ sukṛtasyāhuḥ
sāttvikaṁ nirmalaṁ phalam
rajasas tu phalaṁ duḥkham
ajñānaṁ tamasaḥ phalam

The result of work in goodness is pure. The result of work done in passion leads to misery. The result of work done in ignorance leads to foolishness.

17

सत्त्वात्सञ्जायते ज्ञानं रजसो लोभ एव च ।
प्रमादमोहौ तमसो भवतोऽज्ञानमेव च ॥

sattvāt sañjāyate jñānaṁ
rajaso lobha eva ca

pramāda-mohau tamaso
bhavato 'jñānam eva ca

Mode of goodness gives birth to knowledge. Mode of passion gives birth to greed. Mode of ignorance gives birth to mistakes, madness and illusion.

18

ऊर्ध्वं गच्छन्ति सत्त्वस्था मध्ये तिष्ठन्ति राजसाः ।
जघन्यगुणवृत्तिस्था अधो गच्छन्ति तामसाः ॥

ūrdhvaṁ gacchanti sattva-sthā
madhye tiṣṭhanti rājasāḥ
jaghanya-guṇa-vṛtti-sthā
adho gacchanti tāmasāḥ

Mode of goodness people go upwards to the higher planets. Mode of passion people continue to live on the same earthly plane. Mode of ignorance people go downwards to the hellish planets.

19

नान्यं गुणेभ्यः कर्तारं यदा द्रष्टानुपश्यति ।
गुणेभ्यश्च परं वेत्ति मद्भावं सोऽधिगच्छति ॥

nānyaṁ guṇebhyaḥ kartāraṁ
yadā draṣṭānupaśyati
guṇebhyaś ca paraṁ vetti
mad-bhāvaṁ so 'dhigacchati

Perceiving all actions to be carried out under the influence of the three modes of nature and knowing that the Supreme Lord is beyond the influence of the three modes; a soul who knows these two things is released from the influence of the three modes and attains My spiritual nature.

20

गुणानेतानतीत्य त्रीन्देही देहसमुद्भवान् ।
जन्ममृत्युजरादुःखैर्विमुक्तोऽमृतमश्नुते ॥

guṇān etān atītya trīn
dehī deha-samudbhavān
janma-mṛtyu-jarā-duḥkhair
vimukto 'mṛtam aśnute

When a soul residing in the material body is able to overcome the influence of the three modes of nature, he becomes free from birth, death, old age and their associated distress. Such a person is considered to have My spiritual nature and has attained immortality.

21

अर्जुन उवाच
कैर्लिङ्गैस्त्रीन्गुणानेतानतीतो भवति प्रभो ।
किमाचार: कथं चैतांस्त्रीन्गुणानतिवर्तते ॥

arjuna uvāca
kair liṅgais trīn guṇān etān
atīto bhavati prabho
kim ācāraḥ kathaṁ caitāṁs
trīn guṇān ativartate

Arjuna said –

What are the symptoms of a person who has overcome the influence of the three modes of nature? How is his behavior? And how does he actually manage to overcome the influence of the three modes?

22 – 25

श्रीभगवानुवाच
प्रकाशं च प्रवृत्तिं च मोहमेव च पाण्डव ।
न द्वेष्टि सम्प्रवृत्तानि न निवृत्तानि काङ्क्षति ॥
उदासीनवदासीनो गुणैर्यो न विचाल्यते ।
गुणा वर्तन्त इत्येवं योऽवतिष्ठति नेङ्गते ॥
समदुःखसुखः स्वस्थः समलोष्टाश्मकाञ्चनः ।
तुल्यप्रियाप्रियो धीरस्तुल्यनिन्दात्मसंस्तुतिः ॥
मानापमानयोस्तुल्यस्तुल्यो मित्रारिपक्षयोः ।
सर्वारम्भपरित्यागी गुणातीतः स उच्यते ॥

śrī-bhagavān uvāca
prakāśaṁ ca pravṛttiṁ ca
moham eva ca pāṇḍava
na dveṣṭi sampravṛttāni
na nivṛttāni kāṅkṣati
udāsīnavad āsīno
guṇair yo na vicālyate
guṇā vartanta ity evaṁ
yo 'vatiṣṭhati neṅgate
sama-duḥkha-sukhaḥ svasthaḥ
sama-loṣṭāśma-kāñcanaḥ
tulya-priyāpriyo dhīras
tulya-nindātma-saṁstutiḥ
mānāpamānayos tulyas
tulyo mitrāri-pakṣayoḥ

sarvārambha-parityāgī
guṇātītaḥ sa ucyate

Sri Bhagavan said –
A person is said to have overcome the influence of the three modes of nature if he manifests the following symptoms. He should neither be averse to nor hanker for the illuminating knowledge of goodness, the attachment to action of passion and the delusion of ignorance. He should be indifferently undisturbed by any reaction, understanding well the modus operandi of the three modes of nature. He should regard happiness and sorrow equally, desirable and undesirable equally, blame and praise equally, honor and dishonor equally, friend and foe equally. He should be self-satisfied, steadfast and renounced. Such a person should see a chunk of earth, a stone and a piece of gold with an equal vision.

26

मां च योऽव्यभिचारेण भक्तियोगेन सेवते ।
स गुणान्समतीत्यैतान्ब्रह्मभूयाय कल्पते ॥

māṁ ca yo 'vyabhicāreṇa
bhakti-yogena sevate
sa guṇān samatītyaitān
brahma-bhūyāya kalpate

Overcoming the influence of the three modes of nature is not at all difficult for one who is engaged in serving Me with constant loving devotion. Such a person is at once promoted to the level of liberation or *brahmana* platform.

27

ब्रह्मणो हि प्रतिष्ठाहममृतस्याव्ययस्य च ।
शाश्वतस्य च धर्मस्य सुखस्यैकान्तिकस्य च ॥

brahmaṇo hi pratiṣṭhāham
amṛtasyāvyayasya ca
śāśvatasya ca dharmasya
sukhasyaikāntikasya ca

I am the basis of the immortal, imperishable, everlasting and blissful liberation or the *brahmana* platform.

Chapter

15

Purushottama Yoga

Krishna has ended by saying that the modes of nature can be overcome by devotion and for devotion one needs detachment from the material world. Now he continues to explain detachment. He describes an upside down banyan tree, with its root upwards and its branches downwards. The branches of this tree extend simultaneously upwards and downwards. It is said to be getting nourishment from the modes of nature. The twigs are the sense objects. The leaves are the Vedic hymns. The roots are connected to the fruitive actions of humans. The knower of this tree is said to be the knower of the Vedas.

This tree, a reflection of the spiritual tree, cannot be understood. One should instead focus on cutting down this tree of material existence using the axe of detachment. Then one should ardently search for the real tree, the place of no return where one can surrender to the Supreme Lord, the origin of everything. That supreme abode is illuminated not by the sun, moon or fire but is self-illuminous. Anyone who goes there, never returns to this material world.

The living beings in this conditioned world are my eternal fragments. But due to being conditioned by material nature they are struggling, made helpless by the six senses including the mind. They carry their perceptions about life acquired by the senses and the mind, from one body to another.

The foolish never understand how the living being acquires one body after another body under the influence of the three modes. Only the intelligent, the knowledgeable, the spiritualists who are self-realized and who endeavor to see the soul within the body can clearly see all this. But those whose minds are not pure and who are not self-realized cannot see anything though they try.

If not directly, God can be perceived indirectly too. He is the radiance of the sun that eliminates darkness in this world; he is the splendor of the moon and fire. He sustains each living being with his energy. As the moon he nourishes all vegetables by supplying them the juice of life thus giving them taste. He is the fire of digestion necessary for sustenance. From him comes remembrance, knowledge and forgetfulness also. For those who study the Vedas, he is the object of that knowledge. He is the compiler of Vedanta and also its knower.

The Vedas mention two types of beings, the fallible in the material world and the infallible in the spiritual world. Apart from these two, there is the Supersoul who is the imperishable Supreme, the greatest in all worlds and prescribed in the Vedas as the Supreme Person. This, Krishna confides, is the most secret element of the Vedas. Whoever comprehends this knowledge becomes wise and his actions attain perfection through devotion.

1

श्रीभगवानुवाच
ऊर्ध्वमूलमध:शाखमश्वत्थं प्राहुरव्ययम् ।
छन्दांसि यस्य पर्णानि यस्तं वेद स वेदवित् ॥

śrī-bhagavān uvāca
ūrdhva-mūlam adhaḥ-śākham
aśvatthaṁ prāhur avyayam
chandāṁsi yasya parṇāni
yas taṁ veda sa veda-vit

Sri Bhagavan said –
There is said to be an imperishable banyan tree, which is upside down with its root upwards, and its branches downwards. The leaves of this tree are the Vedic hymns. The knower of this tree is said to be the knower of the Vedas.

2

अधश्चोर्ध्वं प्रसृतास्तस्य शाखा
गुणप्रवृद्धा विषयप्रवाला: ।
अधश्च मूलान्यनुसन्ततानि
कर्मानुबन्धीनि मनुष्यलोके ॥

adhaś cordhvaṁ prasṛtās tasya śākhā
guṇa-pravṛddhā viṣaya-pravālāḥ

adhaś ca mūlāny anusantatāni
karmānubandhīni manuṣya-loke

The branches of this tree extend simultaneously upwards and downwards. It is said to be getting nourishment from the modes of nature. The twigs of the tree are the sense objects. The roots of the tree are connected to the fruitive actions of humans.

3 – 4

न रूपमस्येह तथोपलभ्यते
नान्तो न चादिर्न च सम्प्रतिष्ठा ।
अश्वत्थमेनं सुविरूढमूल-
मसङ्गशस्त्रेण दृढेन छित्त्वा ॥
ततः पदं तत्परिमार्गितव्यं
यस्मिन्गता न निवर्तन्ति भूयः ।
तमेव चाद्यं पुरुषं प्रपद्ये
यतः प्रवृत्तिः प्रसृता पुराणी ॥

na rūpam asyeha tathopalabhyate
nānto na cādir na ca sampratiṣṭhā
aśvattham enaṁ su-virūḍha-mūlam
asaṅga-śastreṇa dṛḍhena chittvā
tataḥ padaṁ tat parimārgitavyaṁ
yasmin gatā na nivartanti bhūyaḥ

tam eva cādyaṁ puruṣaṁ prapadye
yataḥ pravṛttiḥ prasṛtā purāṇī

This tree cannot be perceived in reality within this world. One should instead focus on cutting down this tree whose roots are spreading far and wide. Using the axe of detachment sharpened by the discrimination through knowledge to cut the tree of material existence. Then one should ardently search for that treasure which once attained helps you reach the place of no return. Once there, one should offer oneself to the Supreme Lord from whom everything had originated.

5

निर्मानमोहा जितसङ्गदोषा
अध्यात्मनित्या विनिवृत्तकामाः ।
द्वन्द्वैर्विमुक्ताः सुखदुःखसंज्ञै-
र्गच्छन्त्यमूढाः पदमव्ययं तत् ॥

nirmāna-mohā jita-saṅga-doṣā
adhyātma-nityā vinivṛtta-kāmāḥ
dvandvair vimuktāḥ sukha-duḥkha-saṁjñair
gacchanty amūḍhāḥ padam avyayaṁ tat

A person who attains the eternal spiritual kingdom has the following qualifications. He is *nirmana* or devoid of pride, unaffected by the tricks of the illusory energy, uninfluenced by the wrong company of people, having knowledge of the eternal self, fed up of the prospects of material enjoyment, freed from being affected by dualities like happiness and distress and finally, he knows how to surrender to the Supreme Person.

6

न तद्भासयते सूर्यो न शशाङ्को न पावकः ।
यद्गत्वा न निवर्तन्ते तद्धाम परमं मम ॥

na tad bhāsayate sūryo
na śaśāṅko na pāvakaḥ
yad gatvā na nivartante
tad dhāma paramaṁ mama

Let Me tell you more about the nature of that spiritual kingdom. That supreme abode is not illuminated by the sun, moon or fire. Anyone who goes there, never returns to this material world.

7

मममैवांशो जीवलोके जीवभूतः सनातनः ।
मनःषष्ठानीन्द्रियाणि प्रकृतिस्थानि कर्षति ॥

mamaivāṁśo jīva-loke
jīva-bhūtaḥ sanātanaḥ
manaḥ ṣaṣṭhānīndriyāṇi
prakṛti-sthāni karṣati

As much as that spiritual abode is Mine, that much the living beings in this conditioned world are Mine. They are in fact My eternal fragments. But due to being conditioned by material nature they are struggling very hard, dragged all over by the six senses including the mind.

8

शरीरं यदवाप्नोति यच्चाप्युत्क्रामतीश्वरः ।
गृहीत्वैतानि संयाति वायुर्गन्धानिवाशयात् ॥

śarīraṁ yad avāpnoti
yac cāpy utkrāmatīśvaraḥ
gṛhītvaitāni saṁyāti
vāyur gandhān ivāśayāt

Just like air carries aromas from one place to another, similarly the living beings carry their perceptions about life acquired by the senses and the mind, from one body to another.

9

श्रोत्रं चक्षुः स्पर्शनं च रसनं घ्राणमेव च ।
अधिष्ठाय मनश्चायं विषयानुपसेवते ॥

śrotraṁ cakṣuḥ sparśanaṁ ca
rasanaṁ ghrāṇam eva ca
adhiṣṭhāya manaś cāyaṁ
viṣayān upasevate

Giving up one and taking up another gross body, the living being enjoys sense objects using the six senses namely the ears, the eyes, the nose, the tongue and the sense of touch all centered around the mind.

10

उत्क्रामन्तं स्थितं वाऽपि भुञ्जानं वा गुणान्वितम्।
विमूढा नानुपश्यन्ति पश्यन्ति ज्ञानचक्षुषः॥

utkrāmantaṁ sthitaṁ vāpi
bhuñjānaṁ vā guṇānvitam

vimūḍhā nānupaśyanti
paśyanti jñāna-cakṣuṣaḥ

Unintelligent, foolish people cannot comprehend how a living being gives up one body nor can they understand how the living being acquires another body under the influence of the three modes. But those whose eyes are trained by knowledge can see everything clearly.

11

यतन्तो योगिनश्चैनं पश्यन्त्यात्मन्यवस्थितम् ।
यतन्तोऽप्यकृतात्मानो नैनं पश्यन्त्यचेतसः ॥

yatanto yoginaś cainaṁ
paśyanty ātmany avasthitam
yatanto 'py akṛtātmāno
nainaṁ paśyanty acetasaḥ

The spiritualists who are self-realized and who endeavor to see the soul within the body can clearly see all this. But those whose minds are not pure and who are not self-realized cannot see anything though they try.

12

यदादित्यगतं तेजो जगद्भासयतेऽखिलम् ।
यच्चन्द्रमसि यच्चाग्नौ तत्तेजो विद्धि मामकम् ॥

yad āditya-gataṁ tejo
jagad bhāsayate 'khilam
yac candramasi yac cāgnau
tat tejo viddhi māmakam

Those who cannot see Me directly, can perceive Me indirectly through My influence in the world. The radiance of the sun that eliminates darkness in this world comes from Me. The splendor of the moon and fire also comes from Me.

13

गामाविश्य च भूतानि धारयाम्यहमोजसा ।
पुष्णामि चौषधीः सर्वाः सोमो भूत्वा रसात्मकः ॥

gām āviśya ca bhūtāni
dhārayāmy aham ojasā
puṣṇāmi cauṣadhīḥ sarvāḥ
somo bhūtvā rasātmakaḥ

It is Me who enters into each planet and sustains the living beings there with My energy. I become the moon and nourish all vegetables by supplying them the juice of life, thus giving them taste.

14

अहं वैश्वानरो भूत्वा प्राणिनां देहमाश्रितः ।
प्राणापानसमायुक्तः पचाम्यन्नं चतुर्विधम् ॥

ahaṁ vaiśvānaro bhūtvā
prāṇināṁ deham āśritaḥ
prāṇāpāna-samāyuktaḥ
pacāmy annaṁ catur-vidham

I am the fire of digestion in the bodies of living beings. By joining with the incoming and outgoing life airs, I help digest the four kinds of foods that are eaten.

15

सर्वस्य चाहं हृदि सन्निविष्टो
मत्तः स्मृतिर्ज्ञानमपोहनं च ।
वेदैश्च सर्वैरहमेव वेद्यो
वेदान्तकृद्वेदविदेव चाहम्॥

sarvasya cāhaṁ hṛdi sanniviṣṭo
mattaḥ smṛtir jñānam apohanaṁ ca

vedaiś ca sarvair aham eva vedyo
vedānta-kṛd veda-vid eva cāham

I am also present in everyone's heart and from Me comes remembrance, knowledge and forgetfulness also. I am the essence of all the Vedas and for those who study the Vedas I am the object of that knowledge. Not just that, I am also the compiler of the Vedanta and also its knower.

16

द्वाविमौ पुरुषौ लोके क्षरश्चाक्षर एव च ।
क्षर: सर्वाणि भूतानि कूटस्थोऽक्षर उच्यते ॥

dvāv imau puruṣau loke
kṣaraś cākṣara eva ca
kṣaraḥ sarvāṇi bhūtāni
kūṭa-stho 'kṣara ucyate

In the Vedas there are two types of conscious beings mentioned, namely the fallible and the infallible. In the material world, every living being falls in the category of fallible beings. In the spiritual world, every living being falls in the category of infallible beings.

17

उत्तमः पुरुषस्त्वन्यः परमात्मेत्युदाहृतः ।
यो लोकत्रयमाविश्य बिभर्त्यव्यय ईश्वरः ॥

uttamaḥ puruṣas tv anyaḥ
paramātmety udāhṛtaḥ
yo loka-trayam āviśya
bibharty avyaya īśvaraḥ

Apart from these two types of beings, there is another higher personality called the Supersoul who is the imperishable Supreme Lord that enters into the three worlds and supports it.

18

यस्मात्क्षरमतीतोऽहमक्षरादपि चोत्तमः ।
अतोऽस्मि लोके वेदे च प्रथितः पुरुषोत्तमः ॥

yasmāt kṣaram atīto 'ham
akṣarād api cottamaḥ
ato 'smi loke vede ca
prathitaḥ puruṣottamaḥ

Since I am beyond the purview of both the fallible and the infallible, and since I am the greatest, I am known in all the worlds and prescribed in the Vedas as the Supreme Person.

19

यो मामेवमसम्मूढो जानाति पुरुषोत्तमम् ।
स सर्वविद्भजति मां सर्वभावेन भारत ॥

yo mām evam asammūḍho
jānāti puruṣottamam
sa sarva-vid bhajati māṁ
sarva-bhāvena bhārata

Anyone who knows Me as the Supreme Person without a doubt and undeluded, knows everything. Having this clarity, he completely engages himself in devotional service to Me and worships Me with his entire being.

20

इति गुह्यतमं शास्त्रमिदमुक्तं मयानघ ।
एतद्बुद्ध्वा बुद्धिमान्स्यात्कृतकृत्यश्च भारत ॥

iti guhyatamaṁ śāstram
idam uktaṁ mayānagha
etad buddhvā buddhimān syāt
kṛta-kṛtyaś ca bhārata

I have revealed to you the most secret element of the Vedas. Whoever comprehends this knowledge becomes wise and his actions attain perfection.

Chapter 16

Daivasura Sampada Vibhaga Yoga

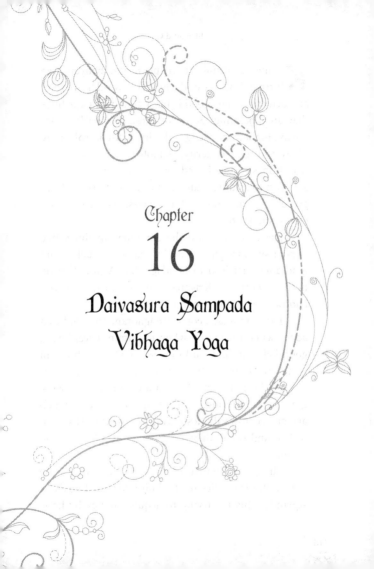

Krishna continues to explain the banyan tree further. The tree of the material world bears good and bad fruits. The good fruits are 26 divine qualities that are liberating. Some of these are fearlessness, purity, higher knowledge, charity, self-control, study of scriptures, austerity, simplicity, non-violence, truthfulness, unaffected by anger, peacefulness, aversion to finding faults, compassion, freedom from greed, determination, forgiveness, courage, non-enviousness, etc.

The bad fruits are the demoniac qualities like hypocrisy, arrogance, vanity, anger, cruelty and ignorance that lead to bondage. But Arjuna had no need to worry, as Krishna assured him that he was endowed with divine qualities.

The demoniac people are ignorant and confused about when to act and when to refrain. Cleanliness, good behavior and truthfulness are almost absent in them. According to them it is not God who controls the world but lust. Thus they indulge in sense gratification through violent and cruel acts which are geared towards destroying the world. Absorbed in lust and pride, they are attracted to illusions and wrong deeds.

The prime motive of a demoniac person's life is to fulfill every desire. To fulfill degraded goals he squanders his life trying to acquire money by hook or by crook which leads to immeasurable anxieties till the end of life. Never ever satisfied with what he gets, he continues scheming for greater future gains. Intoxicated by success, wealth and high birth, he is convinced that no one can be equal to him in being the master, the enjoyer and the controller. Firmly addicted to selfish desires, he drops into a hellish existence.

Even in performing sacrifices and offering charity, his agenda is to secure future happiness by such acts. Such hypocritical rituals and sacrifices are not in alignment with Vedic instructions and are simply a by-product of their imagination. Because of their false pride and arrogance, they envy God and find illogical faults in both the Vedas as well as God. Such demons are forced to take repeated births into ungodly, violent demoniac lives. Not only will they not attain God, they will not attain a human form either.

However, if one wants, these demoniac qualities can be at once given up by giving up just three things that are considered to be gateways to hell—lust, anger and greed. These three lead to serious degradation of consciousness. By sincerely following rules and regulations recommended by the scriptures, one gradually gets elevated in consciousness. Accepting the authority of the scriptures, one must try to comprehend what qualify as duties and what does not qualify as duties. Giving up lust, anger and greed, following scriptures and focusing on self-realization, one certainly attains the supreme goal eventually.

1 – 3

श्रीभगवानुवाच
अभयं सत्त्वसंशुद्धिर्ज्ञानयोगव्यवस्थितिः ।
दानं दमश्च यज्ञश्च स्वाध्यायस्तप आर्जवम् ॥
अहिंसा सत्यमक्रोधस्त्यागः शान्तिरपैशुनम् ।
दया भूतेष्वलोलुप्त्वं मार्दवं ह्रीरचापलम् ॥
तेजः क्षमा धृतिः शौचमद्रोहो नातिमानिता ।
भवन्ति सम्पदं दैवीमभिजातस्य भारत ॥

śrī-bhagavān uvāca
abhayaṁ sattva-saṁśuddhir
jñāna-yoga-vyavasthitiḥ
dānaṁ damaś ca yajñaś ca
svādhyāyas tapa ārjavam
ahiṁsā satyam akrodhas
tyāgaḥ śāntir apaiśunam
dayā bhūteṣv aloluptvaṁ
mārdavaṁ hrīr acāpalam
tejaḥ kṣamā dhṛtiḥ śaucam
adroho nātimānitā
bhavanti sampadaṁ daivīm
abhijātasya bhārata

The imperishable tree of the material world has good and bad fruits. The good fruits are in the form of the following 26 divine qualities. Fearlessness, internal purity, higher knowledge, charity, self-control, performance of sacrifices, study of scriptures, austerity, simplicity, non-violence, truthfulness, unaffected by anger, renunciation, peacefulness, aversion to finding faults, compassion to all beings, freedom from greed, gentleness, determination, exuberance, forgiveness, courage, cleanliness, non-enviousness and absence of hankering for honor.

4

दम्भो दर्पोऽभिमानश्च क्रोधः पारुष्यमेव च ।
अज्ञानं चाभिजातस्य पार्थ सम्पदमासुरीम् ॥

dambho darpo 'bhimānaś ca
krodhaḥ pāruṣyam eva ca
ajñānaṁ cābhijātasya
pārtha sampadam āsurīm

The bad fruits are in the form of the following demoniac qualities. Hypocrisy, arrogance, vanity, anger, cruelty and ignorance.

5

दैवी सम्पद्विमोक्षाय निबन्धायासुरी मता ।
मा शुचः सम्पदं दैवीमभिजातोऽसि पाण्डव ॥

daivī sampad vimokṣāya
nibandhāyāsurī matā
mā śucaḥ sampadaṁ daivīm
abhijāto 'si pāṇḍava

The divine qualities are highly conducive to ensure liberation. While the demoniac qualities guarantee a life of bondage. O son of Pandu, you don't need to worry, as you are endowed with divine qualities.

6

द्वौ भूतसर्गौ लोकेऽस्मिन्दैव आसुर एव च ।
दैवो विस्तरशः प्रोक्त आसुरं पार्थ मे शृणु ॥

dvau bhūta-sargau loke 'smin
daiva āsura eva ca
daivo vistaraśaḥ prokta
āsuraṁ pārtha me śṛṇ

This world is filled primarily with two categories of beings, the divine and the demoniac. So far I have explained to you at length the virtues of those blessed with divine qualities. Let me now elaborate about those possessing demoniac qualities.

7

प्रवृत्तिं च निवृत्तिं च जना न विदुरासुराः ।
न शौचं नापि चाचारो न सत्यं तेषु विद्यते ॥

pravṛttiṁ ca nivṛttiṁ ca
janā na vidur āsurāḥ
na śaucaṁ nāpi cācāro
na satyaṁ teṣu vidyate

The demoniac people are ignorant about action and inaction. They are always confused about when to act and when to refrain. Cleanliness, good behavior and truthfulness are almost absent in them.

8

असत्यमप्रतिष्ठं ते जगदाहुरनीश्वरम् ।
अपरस्परसम्भूतं किमन्यत्कामहैतुकम् ॥

asatyam apratiṣṭhaṁ te
jagad āhur anīśvaram
aparaspara-sambhūtaṁ
kim anyat kāma-haitukam

According to demoniac people, this world is illusory, having no basis and without a God in control. In their opinion, it is just a product of lust and nothing more.

9

एतां दृष्टिमवष्टभ्य नष्टात्मानोऽल्पबुद्धयः ।
प्रभवन्त्युग्रकर्माणः क्षयाय जगतोऽहिताः ॥

etāṁ dṛṣṭim avaṣṭabhya
naṣṭātmāno 'lpa-buddhayaḥ
prabhavanty ugra-karmāṇaḥ
kṣayāya jagato 'hitāḥ

Driven strongly by this opinion, the less intelligent demoniac people participate in unbeneficial cruel actions that are geared towards destroying the world.

10

काममाश्रित्य दुष्पूरं दम्भमानमदान्विताः ।
मोहाद्गृहीत्वासद्ग्राहान्प्रवर्तन्तेऽशुचिव्रताः ॥

kāmam āśritya duṣpūraṁ
dambha-māna-madānvitāḥ
mohād gṛhītvāsad-grāhān
pravartante 'śuci-vratāḥ

Powered by lust, characterized by proud arrogance, proudly taking up wrong deeds being influenced by illusion and mad attraction towards impermanent things, these are the symptoms that distinguish demoniac people.

11 – 12

चिन्तामपरिमेयां च प्रलयान्तामुपाश्रिताः ।
कामोपभोगपरमा एतावदिति निश्चिताः ॥
आशापाशशतैर्बद्धाः कामक्रोधपरायणाः ।
ईहन्ते कामभोगार्थमन्यायेनार्थसञ्चयान् ॥

cintām aparimeyāṁ ca
pralayāntām upāśritāḥ
kāmopabhoga-paramā
etāvad iti niścitāḥ
āśā-pāśa-śatair baddhāḥ
kāma-krodha-parāyaṇāḥ
īhante kāma-bhogārtham
anyāyenārtha-sañcayān

The demoniac people believe in squeezing out all the pleasure the senses can offer to fulfill every desire as the prime motive of life. To cater to this motive of fulfilling the plethora of desires they have, they build a castle of hope that oscillates between lust and anger. Such people finally end up being caught in a whirlpool of immeasurable anxieties till the end of their lives trying to acquire money through unlawful means to fulfill their degraded goals.

13 – 15

इदमद्य मया लब्धमिमं प्राप्स्ये मनोरथम् ।
इदमस्तीदमपि मे भविष्यति पुनर्धनम्॥
असौ मया हतः शत्रुर्हनिष्ये चापरानपि ।
ईश्वरोऽहमहं भोगी सिद्धोऽहं बलवान्सुखी॥
आढ्योऽभिजनवानस्मि कोऽन्योऽस्ति सदृशो मया ।
यक्ष्ये दास्यामि मोदिष्य इत्यज्ञानविमोहिताः ॥

idam adya mayā labdham
imaṁ prāpsye manoratham
idam astīdam api me
bhaviṣyati punar dhanam
asau mayā hataḥ śatrur
haniṣye cāparān api
īśvaro 'ham ahaṁ bhogī
siddho 'haṁ balavān sukhī
āḍhyo 'bhijanavān asmi
ko'nyo'sti sadṛśo mayā
yakṣye dāsyāmi modiṣya
ity ajñāna-vimohitāḥ

Sunk deeply into ignorance, a demoniac person constantly plots. He is never contented with how much he has managed to accumulate today. He is always scheming for greater future gains. Thus he is totally into increasing what is "mine". Categorizing people into friends and enemies, he aims towards eliminating his enemies and securing his future. Intoxicated by success, wealth and high birth, he is convinced that no one can be equal to him in being the Lord, the enjoyer and the controller. Even in performing sacrifices and offering charity, his agenda is to secure his future happiness by such acts.

16

अनेकचित्तविभ्रान्ता मोहजालसमावृता: ।
प्रसक्ता: कामभोगेषु पतन्ति नरकेऽशुचौ ॥

aneka-citta-vibhrāntā
moha-jāla-samāvṛtāḥ
prasaktāḥ kāma-bhogeṣu
patanti narake 'śucau

Clouded by unlimited anxieties and strongly influenced by a super complex network of illusions, such people become addicted to selfish desires and drop into a hellish existence.

17

आत्मसम्भाविताः स्तब्धा धनमानमदान्विताः ।
यजन्ते नामयज्ञैस्ते दम्भेनाविधिपूर्वकम् ॥

ātma-sambhāvitāḥ stabdhā
dhana-māna-madānvitāḥ
yajante nāma-yajñais te
dambhenāvidhi-pūrvakam

Filled with so much complacency, stubbornness, pride, intense desire for wealth, even if they engage in rituals, it is only an external show without real substance. Such hypocritical sacrifices are not in alignment with Vedic instructions and are simply a by-product of their concoctions.

18

अहङ्कारं बलं दर्पं कामं क्रोधं च संश्रिताः ।
मामात्मपरदेहेषु प्रद्विषन्तोऽभ्यसूयकाः ॥

ahaṅkāraṁ balaṁ darpaṁ
kāmaṁ krodhaṁ ca saṁśritāḥ
mām ātma-para-deheṣu
pradviṣanto 'bhyasūyakāḥ

The ultimate end result of such bloated egos, power struggles, arrogance, lust and anger is that these people envy Me. Even though I am seated in their own hearts as well as in those of others, these envious people expertize in finding illogical faults in both the Vedas as well as Me.

19

तानहं द्विषतः क्रूरान्संसारेषु नराधमान् ।
क्षिपाम्यजस्रमशुभानासुरीष्वेव योनिषु ॥

tān ahaṁ dviṣataḥ krūrān
saṁsāreṣu narādhamān
kṣipāmy ajasram aśubhān
āsurīṣv eva yoniṣu

The fate of such cruel envious demons is that they are forced to take repeated rebirth into ungodly, violent demoniac lives.

20

आसुरीं योनिमापन्ना मूढा जन्मनि जन्मनि ।
मामप्राप्यैव कौन्तेय ततो यान्त्यधमां गतिम् ॥

āsurīṁ yonim āpannā
mūḍhā janmani janmani
mām aprāpyaiva kaunteya
tato yānty adhamāṁ gatim

What to speak of attaining Me, such people will not even attain birth in human form of life but rather take birth in ungodly deluded species of life.

21

त्रिविधं नरकस्येदं द्वारं नाशनमात्मनः ।
कामः क्रोधस्तथा लोभस्तस्मादेतत्त्रयं त्यजेत् ॥

tri-vidhaṁ narakasyedaṁ
dvāraṁ nāśanam ātmanaḥ
kāmaḥ krodhas tathā lobhas
tasmād etat trayaṁ tyajet

All these demoniac qualities can be at once given up by giving up just three things that are considered to be gateways to hell—lust, anger and greed. These three lead to a serious degradation of consciousness.

22

एतैर्विमुक्तः कौन्तेय तमोद्वारैस्त्रिभिर्नरः ।
आचरत्यात्मनः श्रेयस्ततो याति परां गतिम् ॥

etair vimuktaḥ kaunteya
tamo-dvārais tribhir naraḥ
ācaraty ātmanaḥ śreyas
tato yāti parāṁ gatim

A person who has successfully managed not to enter these three gateways to hell and focus on self-realization, certainly attains the supreme goal eventually.

23

यः शास्त्रविधिमुत्सृज्य वर्तते कामकारतः ।
न स सिद्धिमवाप्नोति न सुखं न परां गतिम् ॥

yaḥ śāstra-vidhim utsṛjya
vartate kāma-kārataḥ
na sa siddhim avāpnoti
na sukhaṁ na parāṁ gatim

Abandoning the injunctions of the scriptures, if one chooses to follow the whims of his own mind, such a person will neither reach the stage of perfection, nor experience happiness nor achieve the ultimate goal of life.

24

तस्माच्छास्त्रं प्रमाणं ते कार्याकार्यव्यवस्थितौ ।
ज्ञात्वा शास्त्रविधानोक्तं कर्म कर्तुमिहार्हसि ॥

tasmāc chāstraṁ pramāṇaṁ te
kāryākārya-vyavasthitau
jñātvā śāstra-vidhānoktaṁ
karma kartum ihārhasi

Accepting the authority of the scriptures, one must try to comprehend what is prescribed in the scriptures as one's duties and what does not qualify as duties. By sincerely following rules and regulations recommended by the scriptures, one gradually gets elevated in his consciousness.

Chapter

17

Shraddha Tarya Vibhaga Yoga

Arjuna expresses his doubt to Krishna that there are some people who study the Vedas but instead of following the scriptures they follow a different kind of worship according to their imagined understanding. What mode do such people fall in? Are they in the mode of goodness, passion or ignorance?

Krishna opines that faith is governed by the predominating mode of nature, the mode of ignorance, passion or goodness, which in turn is determined by previous conditionings. Faith depends on the state of mind and state of mind is simply a reflection of the predominant mode of nature that governs a person.

It's easy to understand which mode governs a person, simply by inspecting whom he is worshipping. Those governed by the mode of goodness, worship demigods. Those presided by mode of passion, worship demoniac people. Those influenced by the mode of ignorance worship ghosts and spirits.

When one undertakes intense austerities as an exhibition of pride and ego and impelled by foolish desires and attachments, they end up torturing their own bodies as well as the Supersoul dwelling in their hearts by disregarding the instructions given in the scriptures.

Not just the type of faith but also the type of food one eats, the types of sacrifices, austerities and charities one undertakes, indicates the mode of nature a person is situated in.

In the mode of goodness, food is juicy, mild, wholesome and beneficial. Eating such food prolongs life span, purifies one, increases vitality, immunizes from diseases, increases happiness levels and improves appetite. Mode of goodness sacrifices are those that are performed as per scriptural injunctions simply as a matter of duty. Mode of goodness charity is that with no expectation of any benefit. Charity given at an appropriate time, an appropriate place and to an appropriate person, purifies the heart.

Foods that are extreme in bitterness, sourness, saltiness, dryness and fieriness are considered to be mode of passion foods. Consuming such food causes pain, misery and unhealthiness. Mode of passion sacrifices are those that are performed largely to enjoy the benefits of the sacrifice and as a boastful exhibition of religiosity. Mode of passion charity is that where the charity is either performed with greed for resulting rewards or performed in a disgruntled spirit.

Mode of ignorance food is stale, foul smelling, tasteless, putrid, remnants of others, and unfit to be offered in sacrifices. Mode of ignorance sacrifices are either contrary to or without scriptural direction. Mode of ignorance charity is that which is given at the wrong place, to a wrong person, at the wrong time and in a disrespectful manner.

Austerities are of body, speech and mind. Austerity of the body comprises worship of the Supreme Lord, knowledgeable men, the spiritual master and other superiors. Also includes maintaining cleanliness, simplicity, celibacy and non-violence. Austerity of speech is in speaking non-agitating words, truthful words, pleasing words, and words that are upheld by the scriptures. Austerity of mind is in cultivating satisfaction, simplicity, gravity, self-restraint and purity.

Mode of goodness austerities are those three-fold austerities done only for the sake of pleasing the Supreme Lord and not with any expectation of selfish gains. Mode of passion austerities are driven by pride, respect, honor and worship. Mode of ignorance austerities are those out of sheer foolishness or with an intention to cause pain to oneself or others.

After recognizing the predominant mode that is binding, Krishna explains the three words *Om tat sat*, the symbolic representation of the absolute truth used during sacrifices for the pleasure of the Supreme Lord.

Vedic spiritualists performing sacrifices, charities and penances in accordance with the scriptural injunctions always begin by chanting the sacred syllable *Om*, in order to purify the defects that may accrue into their performances. They utter the syllable tat to get freedom from material bondage and to achieve liberation. *Sat* refers to the object of sacrifice, the Supreme Lord. All three, namely the Lord, the devotee and devotional actions are all of absolute nature and therefore addressed as sat. Sacrifices, austerities and charities that are performed without faith in the Supreme Lord are called *asat*. Such impious acts are useless, in this life as well as next.

1

अर्जुन उवाच
ये शास्त्रविधिमुत्सृज्य यजन्ते श्रद्धयान्विता: ।
तेषां निष्ठा तु का कृष्ण सत्त्वमाहो रजस्तम: ॥

arjuna uvāca
ye śāstra-vidhim utsṛjya
yajante śraddhayānvitāḥ
teṣāṁ niṣṭhā tu kā kṛṣṇa
sattvam āho rajas tamaḥ

Arjuna said –

After understanding the divine and demoniac nature, my doubt is that there are some people who study the Vedas but do not follow the instructions of their teachers; instead they adopt some kind of worship according to their imagined understanding. What mode do such people fall in? Are they in the mode of goodness, passion or ignorance?

2

श्रीभगवानुवाच
त्रिविधा भवति श्रद्धा देहिनां सा स्वभावजा ।
सात्त्विकी राजसी चैव तामसी चेति तां शृणु ॥

śrī-bhagavān uvāca
tri-vidhā bhavati śraddhā
dehināṁ sā svabhāva-jā
sāttvikī rājasī caiva
tāmasī ceti tāṁ śṛṇu

Sri Bhagavan said –
Faith in humans is of three types according to the mode of nature one is predominantly governed by, which in turn is determined by previous conditionings. Depending on this, the three types of faith are in the mode of ignorance, passion or goodness.

3

सत्त्वानुरूपा सर्वस्य श्रद्धा भवति भारत ।
श्रद्धामयोऽयं पुरुषो यो यच्छ्रद्धः स एव सः ॥

sattvānurūpā sarvasya
śraddhā bhavati bhārata
śraddhā-mayo 'yaṁ puruṣo
yo yac-chraddhaḥ sa eva saḥ

The quality of faith is directly dependent on the state of mind and state of mind is simply a reflection of the predominant mode of nature that governs a person.

4

यजन्ते सात्त्विका देवान्यक्षरक्षांसि राजसाः ।
प्रेतान्भूतगणांश्चान्ये यजन्ते तामसा जनाः ॥

yajante sāttvikā devān
yakṣa-rakṣāṁsi rājasāḥ
pretān bhūta-gaṇāṁś cānye
yajante tāmasā janāḥ

In order to understand which mode governs a person, simply inspect whom he is worshipping. Those governed by the mode of goodness, worship the demigods. Those presided by mode of passion, worship demoniac people. Those influenced by the mode of ignorance worship ghosts and spirits.

5 – 6

अशास्त्रविहितं घोरं तप्यन्ते ये तपो जनाः ।
दम्भाहङ्कारसंयुक्ताः कामरागबलान्विताः ॥
कर्षयन्तः शरीरस्थं भूतग्राममचेतसः ।
मां चैवान्तः शरीरस्थं तान्विद्ध्यासुरनिश्चयान् ॥

aśāstra-vihitaṁ ghoraṁ
tapyante ye tapo janāḥ
dambhāhaṅkāra-saṁyuktāḥ
kāma-rāga-balānvitāḥ
karṣayantaḥ śarīra-sthaṁ
bhūta-grāmam acetasaḥ
māṁ caivāntaḥ śarīra-sthaṁ
tān viddhy āsura-niścayān

Many people undertake intense austerities, simply as an exhibition of their pride and ego. Though these penances are not recommended in the scriptures, they still perform them impelled by foolish desires and attachments. They end up torturing their own bodies physically as well as the Supersoul dwelling in their hearts by not following the instructions given by Him in the scriptures.

7

आहारस्त्वपि सर्वस्य त्रिविधो भवति प्रिय: ।
यज्ञस्तपस्तथा दानं तेषां भेदमिमं शृणु ॥

āhāras tv api sarvasya
tri-vidho bhavati priyaḥ
yajñas tapas tathā dānaṁ
teṣāṁ bhedam imaṁ śṛṇu

Not only the types of faith, but also the type of food one eats is divided into three categories depending on the mode one is situated in. Apart from food, the types of sacrifices, austerities and charities one undertakes, also depend on the mode of nature a person is situated in. I will explain the differences between them now.

8

आयु: सत्त्वबलारोग्यसुखप्रीतिविवर्धना: ।
रस्या: स्निग्धा: स्थिरा हृद्या आहारा: सात्त्विकप्रिया: ॥

āyuḥ sattva-balārogyasukha-
prīti-vivardhanāḥ
rasyāḥ snigdhāḥ sthirā hṛdyā
āhārāḥ sāttvika-priyāḥ

Mode of goodness foods is said to be that which is juicy, mild, wholesome and beneficial. Eating such foods prolongs life span, purifies one, increases vitality, immunizes from diseases, increases happiness levels and improves appetite.

9

कट्वम्ललवणात्युष्णतीक्ष्णरूक्षविदाहिनः ।
आहारा राजसस्येष्टा दुःखशोकामयप्रदाः ॥

kaṭv-amla-lavaṇāty-uṣṇa-tīkṣṇa-
rūkṣa-vidāhinaḥ
āhārā rājasasyeṣṭā
duḥkha-śokāmaya-pradāḥ

Foods that are extreme in bitterness, sourness, saltiness, hotness, pungence, dryness and fieriness are considered to be mode of passion foods. Consuming such food causes pain, misery and unhealthiness.

10

यातयामं गतरसं पूति पर्युषितं च यत् ।
उच्छिष्टमपि चामेध्यं भोजनं तामसप्रियम् ॥

yāta-yāmaṁ gata-rasaṁ
pūti paryuṣitaṁ ca yat
ucchiṣṭam api cāmedhyaṁ
bhojanaṁ tāmasa-priyam

Mode of ignorance foods are those that are stale, foul smelling, tasteless, putrid, remnants of others, and foodstuff that is unfit to be offered in sacrifices.

11

अफलाकाङ्क्षिभिर्यज्ञो विधिदिष्टो य इज्यते ।
यष्टव्यमेवेति मनः समाधाय स सात्त्विकः ॥

aphalākāṇkṣibhir yajño
vidhi-dṛṣṭo ya ijyate
yaṣṭavyam eveti manaḥ
samādhāya sa sāttvikaḥ

Mode of goodness sacrifices are those that are performed in strict accordance with the scriptural injunctions by those who are detached from results and who perform it simply as a matter of duty.

12

अभिसन्धाय तु फलं दम्भार्थमपि चैव यत् ।
इज्यते भरतश्रेष्ठ तं यज्ञं विद्धि राजसम् ॥

abhisandhāya tu phalaṁ
dambhārtham api caiva yat
ijyate bharata-śreṣṭha
taṁ yajñaṁ viddhi rājasam

Mode of passion sacrifices are those that are performed largely to enjoy the benefits of the sacrifice and as a boastful exhibition of religiosity.

13

विधिहीनमसृष्टान्नं मन्त्रहीनमदक्षिणम् ।
श्रद्धाविरहितं यज्ञं तामसं परिचक्षते ॥

vidhi-hīnam asṛṣṭānnaṁ
mantra-hīnam adakṣiṇam
śraddhā-virahitaṁ yajñam
tāmasaṁ paricakṣate

Mode of ignorance sacrifices are those that are either contrary to the scriptural injunctions or without the basis of any scriptural direction. In such sacrifices, there is no giving away of sanctified foodstuffs; there is either absolutely none or at worst, wrong chanting of Vedic hymns. There is no grateful remuneration for performers of the rituals and there is absolutely no faith.

14

देवद्विजगुरुप्राज्ञपूजनं शौचमार्जवम् ।
ब्रह्मचर्यमहिंसा च शारीरं तप उच्यते ॥

deva-dvija-guru-prājña
pūjanaṁ śaucam ārjavam
brahmacaryam ahiṁsā ca
śārīraṁ tapa ucyate

Austerity of the body comprises worship of the Supreme Lord, knowledgeable men, the spiritual master and other superiors. In addition to this, maintaining cleanliness, simplicity, celibacy and non-violence are considered austerities of the body.

15

अनुद्वेगकरं वाक्यं सत्यं प्रियहितं च यत् ।
स्वाध्यायाभ्यसनं चैव वाङ्मयं तप उच्यते ॥

anudvega-karaṁ vākyaṁ
satyaṁ priya-hitaṁ ca yat
svādhyāyābhyasanaṁ caiva
vāṅ-mayaṁ tapa ucyate

Austerity of speech is considered to be in speaking non-agitating words, truthful words, pleasing words, beneficial words and words that are upheld by the scriptures.

16

मन:प्रसाद: सौम्यत्वं मौनमात्मविनिग्रह: ।
भावसंशुद्धिरित्येतत्तपो मानसमुच्यते ॥

manaḥ-prasādaḥ saumyatvaṁ
maunam ātma-vinigrahaḥ
bhāva-saṁśuddhir ity etat
tapo mānasam ucyate

Austerity of mind is considered to be in cultivating satisfaction, simplicity, gravity, self-restraint and purity.

17

श्रद्धया परया तप्तं तपस्तत्त्रिविधं नरैः ।
अफलाकाङ्क्षिभिर्युक्तैः सात्त्विकं परिचक्षते ॥

śraddhayā parayā taptaṁ
tapas tat tri-vidhaṁ naraiḥ
aphalākāṅkṣibhir yuktaiḥ
sāttvikaṁ paricakṣate

Mode of goodness austerities are those where the performer performs the above mentioned three-fold austerities with great faith only for the sake of pleasing the Supreme Lord and not with any expectation of selfish gains.

18

सत्कारमानपूजार्थं तपो दम्भेन चैव यत् ।
क्रियते तदिह प्रोक्तं राजसं चलमध्रुवम् ॥

satkāra-māna-pūjārtham
tapo dambhena caiva yat
kriyate tad iha proktaṁ
rājasaṁ calam adhruvam

Mode of passion austerities are those where the performer performs the austerities driven by pride while desiring respect, honor and worship. The results of such performance of austerities is neither stable nor lasting.

19

मूढग्राहेणात्मनो यत्पीडया क्रियते तपः ।
परस्योत्सादनार्थं वा तत्तामसमुदाहृतम् ॥

mūḍha-grāheṇātmanaḥ yat
pīḍayā kriyate tapaḥ
parasyotsādanārthaṁ vā
tat tāmasam udāhṛtam

Mode of ignorance austerities are those where the performer performs the austerities out of sheer foolishness or with an intention to cause pain to oneself or others.

20

दातव्यमिति यद्दानं दीयतेऽनुपकारिणे ।
देशे काले च पात्रे च तद्दानं सात्त्विकं स्मृतम् ॥

dātavyam iti yad dānaṁ
dīyate 'nupakāriṇe

deśe kāle ca pātre ca
tad dānaṁ sāttvikaṁ smṛtam

Mode of goodness charity is that where the charity is performed simply as a matter of duty, with no expectation of any benefit. Such charity given at an appropriate time, an appropriate place and to an appropriate person, purifies the heart.

21

यत्तु प्रत्युपकारार्थं फलमुद्दिश्य वा पुनः ।
दीयते च परिक्लिष्टं तद्दानं राजसं स्मृतम् ॥

yat tu pratyupakārārthaṁ
phalam uddiśya vā punaḥ
dīyate ca parikliṣṭaṁ
tad dānaṁ rājasaṁ smṛtam

Mode of passion charity is that where the charity is either performed with greed for resulting rewards or performed in a disgruntled spirit.

22

अदेशकाले यद्दानमपात्रेभ्यश्च दीयते ।
असत्कृतमवज्ञातं तत्तामसमुदाहृतम् ॥

adeśa-kāle yad dānam
apātrebhyaś ca dīyate
asatkṛtam avajñātaṁ
tat tāmasam udāhṛtam

Mode of ignorance charity is that which is given at the wrong place, to a wrong person, at the wrong time and in a disrespectful manner.

23

ॐ तत्सदिति निर्देशो ब्रह्मणस्त्रिविधः स्मृतः ।
ब्राह्मणास्तेन वेदाश्च यज्ञाश्च विहिताः पुरा ॥

om-tat-sad iti nirdeśo
brahmaṇas tri-vidhaḥ smṛtaḥ
brāhmaṇās tena vedāś ca
yajñāś ca vihitāḥ purā

The three words *Om tat sat,* the symbolic representation of the absolute truth, were used by *brahmanas* during the performance of sacrifices for the pleasure of the Supreme Lord.

24

तस्माद्‌ॐ इत्युदाहृत्य यज्ञदानतप:क्रिया: ।
प्रवर्तन्ते विधानोक्ता: सततं ब्रह्मवादिनाम् ॥

tasmād om ity udāhṛtya
yajña-dāna-tapaḥ-kriyāḥ
pravartante vidhānoktāḥ
satataṁ brahma-vādinām

The Vedic spiritualists who participate in sacrifices, charities and penances that are in accordance with the scriptural injunctions always begin the performance by chanting the sacred syllable *Om*, in order to purify the defects that may accrue into their performances.

25

तदित्यनभिसन्धाय फलं यज्ञतप:क्रिया: ।
दानक्रियाश्च विविधा: क्रियन्ते मोक्षकाङ्‌क्षिभि: ॥

tad ity anabhisandhāya
phalaṁ yajña-tapaḥ-kriyāḥ
dāna-kriyāś ca vividhāḥ
kriyante mokṣa-kāṅkṣibhiḥ

Desiring to get freed from material bondage and to achieve liberation, the spiritualists utter the syllable *tat* while performing selfless sacrifices, austerities and charities.

26 – 27

सद्भावे साधुभावे च सदित्येतत्प्रयुज्यते ।
प्रशस्ते कर्मणि तथा सच्छब्दः पार्थ युज्यते ॥
यज्ञे तपसि दाने च स्थितिः सदिति चोच्यते ।
कर्म चैव तदर्थीयं सदित्येवाभिधीयते ॥

sad-bhāve sādhu-bhāve ca
sad ity etat prayujyate
praśaste karmaṇi tathā
sac-chabdaḥ pārtha yujyate
yajñe tapasi dāne ca
sthitiḥ sad iti cocyate
karma caiva tad-arthīyaṁ
sad ity evābhidhīyate

The Supreme Lord who is the object of sacrifices, austerities and charities is called *sat*. The performer of such sacrifices, austerities and charities is also referred to as *sat*. The very sacrifices, austerities and charities that are performed are also *sat*. All the three, namely the Lord, the devotee performer and the devotional actions are all of absolute nature and therefore addressed as *sat*.

~ 28 ~

अश्रद्धया हुतं दत्तं तपस्तप्तं कृतं च यत् ।
असदित्युच्यते पार्थ न च तत्प्रेत्य नो इह ॥

aśraddhayā hutaṁ dattaṁ
tapas taptaṁ kṛtaṁ ca yat
asad ity ucyate pārtha
na ca tat pretya no iha

Sacrifices, austerities and charities that are performed without faith in the Supreme Lord are called *asat* or impermanent. Such impious acts are useless, in this life as well as next.

Chapter

18

Moksha Sannyasa Yoga

In the concluding chapter, Krishna reinforces all that he has said to Arjuna. Arjuna has one last question. He wants to know how to differentiate renunciation or *tyaga* from the renounced order of life or *sanyasa*.

Krishna explains that giving up all those activities that are driven by a desire to enjoy, that detachment refers to *sanyasa*. But giving up the desire to enjoy the results of all activities, that detachment is called renunciation or *tyaga*.

Activities of sacrifice, charity and penance should never ever be abandoned since these activities are purifying if done with no expectations of personal profits, but simply as a matter of duty.

Renunciation of assigned duties due to illusion is considered to be renunciation in the mode of ignorance. Renunciation of assigned duties considering them bothersome or discomforting is considered to be renunciation in the mode of passion. When assigned duties are performed as a matter of duty with zero attachment to result, it is considered to be renunciation in the mode of goodness.

It is impossible to renounce activities all together. But what is definitely possible is giving up attachment to the results of the activities and one who does that is considered a true renunciant.

For one who is attached to the results of one's activities, will have to face the reactions of his actions after death. But those who remain detached to the results of activities have no such reactions to their actions and thus no dilemmas to enjoy or suffer.

Any action has five factors influencing it. They are—the place where the action is carried out, the person who is performing the action, the instruments that are used to carry out the action, different types of efforts put to complete the action and the final factor, the Supersoul. These five factors govern every action a person performs with his body, mind and words, whether the action is right or wrong.

When a person driven by ego is convinced that he is the only doer of all action, conveniently neglecting to see the influence of other four factors, he is unintelligent. On the other hand, a person who believes that he is not the doer of actions is clearly intelligent and not bound by his actions.

There are three motivators of action—knowledge, object of knowledge and the knower. And three practical factors, the senses, the work itself and the performer of work. Krishna explains this in greater details.

Knowledge in the mode of goodness is that by which one perceives the spiritual nature in all living beings irrespective of external differences. Knowledge in the mode of passion is that by which one perceives only differences at all levels in all living beings. Knowledge in the mode of ignorance is that by which one gets attached to a particular type of insignificant work, not knowing the truth in totality.

Action in the mode of goodness is that which is carried out in a balanced way, done with no attachment to results and performed with neither love nor hatred. Action in the mode of passion is that in which there is a Herculean endeavor and is aimed to seek gratification of desires. Such an action is driven by the false ego. Action in the mode of ignorance is that in which there is no respect for scriptural instructions, there is no concern for reactions or consequences and there is no concern for cruelty or pain caused to others.

Doer in mode of goodness is one who acts without false ego, being unaffected by success or failure and with great enthusiasm combined with determination. Doer in mode of passion is attached to action and its results; one who desires to enjoy the results of actions is always greedy, envious, impure and always affected by joy and sorrow. Doer in mode of ignorance is one who acts opposed to scriptural recommendations. Such a person is avaricious, stubborn, deceitful, abusive, lethargic, always surly and a perpetual procrastinator.

Understanding in the mode of goodness is that by which one can clearly decipher what should be done and what shouldn't, what binds and what doesn't. Understanding in the mode of passion is that by which one can never differentiate between religion and irreligion, between action that ought to be done and that which ought not be done. Understanding in the mode of ignorance is that by which one confuses religion to be irreligion and vice versa as a result of which one naturally digresses into the wrong direction.

Determination in mode of goodness is that which is enduring, sustained by yogic practice and which controls the mind, life and the senses. Determination in mode of passion is that which causes attachment to results of actions in the areas of religiosity, economic development and sense enjoyment. Determination in mode of ignorance is that by which one cannot progress beyond dreaming, fear, lamentation, sadness and illusion.

Happiness in the mode of goodness is that which is poison in the beginning but nectar in the end since it eventually results in self-realization. Happiness in the mode of passion is that which is nectar in the beginning but becomes poison in the end since it is borne of sense gratification. Happiness in the mode of ignorance is that which is delusion from the beginning to the end since it makes one blind to the need for self-realization. Such happiness arises out of sleep, laziness and illusion.

Everyone in this world, including the demigods in the higher planets, are bound by the influence of the three modes of nature. In fact which *varna*, Brahmana, Kshatriya, Vaishya or Sudra, one belongs to is also determined by which mode of nature one is influenced by. A man can perfect his life by being true to one's natural propensity to work. Performance of such work is not affected by sinful reactions. Better to remain engaged in one's own duties even if performed imperfectly, than to perform someone else's duties perfectly.

By practicing self-control, detachment from material pleasures and practice of renunciation, one can obtain freedom from reactions. He thus progressively attains pure devotion for Krishna. By dint of devotional service, he becomes eligible to enter the kingdom of God.

Krishna advises Arjuna again to completely depend on him, to work under his protection and always remain fully conscious of him. But if he does not heed Krishna's advice to work in higher consciousness but acts through the influence of the ego then he will be a lost soul, controlled by material nature. How will he overpower his very nature and mind that would force him to fight even though he refuses to do so now?

Krishna has nothing more to say to Arjuna and only requests him to ruminate on this knowledge intensely and then act as per his own desire.

As a final word of advice, Krishna goads Arjuna to offer worship and respects to him, to become his devotee so then he will surely come to him. To give up all varieties of religion and duties, and choose to take shelter of him. To become free from all sinful reactions. Do not fear. It is Krishna's assurance to Arjuna, his dear friend.

He forbids Arjuna to share this confidential knowledge with those who do not practice devotional service or those who envy him. But it can be shared with devotees. In fact there is no one in this world more dear to him than one who spreads this knowledge of Krishna. Anyone who studies this sacred conversation, anyone who listens to this conversation between Krishna and Arjuna with faith and with no envy in the heart, soon becomes freed of all sins and attains an auspicious planet where exalted personalities reside.

Arjuna finally responds to Krishna. He says that his illusion is dispelled and he is now very clear and completely free from doubts and fully prepared to carry out Krishna's instructions without any hesitation.

The Bhagavad Gita concludes with Sanjaya feeling fortunate having heard this conversation between two great personalities, Krishna and Arjuna thanks to the grace of his guru Vyas. He declares to Dhritarashtra that wherever Lord Krishna, the master mystic is present and wherever Arjuna, the supreme bowman is present, there will surely follow opulence, victory, unbelievable power and morality.

1

अर्जुन उवाच
सन्न्यासस्य महाबाहो तत्त्वमिच्छामि वेदितुम् ।
त्यागस्य च हृषीकेश पृथक्केशिनिषूदन ॥

arjuna uvāca
sannyāsasya mahābāho
tattvam icchāmi veditum
tyāgasya ca hṛṣīkeśa
pṛthak keśī-niṣūdana

Arjuna said –
O Krishna, kindly dispel this doubt that I have in my mind. I want to know the commonality and differences between the concept of renunciation or *tyaga* and the formal renounced order of life or *sanyasa*.

2

श्रीभगवानुवाच
काम्यानां कर्मणां न्यासं सन्न्यासं कवयो विदुः ।
सर्वकर्मफलत्यागं प्राहुस्त्यागं विचक्षणाः ॥

śrī-bhagavān uvāca
kāmyānāṁ karmaṇāṁ nyāsaṁ
sannyāsaṁ kavayo viduḥ

sarva-karma-phala-tyāgaṁ
prāhus tyāgaṁ vicakṣaṇāḥ

Sri Bhagavan said –
When a person gives up all those activities that are driven by a desire to enjoy, that detachment is called renounced order of life or *sanyasa*. When a person gives up the desire to enjoy the results of all activities, that detachment is called renunciation or *tyaga*.

3

त्याज्यं दोषवदित्येके कर्म प्राहुर्मनीषिणः ।
यज्ञदानतपःकर्म न त्याज्यमिति चापरे ॥

tyājyaṁ doṣavad ity eke
karma prāhur manīṣiṇaḥ
yajña-dāna-tapaḥ-karma
na tyājyam iti cāpare

Many wise people consider all types of activities as bad. But there are others who believe that at no cost, activities of sacrifices, charity and penances should be given up as bad.

4

निश्चयं शृणु मे तत्र त्यागे भरतसत्तम ।
त्यागो हि पुरुषव्याघ्र त्रिविधः सम्प्रकीर्तितः ॥

niścayaṁ śṛṇu me tatra
tyāge bharata-sattama
tyāgo hi puruṣa-vyāghra
tri-vidhaḥ samprakīrtitaḥ

Let Me now share with you My opinion about renunciation. Renunciation is also considered to be of three types.

5

यज्ञदानतपःकर्म न त्याज्यं कार्यमेव तत् ।
यज्ञो दानं तपश्चैव पावनानि मनीषिणाम् ॥

yajña-dāna-tapaḥ-karma
na tyājyaṁ kāryam eva tat
yajño dānaṁ tapaś caiva
pāvanāni manīṣiṇām

Activities of sacrifices, charity and penances should never ever be abandoned since these activities are purifying even for divine personalities.

6

एतान्यपि तु कर्माणि सङ्गं त्यक्त्वा फलानि च ।
कर्तव्यानीति मे पार्थ निश्चितं मतमुत्तमम् ॥

etāny api tu karmāṇi
saṅgaṁ tyaktvā phalāni ca
kartavyānīti me pārtha
niścitaṁ matam uttamam

But these three activities must be done with no expectations of personal profits, but rather simply as a matter of duty. This is My ultimate opinion.

7

नियतस्य तु सन्न्यास: कर्मणो नोपपद्यते ।
मोहात्तस्य परित्यागस्तामस: परिकीर्तित: ॥

niyatasya tu sannyāsaḥ
karmaṇo nopapadyate
mohāt tasya parityāgas
tāmasaḥ parikīrtitaḥ

Of the three types of renunciation, the one in which recommended assigned duties are abandoned due to illusion is considered to be renunciation in the mode of ignorance.

8

दु:खमित्येव यत्कर्म कायक्लेशभयात्त्यजेत् ।
स कृत्वा राजसं त्यागं नैव त्यागफलं लभेत् ॥

duḥkham ity eva yat karma
kāya-kleśa-bhayāt tyajet
sa kṛtvā rājasaṁ tyāgaṁ
naiva tyāga-phalaṁ labhet

The one in which recommended assigned duties are abandoned considering it bothersome or discomforting, is considered to be renunciation in the mode of passion. Such renunciation is not considered to be respectful and he does not attain the intended result of renunciation.

9

कार्यमित्येव यत्कर्म नियतं क्रियतेऽर्जुन ।
सङ्गं त्यक्त्वा फलं चैव स त्याग: सात्त्विको मत: ॥

kāryam ity eva yat karma
niyataṁ kriyate 'rjuna
saṅgaṁ tyaktvā phalaṁ caiva
sa tyāgaḥ sāttviko mataḥ

The one in which recommended assigned duties are performed as a matter of duty only with nil attachment to the result is considered to be renunciation in the mode of goodness.

10

न द्वेष्ट्यकुशलं कर्म कुशले नानुषज्जते ।
त्यागी सत्त्वसमाविष्टो मेधावी छिन्नसंशयः ॥

na dveṣṭy akuśalaṁ karma
kuśale nānuṣajjate
tyāgī sattva-samāviṣṭo
medhāvī chinna-saṁśayaḥ

A person who performs renunciation in the mode of goodness is intelligent enough to not become too much hateful of unfavorable activities nor overly attached to favorable activities. He knows very well how to act dutifully without any doubts.

11

न हि देहभृता शक्यं त्यक्तुं कर्माण्यशेषतः ।
यस्तु कर्मफलत्यागी स त्यागीत्यभिधीयते ॥

na hi deha-bhṛtā śakyaṁ
tyaktuṁ karmāṇy aśeṣataḥ
yas tu karma-phala-tyāgī
sa tyāgīty abhidhīyate

In reality, complete renunciation of all activities is impossible in this world. But what is definitely possible is giving up attachment to the results of the activities and one who does that is considered a true renunciant.

12

अनिष्टमिष्टं मिश्रं च त्रिविधं कर्मणः फलम् ।
भवत्यत्यागिनां प्रेत्य न तु सन्न्यासिनां क्वचित् ॥

aniṣṭam iṣṭaṁ miśraṁ ca
tri-vidhaṁ karmaṇaḥ phalam
bhavaty atyāginām pretya
na tu sannyāsinām kvacit

For one who is attached to the results of one's activities, will have to face the reactions of his actions after death. Reactions may be good, bad or mixed. But those who remain detached to the results of activities have no such reactions to their actions and thus no dilemmas to enjoy or suffer.

13

पञ्चैतानि महाबाहो कारणानि निबोध मे ।
सांख्ये कृतान्ते प्रोक्तानि सिद्धये सर्वकर्मणाम् ॥

pañcaitāni mahā-bāho
kāraṇāni nibodha me
sāṅkhye kṛtānte proktāni
siddhaye sarva-karmaṇām

Any action performed in this world has five causes influencing it. Let Me now explain to you these five influencers.

14

अधिष्ठानं तथा कर्ता करणं च पृथग्विधम् ।
विविधाश्च पृथक्चेष्टा दैवं चैवात्र पञ्चमम् ॥

adhiṣṭhānaṁ tathā kartā
karaṇaṁ ca pṛthag-vidham

vividhāś ca pṛthak ceṣṭā
daivaṁ caivātra pañcamam

The five factors influencing every action that one does are, the place where the action is carried out, the person who is performing the action, the instruments that are used to carry out the action, different types of efforts put to complete the action and the final factor, the Supersoul.

15

शरीरवाङ्मनोभिर्यत्कर्म प्रारभते नरः ।
न्याय्यं वा विपरीतं वा पञ्चैते तस्य हेतवः ॥

śarīra-vāṅ-manobhir yat
karma prārabhate naraḥ
nyāyyaṁ vā viparītaṁ vā
pañcaite tasya hetavaḥ

These five factors govern every action a person performs with his body, mind and words, whether the action is right or wrong.

16

तत्रैवं सति कर्तारमात्मानं केवलं तु यः ।
पश्यत्यकृतबुद्धित्वान्न स पश्यति दुर्मतिः ॥

tatraivaṁ sati kartāram
ātmānaṁ kevalaṁ tu yaḥ
paśyaty akṛta-buddhitvān
na sa paśyati durmatiḥ

Governed by the ego, when a person is convinced that he is the only doer of all action, conveniently neglecting to see the influence of these five factors, is foolish and does not have clarity.

17

यस्य नाहङ्कृतो भावो बुद्धिर्यस्य न लिप्यते ।
हत्वापि स इमाँल्लोकान्न हन्ति न निबध्यते ॥

yasya nāhaṅkṛto bhāvo
buddhir yasya na lipyate
hatvāpi sa imāl̐ lokān
na hanti na nibadhyate

On the other hand, a person who is not driven by false ego to believe that he is the doer of actions and one whose intelligence is not garbled, is not bound by his actions.

18

ज्ञानं ज्ञेयं परिज्ञाता त्रिविधा कर्मचोदना ।
करणं कर्म कर्तेति त्रिविधः कर्मसङ्ग्रहः ॥

jñānaṁ jñeyaṁ parijñātā
tri-vidhā karma-codanā
karaṇaṁ karma karteti
tri-vidhaḥ karma saṅgrahaḥ

Action is motivated by three factors, knowledge, object of knowledge and the knower. Action has three practical factors, the senses, the work itself and the performer of work.

19

ज्ञानं कर्म च कर्ता च त्रिधैव गुणभेदतः ।
प्रोच्यते गुणसंख्याने यथावच्छृणु तान्यपि ॥

jñānaṁ karma ca kartā ca
tridhaiva guṇa-bhedataḥ
procyate guṇa-saṅkhyāne
yathāvac chṛṇu tāny api

Now I will explain to you about the three kinds of knowledge, actions and performer of actions, which are divided according to the three modes of nature.

20

सर्वभूतेषु येनैकं भावमव्ययमीक्षते ।
अविभक्तं विभक्तेषु तज्ज्ञानं विद्धि सात्त्विकम् ॥

sarva-bhūteṣu yenaikaṁ
bhāvam avyayam īkṣate
avibhaktaṁ vibhakteṣu
taj jñānaṁ viddhi sāttvikam

Knowledge in the mode of goodness is that by which one perceives equality in all living beings due to similar spiritual nature internally irrespective of differences in forms externally.

21

पृथक्त्वेन तु यज्ज्ञानं नानाभावान्पृथग्विधान् ।
वेत्ति सर्वेषु भूतेषु तज्ज्ञानं विद्धि राजसम् ॥

pṛthaktvena tu yaj jñānaṁ
nānā-bhāvān pṛthag-vidhān
vetti sarveṣu bhūteṣu
taj jñānaṁ viddhi rājasam

Knowledge in the mode of passion is that by which one perceives only differences at all levels in all living beings.

22

यत्तु कृत्स्नवदेकस्मिन्कार्ये सक्तमहैतुकम् ।
अतत्त्वार्थवदल्पं च तत्तामसमुदाहृतम् ॥

yat tu kṛtsna-vad ekasmin
kārye saktam ahaitukam
atattvārthavad alpaṁ ca
tat tāmasam udāhṛtam

Knowledge in the mode of ignorance is that by which one gets attached to a particular type of insignificant work, not knowing the truth in totality.

23

नियतं सङ्गरहितमरागद्वेषतः कृतम् ।
अफलप्रेप्सुना कर्म यत्तत्सात्त्विकमुच्यते ॥

niyataṁ saṅga-rahitam
arāga-dveṣataḥ kṛtam
aphala-prepsunā karma
yat tat sāttvikam ucyate

Action in the mode of goodness is that which is carried out in a balanced way, done with no attachment to results and performed with neither love nor hatred.

24

यत्तु कामेप्सुना कर्म साहङ्कारेण वा पुनः ।
क्रियते बहुलायासं तद्राजसमुदाहृतम् ॥

yat tu kāmepsunā karma
sāhaṅkāreṇa vā punaḥ
kriyate bahulāyāsaṁ
tad rājasam udāhṛtam

Action in the mode of passion is that in which there is a Herculean endeavor and is aimed to seek gratification of desires. Such an action is performed driven by the false ego.

25

अनुबन्धं क्षयं हिंसामनपेक्ष्य च पौरुषम् ।
मोहादारभ्यते कर्म यत्तत्तामसमुच्यते ॥

anubandhaṁ kṣayaṁ hiṁsām
anapekṣya ca pauruṣam
mohād ārabhyate karma
yat tat tāmasam ucyate

Action in the mode of ignorance is that in which there is no respect for scriptural instructions, there is no concern for reactions or consequences and there is no concern for cruelty or pain caused to others.

26

मुक्तसङ्गोऽनहंवादी धृत्युत्साहसमन्वितः ।
सिद्ध्यसिद्ध्योर्निर्विकारः कर्ता सात्त्विक उच्यते ॥

mukta-saṅgo 'nahaṁ-vādī
dhṛty-utsāha-samanvitaḥ
siddhy-asiddhyor nirvikāraḥ
kartā sāttvika ucyate

Performer of action in mode of goodness is one who performs action without false ego, being unaffected by success or failure and with great enthusiasm combined with determination.

27

रागी कर्मफलप्रेप्सुर्लुब्धो हिंसात्मकोऽशुचिः ।
हर्षशोकान्वितः कर्ता राजसः परिकीर्तितः ॥

rāgī karma-phala-prepsur
lubdho hiṁsātmako 'śuciḥ
harṣa-śokānvitaḥ kartā
rājasaḥ parikīrtitaḥ

Performer of action in mode of passion is one who is attached to action and its results. Such a person who desires to enjoy the results of actions is always greedy, envious, impure and always affected by joy and sorrow.

28

अयुक्तः प्राकृतः स्तब्धः शठो नैष्कृतिकोऽलसः ।
विषादी दीर्घसूत्री च कर्ता तामस उच्यते ॥

ayuktaḥ prākṛtaḥ stabdhaḥ
śaṭho naiṣkṛtiko 'lasaḥ
viṣādī dīrgha-sūtrī ca
kartā tāmasa ucyate

Performer of action in mode of ignorance is one who does actions that are opposed to the scriptural recommendations. Such a person is avaricious, stubborn, deceitful, abusive, lethargic, always surly and a perpetual procrastinator.

29

बुद्धेर्भेदं धृतेश्चैव गुणतस्त्रिविधं शृणु ।
प्रोच्यमानमशेषेण पृथक्त्वेन धनञ्जय ॥

buddher bhedaṁ dhṛteś caiva
guṇatas tri-vidhaṁ śṛṇu
procyamānam aśeṣeṇa
pṛthaktvena dhanañjaya

Let Me now share with you three types of understanding and determinations according to the three modes of nature.

30

प्रवृत्तिं च निवृत्तिं च कार्याकार्ये भयाभये ।
बन्धं मोक्षं च या वेत्ति बुद्धिः सा पार्थ सात्त्विकी ॥

pravṛttiṁ ca nivṛttiṁ ca
kāryākārye bhayābhaye
bandhaṁ mokṣaṁ ca yā vetti
buddhiḥ sā pārtha sāttvikī

Understanding in the mode of goodness is that by which one can clearly decipher what should be done and what shouldn't, what should be feared and what shouldn't, what binds and what doesn't.

31

यया धर्ममधर्मं च कार्यं चाकार्यमेव च ।
अयथावत्प्रजानाति बुद्धिः सा पार्थ राजसी ॥

yayā dharmam adharmaṁ ca
kāryaṁ cākāryam eva ca
ayathāvat prajānāti
buddhiḥ sā pārtha rājasī

Understanding in the mode of passion is that by which one can never differentiate between religion and irreligion, between action that ought to be done and that which ought not to be done.

32

अधर्मं धर्ममिति या मन्यते तमसावृता ।
सर्वार्थान्विपरीतांश्च बुद्धिः सा पार्थ तामसी ॥

adharmaṁ dharmam iti yā
manyate tamasāvṛtā
sarvārthān viparītāṁś ca
buddhiḥ sā pārtha tāmasī

Understanding in the mode of ignorance is that by which one confuses religion to be irreligion and irreligion to be religion. Such a person is always affected by illusion and darkness as a result of which one naturally digresses into the wrong direction.

33

धृत्या यया धारयते मनःप्राणेन्द्रियक्रियाः ।
योगेनाव्यभिचारिण्या धृतिः सा पार्थ सात्त्विकी ॥

dhṛtyā yayā dhārayate
manaḥ prāṇendriya-kriyāḥ
yogenāvyabhicāriṇyā
dhṛtiḥ sā pārtha sāttvikī

Determination in mode of goodness is that which is imperishable, sustained by yogic practice and which controls the mind, life and the senses.

34

यया तु धर्मकामार्थान्धृत्या धारयतेऽर्जुन ।
प्रसङ्गेन फलाकाङ्क्षी धृतिः सा पार्थ राजसी ॥

yayā tu dharma-kāmārthān
dhṛtyā dhārayate 'rjuna
prasaṅgena phalākāṅkṣī
dhṛtiḥ sā pārtha rājasī

Determination in mode of passion is that by which one remains very much attached to results of actions in the areas of religiosity, economic development and sense enjoyment.

35

यया स्वप्नं भयं शोकं विषादं मदमेव च ।
न विमुञ्चति दुर्मेधा धृतिः सा पार्थ तामसी ॥

yayā svapnaṁ bhayaṁ śokaṁ
viṣādaṁ madam eva ca
na vimuñcati durmedhā
dhṛtiḥ sā pārtha tāmasī

Determination in mode of ignorance is that by which one cannot progress beyond dreaming, fear, lamentation, sadness and illusion.

36

सुखं त्विदानीं त्रिविधं शृणु मे भरतर्षभ ।
अभ्यासाद्रमते यत्र दुःखान्तं च निगच्छति ॥

sukhaṁ tv idānīṁ tri-vidhaṁ
śṛṇu me bharatarṣabha
abhyāsād ramate yatra
duḥkhāntaṁ ca nigacchati

Let Me now share with you about three kinds of happiness which a living being enjoys and which helps him deal with miseries.

37

यत्तदग्रे विषमिव परिणामेऽमृतोपमम् ।
तत्सुखं सात्त्विकं प्रोक्तमात्मबुद्धिप्रसादजम् ॥

yat tad agre viṣam iva
pariṇāme 'mṛtopamam
tat sukhaṁ sāttvikaṁ proktam
ātma-buddhi-prasāda-jam

Happiness in the mode of goodness is that which is poison in the beginning but nectar in the end since it eventually results in self-realization.

38

विषयेन्द्रियसंयोगाद्यत्तदग्रेऽमृतोपमम् ।
परिणामे विषमिव तत्सुखं राजसं स्मृतम् ॥

viṣayendriya-saṁyogād
yat tad agre 'mṛtopamam
pariṇāme viṣam iva
tat sukhaṁ rājasaṁ smṛtam

Happiness in the mode of passion is that which is nectar in the beginning but becomes poison in the end since it is borne of contact of the senses with the sense objects.

39

यदग्रे चानुबन्धे च सुखं मोहनमात्मनः ।
निद्रालस्यप्रमादोत्थं तत्तामसमुदाहृतम् ॥

yad agre cānubandhe ca
sukhaṁ mohanam ātmanaḥ
nidrālasya-pramādotthaṁ
tat tāmasam udāhṛtam

Happiness in the mode of ignorance is that which is delusion from the beginning to the end since it makes one blind to the need for self-realization. Such happiness arises out of sleep, laziness and illusion.

40

न तदस्ति पृथिव्यां वा दिवि देवेषु वा पुनः ।
सत्त्वं प्रकृतिजैर्मुक्तं यदेभिः स्यात्त्रिभिर्गुणैः ॥

na tad asti pṛthivyāṁ vā
divi deveṣu vā punaḥ
sattvaṁ prakṛti-jair muktaṁ
yad ebhiḥ syāt tribhir guṇaiḥ

Every being in this world, including the demigods in the higher planets, are bound by the influence of the three modes of nature.

41

ब्राह्मणक्षत्रियविशां शूद्राणां च परन्तप ।
कर्माणि प्रविभक्तानि स्वभावप्रभवैर्गुणैः ॥

brāhmaṇa-kṣatriya-viśāṁ
śūdrāṇāṁ ca parantapa
karmāṇi pravibhaktāni
svabhāva-prabhavair guṇaiḥ

In fact which *varna*, Brahmana, Kshatriya, Vaishya or Sudra, one belongs to is also determined by which mode of nature one is influenced by.

42

शमो दमस्तपः शौचं क्षान्तिरार्जवमेव च ।
ज्ञानं विज्ञानमास्तिक्यं ब्रह्मकर्म स्वभावजम् ॥

śamo damas tapaḥ śaucaṁ
kṣāntir ārjavam eva ca
jñānaṁ vijñānam āstikyaṁ
brahma-karma svabhāva-jam

The natural qualities exhibited by a Brahmana are peacefulness, self-control, austerity, purity, tolerance, honesty, knowledge, wisdom and religiosity.

43

शौर्यं तेजो धृतिर्दाक्ष्यं युद्धे चाप्यपलायनम् ।
दानमीश्वरभावश्च क्षात्रं कर्म स्वभावजम् ॥

śauryaṁ tejo dhṛtir dākṣyaṁ
yuddhe cāpy apalāyanam
dānam īśvara-bhāvaś ca
kṣātraṁ karma svabhāva-jam

The natural qualities exhibited by a Kshatriya are heroism, strength, determination, resourcefulness, not shying away from battle, magnanimity and leadership.

44

कृषिगोरक्ष्यवाणिज्यं वैश्यकर्म स्वभावजम् ।
परिचर्यात्मकं कर्म शूद्रस्यापि स्वभावजम् ॥

kṛṣi-go-rakṣya-vāṇijyaṁ
vaiśya-karma svabhāva-jam
paricaryātmakaṁ karma
śūdrasyāpi svabhāva-jam

The natural qualities exhibited by a Vaishya are farming, cow protection and business. The natural qualities exhibited by a Sudra are labor and menial service to others.

45

स्वे स्वे कर्मण्यभिरतः संसिद्धिं लभते नरः ।
स्वकर्मनिरतः सिद्धिं यथा विन्दति तच्छृणु ॥

sve sve karmaṇy abhirataḥ
saṁsiddhiṁ labhate naraḥ
sva-karma-nirataḥ siddhiṁ
yathā vindati tac chṛṇu

By being true to one's natural propensity to work, a man can perfect his life. Let Me now explain to you how this is possible.

46

यतः प्रवृत्तिर्भूतानां येन सर्वमिदं ततम् ।
स्वकर्मणा तमभ्यर्च्य सिद्धिं विन्दति मानवः ॥

yataḥ pravṛttir bhūtānāṁ
yena sarvam idaṁ tatam
sva-karmaṇā tam abhyarcya
siddhiṁ vindati mānavaḥ

Along with carrying out one's work according to natural propensity, if a person worships the all-pervading Lord who is the source of every living being, such a person attains perfection through his work.

47

श्रेयान्स्वधर्मो विगुणः परधर्मात्स्वनुष्ठितात् ।
स्वभावनियतं कर्म कुर्वन्नाप्नोति किल्बिषम् ॥

śreyān sva-dharmo viguṇaḥ
para-dharmāt sv-anuṣṭhitāt
svabhāva-niyataṁ karma
kurvan nāpnoti kilbiṣam

When a person performs duties that are in tandem with his natural propensity, performance of such work is not affected by sinful reactions. Therefore it is always better to remain engaged in one's own duties even if performed imperfectly, than to perform someone else's duties perfectly.

48

सहजं कर्म कौन्तेय सदोषमपि न त्यजेत् ।
सर्वारम्भा हि दोषेण धूमेनाग्निरिवावृताः ॥

saha-jaṁ karma kaunteya
sa-doṣam api na tyajet
sarvārambhā hi doṣeṇa
dhūmenāgnir ivāvṛtāḥ

No matter what you do in this world, there will be some fault associated with that action. All duties have faults. Even fire is always covered by smoke. So even if there is some fault in the work that is assigned to you according to your natural propensity, you should not give it up.

49

असक्तबुद्धिः सर्वत्र जितात्मा विगतस्पृहः ।
नैष्कर्म्यसिद्धिं परमां सन्न्यासेनाधिगच्छति ॥

asakta-buddhiḥ sarvatra
jitātmā vigata-spṛhaḥ
naiṣkarmya-siddhiṁ paramāṁ
sannyāsenādhigacchati

By practicing self-control, detachment from material pleasures, practice of renunciation and having an unattached intelligence, one can obtain freedom from reactions.

50

सिद्धिं प्राप्तो यथा ब्रह्म तथाप्नोति निबोध मे ।
समासेनैव कौन्तेय निष्ठा ज्ञानस्य या परा ॥

siddhiṁ prāpto yathā brahma
tathāpnoti nibodha me
samāsenaiva kaunteya
niṣṭhā jñānasya yā parā

Now I will teach you the practice by which one can achieve this perfection, which is the highest stage of knowledge.

51 – 53

बुद्ध्या विशुद्धया युक्तो धृत्यात्मानं नियम्य च ।
शब्दादीन्विषयांस्त्यक्त्वा रागद्वेषौ व्युदस्य च ॥
विविक्तसेवी लघ्वाशी यतवाक्कायमानसः ।
ध्यानयोगपरो नित्यं वैराग्यं समुपाश्रितः ॥
अहङ्कारं बलं दर्पं कामं क्रोधं परिग्रहम् ।
विमुच्य निर्ममः शान्तो ब्रह्मभूयाय कल्पते ॥

buddhyā viśuddhayā yukto
dhṛtyātmānaṁ niyamya ca
śabdādīn viṣayāṁs tyaktvā
rāga-dveṣau vyudasya ca
vivikta-sevī laghv-āśī
yata-vāk-kāya-mānasaḥ
dhyāna-yoga-paro nityaṁ
vairāgyaṁ samupāśritaḥ
ahaṅkāraṁ balaṁ darpaṁ
kāmaṁ krodhaṁ parigraham
vimucya nirmamaḥ śānto
brahma-bhūyāya kalpate

A person who does the following things attains self-realization. Using his purified intelligence, he controls the mind with determination, gives up selfish enjoyment, frees himself from attachment and aversion, lives in a secluded place, eats minimal, controls the faculties of body, mind and speech, always absorbed in higher consciousness, is detached from mundane things, is free from false ego, false strength, false pride, false proprietorship, lust and anger and is peaceful.

54

ब्रह्मभूत: प्रसन्नात्मा न शोचति न काङ्क्षति ।
सम: सर्वेषु भूतेषु मद्भक्तिं लभते पराम् ॥

brahma-bhūtaḥ prasannātmā
na śocati na kāṅkṣati
samaḥ sarveṣu bhūteṣu
mad-bhaktiṁ labhate parām

A person who lives in this manner and considered to be transcendentally situated, very soon realizes the Supreme Lord and becomes completely blissful. He stops lamenting at losses and hankering for gains. He looks at all living beings with equanimity. He thus attains pure devotion to Me.

55

भक्त्या मामभिजानाति यावान्यश्चास्मि तत्त्वतः ।
ततो मां तत्त्वतो ज्ञात्वा विशते तदनन्तरम् ॥

bhaktyā mām abhijānāti
yāvān yaś cāsmi tattvataḥ
tato māṁ tattvato jñātvā
viśate tad-anantaram

I can only be understood as the Supreme Lord by dint of devotional service. When a person becomes fully conscious of Me by such practice, he becomes eligible to enter the kingdom of God.

56

सर्वकर्माण्यपि सदा कुर्वाणो मद्व्यपाश्रयः ।
मत्प्रसादादवाप्नोति शाश्वतं पदमव्ययम् ॥

sarva-karmāṇy api sadā
kurvāṇo mad-vyapāśrayaḥ
mat-prasādād avāpnoti
śāśvataṁ padam avyayam

Such a pure devotee of Mine who is under My protection, even if engaged in any kind of activity, finally reaches My imperishable abode by My mercy.

57

चेतसा सर्वकर्माणि मयि सन्न्यस्य मत्परः ।
बुद्धियोगमुपाश्रित्य मच्चित्तः सततं भव ॥

cetasā sarva-karmāṇi
mayi sannyasya mat-paraḥ
buddhi-yogam upāśritya
mac-cittaḥ satataṁ bhava

In all your actions, completely depend on Me, work under My protection and always remain fully conscious of Me.

58

मच्चित्तः सर्वदुर्गाणि मत्प्रसादात्तरिष्यसि ।
अथ चेत्त्वमहङ्कारान्न श्रोष्यसि विनङ्क्ष्यसि ॥

mac-cittaḥ sarva-durgāṇi
mat-prasādāt tariṣyasi
atha cet tvam ahaṅkārān
na śroṣyasi vinaṅkṣyasi

If you remain thus conscious of Me, then you will surely overcome all the hurdles of material life by My mercy. But if you do not work in such higher consciousness of Me, but rather act through the influence of the ego and not pay heed to My advice, then you will be a lost soul.

59

यदहङ्कारमाश्रित्य न योत्स्य इति मन्यसे ।
मिथ्यैष व्यवसायस्ते प्रकृतिस्त्वां नियोक्ष्यति ॥

yad ahaṅkāram āśritya
na yotsya iti manyase
mithyaiṣa vyavasāyas te
prakṛtis tvāṁ niyokṣyati

If you do not take to fighting under My direction, then you will be misdirected by your mind and will definitely fight elsewhere since to fight is your inherent nature.

60

स्वभावजेन कौन्तेय निबद्धः स्वेन कर्मणा ।
कर्तुं नेच्छसि यन्मोहात्करिष्यस्यवशोऽपि तत् ॥

svabhāva-jena kaunteya
nibaddhaḥ svena karmaṇā
kartuṁ necchasi yan mohāt
kariṣyasy avaśo 'pi tat

Right now you may refuse to fight according to My instruction being under the influence of illusion. But your very nature will force you to do the same act that you refused. How will you resist at that time?

61

ईश्वरः सर्वभूतानां हृद्देशेऽर्जुन तिष्ठति ।
भ्रामयन्सर्वभूतानि यन्त्रारूढानि मायया ॥

īśvaraḥ sarva-bhūtānāṁ
hṛd-deśe 'rjuna tiṣṭhati
bhrāmayan sarva-bhūtāni
yantrārūḍhāni māyayā

The bodies of living beings are like machines that are fabricated out of material energy and the Supersoul seated within the heart of every living being offers direction to their wanderings by directing these machines or bodies.

62

तमेव शरणं गच्छ सर्वभावेन भारत ।
तत्प्रसादात्परां शान्तिं स्थानं प्राप्स्यसि शाश्वतम् ॥

tam eva śaraṇaṁ gaccha
sarva-bhāvena bhārata

tat-prasādāt parāṁ śāntiṁ
sthānaṁ prāpsyasi śāśvatam

Therefore one should surrender to the Supersoul wholeheartedly. Only by His grace will one attain divine peace and the eternal supreme abode.

63

इति ते ज्ञानमाख्यातं गुह्याद्गुह्यतरं मया ।
विमृश्यैतदशेषेण यथेच्छसि तथा कुरु ॥

iti te jñānam ākhyātaṁ
guhyād guhyataraṁ mayā
vimṛśyaitad aśeṣeṇa
yathecchasi tathā kuru

I have now explained to you the utmost confidential knowledge. I want you to now ruminate on this knowledge intensely and then do what you desire to do.

64

सर्वगुह्यतमं भूयः शृणु मे परमं वचः ।
इष्टोऽसि मे दृढमिति ततो वक्ष्यामि ते हितम् ॥

sarva-guhyatamaṁ bhūyaḥ
śṛṇu me paramaṁ vacaḥ

iṣṭo 'si me dṛḍham iti
tato vakṣyāmi te hitam

I am now going to share with you My ultimate instruction because you are My dearest friend. This is the most confidential of all knowledge that you have heard yet. Hear this from Me as it is only for your benefit.

65

मन्मना भव मद्भक्तो मद्याजी मां नमस्कुरु ।
मामेवैष्यसि सत्यं ते प्रतिजाने प्रियोऽसि मे ॥

man-manā bhava mad-bhakto
mad-yājī māṁ namaskuru
mām evaiṣyasi satyaṁ te
pratijāne priyo 'si me

Always think of Me. Become My devotee. Offer worship to Me and offer your respects to Me. By doing this you will surely come to Me. I assure you this since you are My dearest friend.

66

सर्वधर्मान्परित्यज्य मामेकं शरणं व्रज ।
अहं त्वां सर्वपापेभ्यो मोक्षयिष्यामि मा शुचः ॥

sarva-dharmān parityajya
mām ekaṁ śaraṇaṁ vraja
ahaṁ tvāṁ sarva-pāpebhyo
mokṣayiṣyāmi mā śucaḥ

Giving up all varieties of religion and duties, just take shelter of Me. I will free you from all sinful reactions. Do not fear.

67

इदं ते नातपस्काय नाभक्ताय कदाचन ।
न चाशुश्रूषवे वाच्यं न च मां योऽभ्यसूयति ॥

idaṁ te nātapaskāya
nābhaktāya kadācana
na cāśuśrūṣave vācyaṁ
na ca māṁ yo 'bhyasūyati

This confidential knowledge should never be shared with people, who do not practice restraint, nor with those who do not practice devotional service, nor with those who envy Me.

68

य इदं परमं गुह्यं मद्भक्तेष्वभिधास्यति ।
भक्तिं मयि परां कृत्वा मामेवैष्यत्यसंशयः ॥

ya idaṁ paramaṁ guhyaṁ
mad-bhakteṣv abhidhāsyati
bhaktiṁ mayi parāṁ kṛtvā
mām evaiṣyaty asaṁśayaḥ

But if one shares this supremely secret knowledge with devotees, pure devotional service is guaranteed and at the end of his life, he returns to Me.

69

न च तस्मान्मनुष्येषु कश्चिन्मे प्रियकृत्तमः ।
भविता न च मे तस्मादन्यः प्रियतरो भुवि ॥

na ca tasmān manuṣyeṣu
kaścin me priya-kṛttamaḥ
bhavitā na ca me tasmād
anyaḥ priyataro bhuvi

In fact there is no one in this world more dear to Me than this person and nor will there ever be anyone dearer.

70

अध्येष्यते च य इमं धर्म्यं संवादमावयोः ।
ज्ञानयज्ञेन तेनाहमिष्टः स्यामिति मे मतिः ॥

adhyeṣyate ca ya imaṁ
dharmyaṁ saṁvādam āvayoḥ
jñāna-yajñena tenāham
iṣṭaḥ syām iti me matiḥ

Anyone who with his intelligence studies this sacred conversation between us actually worships Me with his intelligence.

71

श्रद्धावाननसूयश्च शृणुयादपि यो नरः ।
सोऽपि मुक्तः शुभाँल्लोकान्प्राप्नुयात्पुण्यकर्मणाम् ॥

śraddhāvān anasūyaś ca
śṛṇuyād api yo naraḥ
so 'pi muktaḥ śubhāl lokān
prāpnuyāt puṇya-karmaṇām

Anyone who listens to this conversation between us with faith and with no envy in the heart, soon becomes freed of all sins and attains an auspicious planet where exalted personalities reside.

72

कच्चिदेतच्छ्रुतं पार्थ त्वयैकाग्रेण चेतसा ।
कच्चिदज्ञानसम्मोहः प्रणष्टस्ते धनञ्जय ॥

kaccid etac chrutaṁ pārtha
tvayaikāgreṇa cetasā
kaccid ajñāna-sammohaḥ
praṇaṣṭas te dhanañjaya

O Arjuna, have you heard everything that I spoke to you with a focused mind? Is your ignorance and illusion now gone? If you haven't comprehended everything I have shared with you, I am prepared to repeat it yet again.

73

अर्जुन उवाच
नष्टो मोहः स्मृतिर्लब्धा त्वत्प्रसादान्मयाच्युत ।
स्थितोऽस्मि गतसन्देहः करिष्ये वचनं तव ॥

arjuna uvāca
naṣṭo mohaḥ smṛtir labdhā
tvat-prasādān mayācyuta
sthito 'smi gata-sandehaḥ
kariṣye vacanaṁ tava

Arjuna said –

My dear Krishna, my illusion is dispelled and I have regained my composure by Your grace. I am very clear and completely free from doubts and am fully prepared to carry out your instructions unhesitatingly.

74

सञ्जय उवाच
इत्यहं वासुदेवस्य पार्थस्य च महात्मनः ।
संवादमिममश्रौषमद्भुतं रोमहर्षणम् ॥

sañjaya uvāca
ity ahaṁ vāsudevasya
pārthasya ca mahātmanaḥ
saṁvādam imam aśrauṣam
adbhutaṁ roma-harṣaṇam

Sanjaya said –

I am so fortunate that I have heard this conversation between two great personalities, Krishna and Arjuna. The knowledge that I heard is so great that my hair is standing on end in sheer ecstasy and joy.

75

व्यासप्रसादाच्छ्रुतवानेतद्गुह्यमहं परम् ।
योगं योगेश्वरात्कृष्णात्साक्षात्कथयतः स्वयम् ॥

vyāsa-prasādāc chrutavān
etad guhyam ahaṁ param
yogaṁ yogeśvarāt kṛṣṇāt
sākṣāt kathayataḥ svayam

By the grace of my guru Vyas, I have had the fortune of hearing such a highly confidential conversation, that too directly from the mouth of the master of all mysticism, Krishna himself who spoke to Arjuna.

76

राजन्संस्मृत्य संस्मृत्य संवादमिमम‌द्भुतम् ।
केशवार्जुनयोः पुण्यं हृष्यामि च मुहुर्मुहुः ॥

rājan saṁsmṛtya saṁsmṛtya
saṁvādam imam adbhutam
keśavārjunayoḥ puṇyaṁ
hṛṣyāmi ca muhur muhuḥ

Again and again as I recall the deeply intriguing holy discussion between Krishna and Arjuna, I derive immense pleasure and am feeling thrilled at every moment.

77

तच्च संस्मृत्य संस्मृत्य रूपमत्यद्भुतं हरेः ।
विस्मयो मे महान्राजन्हृष्यामि च पुनः पुनः ॥

tac ca saṁsmṛtya saṁsmṛtya
rūpam aty-adbhutaṁ hareḥ
vismayo me mahān rājan
hṛṣyāmi ca punaḥ punaḥ

O King, the more I remember the amazing form of Lord Krishna, the more awestruck and overjoyed I feel repeatedly.

78

यत्र योगेश्वरः कृष्णो यत्र पार्थो धनुर्धरः ।
तत्र श्रीर्विजयो भूतिर्ध्रुवा नीतिर्मतिर्मम ॥

yatra yogeśvaraḥ kṛṣṇo
yatra pārtho dhanur-dharaḥ
tatra śrīr vijayo bhūtir
dhruvā nītir matir mama

Wherever Lord Krishna, the master mystic, is present and wherever Arjuna, the supreme bowman, is present, there surely will follow opulence, victory, unbelievable power and morality. This is my opinion.

Sanskrit Pronunciation Guide

Throughout the centuries, the Sanskrit language has been written in a variety of alphabets. The mode of writing most widely used throughout India, however, is called *devanāgari*, which means, literally, the writing used in "the cities of the demigods." The *devanāgari* alphabet consists of forty-eight characters: thirteen vowels and thirty-five consonants. Ancient Sanskrit grammarians arranged this alphabet according to practical linguistic principles, and this order has been accepted by all Western scholars. The system of transliteration used in this book conforms to a system that scholars in the last fifty years have accepted to indicate the pronunciation of each Sanskrit sound.

Vowels

अ a आ ā इ i ई ī उ u ऊ ū ऋ ṛ

ॠ ṝ ऌ ḷ ए e ऐ ai ओ o औ au

Consonants

Gutturals:	क ka	ख kha	ग ga	घ gha	ङ ṅa
Palatals:	च ca	छ cha	ज ja	झ jha	ञ ña
Cerebrals:	ट ṭa	ठ ṭha	ड ḍa	ढ ḍha	ण ṇa
Dentals:	त ta	थ tha	द da	ध dha	न na
Labians:	प pa	फ pha	ब ba	भ bha	म ma
Semivowels:	य ya	र ra	ल la	व va	
Sibilants:	श śa	ष ṣa	स sa		
Aspirate:	ह ha	Anusvāra: ं ṁ	Visarga: ः ḥ		

Numerals

०-0 १-1 २-2 ३-3 ४-4 ५-5 ६-6 ७-7 ८-8 ९-9

The vowels are written as follows after a consonant:

ा ā ि i ी ī ु u ू ū ृ ṛ ॄ ṝ े e ै ai ो o ौ au

For example: क ka का kā कि ki की kī कु ku कू kū

कृ kṛ कॄ kṝ के ke कै kai को ko कौ kau

Generally, two or more consonants in conjunction are written together in a special form, as for example: क्ष kṣa त्र tra

The vowel "**a**" is implied after a consonant with no vowel symbol.

The symbol *virāma* (्) indicates that there is no final vowel: क्

The vowels are pronounced as follows:

a —as in b**u**t

ā —as in f**a**r but held twice as long as **a**

ai —as in **ai**sle

au —as in h**ow**

e —as in th**ey**

i —as in p**i**n

ī —as in p**i**que but held twice as long as **i**

l — as in **lree**

o —as in **go**

ṛ —as in **ri**m

ṝ —as in **ree**d but held twice as long as **ṛ**

u —as in p**u**sh

ū —as in r**u**le but held twice as long as **u**

The consonants are pronounced as follows:

Gutturals
(pronounced from the throat)

k —as in **k**ite

kh —as in Ec**kh**art

g —as in **g**ive

gh —as in di**g-h**ard

ṅ —as in si**ng**

Labials
(pronounced with the lips)

p —as in **p**ine

ph —as in u**p-h**ill (not **f**)

b —as in **b**ird

bh —as in ru**b-h**ard

m —as in **m**other

Cerebrals
(pronounced with tip of tongue against roof of mouth)

ṭ —as in **t**ub
ṭh —as in ligh**t-h**eart
ḍ —as in **d**ove
ḍh —as in re**d-h**ot
ṇ —as in si**ng**

Dentals
(pronounced as cerebrals but with tongue against teeth)

t —as in **t**ub
th —as in ligh**t-h**eart
d —as in **d**ove
dh —as in re**d-h**ot
n —as in **n**ut

Aspirate

h —as in **h**ome

Anusvāra

ṁ —a resonant nasal sound like in the french worn *bo***n**

Palatals
(pronounced with middle of tongue against palate)

c —as in **ch**air
ch —as in staun**ch-h**eart
j —as in **j**oy
jh —as in he**dgeh**og
ñ —as in ca**ny**on

Semivowels

y —as in **y**es
r —as in **r**un
l —as in **l**ight
v —as in **v**ine, except when preceded in the same syllable by a consonant, then like in s**w**an

Sibilants

ś —as in the German word *sprechen*
ṣ —as in **sh**ine
s —as in **s**un

Visarga

ḥ —as final **h**-sound: **aḥ** is pronounced like **aha**: **iḥ** like **ihi**

There is no strong accentuation of syllables in Sanskrit, or pausing between words in a line, only a flowing of short and long (twice as long as the short) syllables. A long syllable is one whose vowel is long (**ā, ai, au, e, ī, o, ṝ, ū**) or whose short vowel is followed by more than one consonant (including **ḥ** and **ṁ**). Aspirated consonants (consonants followed by an **h**) count as single consonants.